SELF *and* SOCIAL CHANGE

SELF *and* SOCIAL CHANGE

MATTHEW ADAMS

SAGE Publications
Los Angeles ▪ London ▪ New Delhi ▪ Singapore

SAGE Publications Ltd
1 Oliver's Yard
55 City Road
London EC1Y 1SP

SAGE Publications Inc.
2455 Teller Road
Thousand Oaks, California 91320

SAGE Publications India Pvt Ltd
B I/I 1 Mohan Cooperative Industrial Area
Mathura Road
New Delhi 110 044

SAGE Publications Asia-Pacific Pte Ltd
33 Pekin Street #02-01
Far East Square
Singapore 048763

British Library Cataloguing in Publication data

A catalogue record for this book is available from the British Library

ISBN 978-1-4129-0710-1
ISBN 978-1-4129-0711-8 (pbk)

Library of Congress Control Number: 2006929865

Typeset by C&M Digitals (P) Ltd., Chennai, India
Printed in Great Britain by Cromwell Press Ltd, Wiltshire
Printed on paper from sustainable resources

For the one on the way,
as yet unnamed

Contents

Introduction

What do you think are the most significant social changes of the last fifty years? Here are a selection of answers offered by friends and colleagues: the introduction of the contraceptive pill; the proliferation of television ownership; the globalization of capitalism; communications and information technology developments; prolonged dependency of offspring on parents; post-modern pessimism; a shift from production to consumption; reproductive technologies (e.g. IVF); gay visibility; increased opportunities for women and the end of apartheid.

You may or may not have come up with similar answers. In fact what we perceive to be important social changes will vary depending on our personal histories and relationships as well our current context. A social change, such as the fall of the Berlin wall, may have been experienced as tremendously significant for some, but irrelevant to others. Generalizing is difficult from the outset. But they are fascinating examples and invite us to explore the idea of social change further.

How can we make sense of these far-reaching changes? Social theory often attempts to find more general categories of social change to which more specific changes can be allotted. Whilst not losing touch completely with a micro-approach to social change – concern for the specific, localized perception of significant change – we will now turn to macro-approaches to social change. In one of the few existing overviews, Jordan and Pile describe the sociology of social change as 'the investigation of the times and places when and where society becomes different... [as] necessarily dealing with situations when things are strange, when the new and the old rub up against each other or evolve into another social form' (Jordan and Pile, 2002: xiv). This is a suitably broad description for a phenomenon as nebulous as social change, and it will serve as a working definition for the purposes of this book.

An overview of sociological accounts of social change is an intimidating prospect. So much sociology attempts to indicate what is new, emerging, or soon-to-be-common. Of course at the same time the light of the new casts a descriptive glow over what is lost; the soon to be distant memories of established patterns, the unravelling of once-familiar social habits, the now-you-mention-it obsolescence of formerly taken-for-granted practices and institutions. The process is rarely envisaged as simply one of the new replacing the old however. Social theorizing often posits a more subtle and sophisticated co-existence of old and new patterns in the social fabric (e.g. Heelas *et al.*, 1996; Rojek, 1995; Beck and Willms, 2004), from which social change emerges as a dynamic force.

In the sociological imagination a key dimension of significant social change is often argued to be its contemporariness. It is often argued that our current period is one of substantial social change against which the claims for change of previous eras fade by comparison. Hence Giddens argues that modernity was another form of traditional society until it finally shed its chrysalis and emerged as late modernity or post-traditional society: 'For most of its history, modernity has rebuilt tradition as it has dissolved it...the persistence and recreation of tradition was central....' (Giddens, 1994: 56). Despite this theoretical tendency radical upheaval has long been seen to be an inherent dynamism of society, *now* so often the point of crescendo. In the West, announcements of social discontinuity have coalesced to some extent around *fin de siecle* theorizing of the nineteenth and twentieth centuries (Alexander, 1995), additionally punctuated by the aftermath of two world wars. Hence others are far more cautious in perceiving social transformation, emphasizing instead continuity, in terms of traditions, inequalities and broader social relations.

Amidst such breadth the scope of this book is modest, and will largely limit itself to more recent accounts of social change as utilized by prominent sociological theories of identity. The focus is the general mechanisms of the relationship between social change and self-identity and what they can reveal about their mutual nature, rather than the details of specific changes. More specifically, one of a number of dominant tropes will be the focus of each chapter. These tropes can be broadly defined in terms of the psychosocial processes they place at the heart of their analysis: psychosocial fragmentation in chapter two, extended reflexivity in chapter three, discursive regulation in chapter four, and cultural pathology in chapter five. Chapter six is an attempt to draw together some of the main critical points from the preceding chapters and develop a socially situated analysis of selfhood.

Book Structure

Before engaging with these specific tropes in detail, an attempt will be made in the first chapter to broadly portray some of the kinds of transformations which tend to be assumed in any discussion of social change. Such a rudimentary sketch does not attempt to do justice to the many differences between key theorists of social change. The accounts of self in relation to social change tackled in subsequent chapters differ in important respects: in the kinds of social change they emphasize over others, the positive or negative value attributed to them, and the extent to which they signify a break from the past. These differences will be pursued as they become relevant. With these caveats in mind, it is possible to consider a number of social changes which have been argued to shape the recent and emerging history of the globe.

The theories of psychosocial fragmentation discussed in chapter two are perhaps the furthest removed from an explicit account of self-reflexivity, though they provide an important starting point. The key claim made there is that the self has become severed from its meaningful points of anchorage and ends up drifting in a sea of uncertainty and alienation. Accounts of psychosocial fragmentation have provided us with abundant accounts of social changes we are supposedly encountering, often with a polemical eloquence which is convincingly damning. Its influence is felt in almost all sociological accounts of self-identity. As illustrated in chapter two, as a trope on the sociological landscape the significance of theses of fragmentation has not waned, invigorated as it has been by the impact of post-modern perspectives. Nonetheless in its unreconstructed forms it rests on a one-dimensional understanding of agency and the social-psychological inter-relationship: social order fragments, the self fragments, alienating itself from itself in the process. Critical difficulties lie here in the dangers of conservatism and essentialism amongst others. Thus the formation of new communities, perhaps along different lines to those of more 'traditional' times are missed or marginalized; opportunities for more relational, less individualistic constructions of self-identity are unnecessarily denigrated; and creative and varied responses are portrayed as homogenous and passive. Such criticism forms the backdrop for a discussion of the extended reflexivity thesis in chapter three.

The extended reflexivity thesis is an attempt to flesh out a more dilemmatic approach to the psychological dynamics of psychosocial fragmentation. Giddens's work in particular, taken as a whole, is a sophisticated attempt to conceptualize a tripartite model of self (unconscious, practical consciousness, reflexivity) and the ways in which it is intertwined with changing social structures – structuration. Extended self-reflexivity is argued to be the ambivalent fruit of social change overlooked by standard accounts of psychosocial fragmentation. Whilst it may contain the potentially self-ruinous seeds of excessive uncertainty, meaninglessness, addiction, obsessiveness and narcissism, it also holds out hope for day-to-day reconstitution of institutions and the reappropriation of spheres of meaning, along reflexively organized lines rather than the ascribed doxa of previous socio-cultural eras. The thesis is summarized before moving on to a survey of its critical reception.

The extended reflexivity thesis is thought by some to have neglected the reality of relational, embodied selves with complex psychic structures. Giddens's version of unconscious and emotional life was claimed to be excessively 'tidy' and individualized, possibly in order to more easily accommodate his vision of extended reflexivity. The self-reflexive process is thus claimed to be a more partial, ambiguous and contradictory phenomenon than the extended reflexivity thesis tends to allow for. A more complex and multivious account of psychic life can arguably be found in psychoanalysis and this critical point is expanded upon here and underpins the later discussions in chapter five.

Critical commentary has also focused upon the extent to which the extended reflexivity thesis utilizes an unduly weakened concept of social structure. According to this counter-argument, social structures still differentially shape the ability of different social groups to be reflexive, and to connect reflexivity with genuine choices. This is an important argument pursued in some detail in chapter three and throughout this book. Finally, critical voices have suggested the analysis of reflexivity as an emerging process of self-identity transcending cultural boundaries masks its origins in, and perpetuation of, normative discourses of rationality, individualization and autonomy which now elide smoothly with the neo-liberal politics and policies of contemporary capitalism. This interpretation forms the basis for a critical dialogue between the extended reflexivity thesis and Foucaultian analyses of self-identity in the context of social change, discussed in chapter four.

Discursive accounts of regulation which draw on Foucault at first appear to have little in common with the extended reflexivity thesis. Theirs is a very different portrayal of social change and the subject, emphasizing the primacy of language, the ways in which discourses intermesh to form reality and the subsequent construction of socially differentiated subjects. Out of discursive formations emerges the particular shape of an embodied subjectivity, folding discourses into the reality of its own constitution through the techniques made available to it, always pre-existing it. However, Foucaultian accounts of governmentality have pointed to the emergence of self-surveillance as a historically contingent technology for regulating people in contemporary societies. According to this understanding individuals are increasingly invited to scrutinize themselves, according to principles of autonomy, self-realisation and self-mastery. It is such an invitation that brings a Foucaultian analysis into contact with the extended reflexivity thesis, for the phenomena of self-scrutiny and self-reflexivity overlap a great deal. The important critical difference is that for Foucaultian analyses, the reflexive process is embedded in the dominant discourses of a particular social order, rather than being capable of standing apart from and reworking them. As the examples of employee-identity illustrates there is argued to be a hijacking of self-reflexivity by state and corporate powers with the aim of ensuring a docile and compliant consumer-worker-citizen.

Criticisms of Foucault's over-determinism lead to a re-emergence of questions of agency and the possibility of reflexive autonomy. Despite offering a compelling critical inversion of the extended reflexivity thesis, modernist assumptions concerning the 'self' as origin of an awareness which transcends cultural constructions and interpolations resurface. Foucaultian analyses tend to do one of two contradictory things: either they deny the subject any interiority at all, frustrating a meaningful examination of the psychic power people invest in, and form attachments, to particular regimes of truth, forms of governmentality or techniques of self over another, which presumably play a key part in social differentiation; or they offer the hope of a critical self-reflexivity as an implicit or explicit ideal, whilst critical of present manifestations of it as historically contingent discursive constructions. Furthermore, this invitation to self-mastery is as in danger of slipping into gendered and class-based notions of the bounded subject as those at the fore of the extended reflexivity thesis. The search for a model of selfhood which acknowledges and theorizes the investments and attachments which mutually bind self-identity and social structure, without valorizing processes of self-reflexivity, leads to an exploration of the concept of narcissism from a psychodynamic perspective.

Sociological accounts of narcissism parallel a Foucaultian emphasis upon the appropriation of intimate processes of subjectivity by dominant socio-cultural processes. A psychoanalytic framework brings a different inflection to the psychological processes involved however. According to this approach, early interactions with significant others forms the basis for one's psychological make-up amidst complex process of psychical inter-penetration. The unconscious internalization of these early relations forms the basis of a self and continues to shape those relations across the life-span. The particular relational dynamics involved in the aetiology of narcissistic disorders have long been highlighted and continue to be refined in clinical literature.

Christopher Lasch and others have argued that the social changes we are now familiar with reproduce these dynamics at the level of individual families. They undermine the relations necessary to develop an individu-ated sense of self, 'fixing' the psyche in a narcissistic nexus into which the demands and seductions of late capitalist society steps, consolidating nar-cissistic disorders and initiating a cycle of narcissism as narcissistic adults go on to bring up narcissistic children. The characteristics of narcissism are thus argued to be familiar aspects of contemporary consumer culture: fear of death and old age, constant solicitation of the admiration of others, fear of dependence and so on. Some aspects of narcissism seem closely allied to what is elsewhere referred to as the reflexive project of selfhood such as pervasive self-scrutiny, a concern with self-actualisation, and a contractual approach to relationships. It is at this point of conjuncture that a Laschian analysis appears to invert self-reflexivity by portraying it as a pathological, disempowered response to a dominant social structure, draining the concept of the balanced ambivalence with which it is invested by Giddens and others.

The wedding of psychoanalysis and critical theory in Lasch's analysis, though by no means novel, serves as an example of the possibility of con-ceptualizing psychic life as it interpenetrates changing social structures without losing sight of either. Despite the potential of a creative use of object relations theory however, Lasch, like earlier theorists of psychoso-cial fragmentation, has been criticized for an excessively nostalgic view of the past and an excessively pessimistic view of the present in his broader cultural analyses. Consequently it is argued that he does not give ade-quate ground to the spaces for agency opened up by individuals and groups in the fissures of an eroding order, nor to the differential impact of the culture he decimates so thoroughly. Furthermore, in the denigration of the psychodynamics of narcissism, he has been perceived to have reproduced the normative ideal of masculine individualism at the expense of the psychological value of relatedness. Lasch's account leads us to a more specific affirmation of what should be *valued* in the struggle for selfhood perhaps more explicitly and more thoroughly than most accounts covered in this book, but it is uncertain whether the problems which accompany such an affirmation outweigh its benefits.

While certain elements of all of the approaches discussed are of value, none of them alone capture the complexity of modern identity, and all of them contain some vital absences. The final chapter takes up the analysis of selfhood in terms of the notion of extended reflexivity again. It is an attempt to explore in more detail the social structuring and cultural situatedness of self-reflexive processes to create a more particularized account of the nature of contemporary identities. The importance of a global economic and employment structure is discussed, with an accompanying return to the issue of polarization, and the relationship between identity and the social allocation of resources is reassessed. What emerges in this final chapter is a heavily qualified version of the 'reflexive project of selfhood'. The specific limitations argued to be inseparable from that conceptualization draw to some degree on the arguments and critiques raised in the previous chapters, but the account of identity outlined here also reiterates some of their limitations, and attempts to move beyond them.

Acknowledgements

Thanks to all my colleagues in the School of Applied Social Sciences at the University of Brighton for providing a convivial and dialogical environment in which to work; and to my old colleagues at Nottingham Trent who offered guidance, passion and inspiration stretching back to my undergraduate days. Thanks to my old friends, particularly Mat, Steve, Rik, Bobby, Fraser and John who still know how to get by in good faith and get together in good spirits. And in memory of Darren Cossou and all that he was in that short time. Thanks for the support of Viv and Steve Adams, and Sam and Eve along the way, who through an abundance of love; care; humility; good faith and healthy scepticism have provided living examples of the best kind of situated selfhood I can only aspire to. Thanks especially to Clare, Amelie and Dylan, whose love makes it all happen day in, day out. All this taken together is the guiding light behind everything that goes into this book; its shortcomings however, are all my own.

Only through the accounts of others have we come to know of our unity. On the thread of our history as told by the others, year by year, we end up resembling ourselves.

Gaston Bachelard

1

Self and Social Change

The story of social change in the late twentieth and early twenty-first centuries is a complex and contested one. It is worth stating at the outset that attempting to separate out social changes is an analytic process. As soon as we pull them apart they snap back into a complex inter-related whole. 'Social change is both a specific and a multifaceted phenomenon' states one commentator (Jordan, 2002: 300). It might be fruitful to consider the elements of social change described below in a way similar to Donna Haraway (1997). Although she categorizes change slightly differently, the main areas are described as multiple 'horns' of a 'wormhole'. Haraway's language is characteristically vivid here; the metaphor of a wormhole is taken to indicate how aspects of each area of social change appear and disappear in the fabric of one another (Jordan, 2002: 292). Thus it is impossible to conceive of social change in its totality, but inaccurate to consider it as made up of discreet and compatible units.

Take one example of a relatively mundane development in social communication, video conferencing, which is still an emerging technology at the time of writing. We might want to place this in a social change category of 'communication'. However, its central function might yet be in transforming the workplace, making travel less necessary and home-based employment more of a possibility. So we are tempted to put it in the 'work' category. However, the fact that people can communicate in the same physical 'space' whilst being in different spaces and time zones may suggest a profound change in our experience of time/space. So maybe video conferencing should go in a 'time/space' category? The same applies to many examples. Thus it is worth remembering that what are discussed as separate social changes and categories of social change relate closely to each other and co-exist in complex ways.

Despite complexities and controversies, social transformations have repeatedly been flagged up using the following terms and ideas to indicate (or contest) the general shift to post-traditional society: globalization, technology, the body, reflexivity, time and space, homogenization, transnational corporations, individualization, polarization and gender.

Globalization

> There has been a 'globalisation' of economic, social and political relationships which have undermined the coherence, wholeness and unity of individual societies.
>
> (John Urry, 1989: 97)

The globe as an organizing principle entered the popular imagination in the early 1960s with Mcluhan's vivid portrayal of a 'global village' (McLuhan, 1964). Globalization has since become the chosen term of many social theorists to capture the multiple, dialectical dynamics and outcomes of recent social change. At its most basic, globalization refers to 'the multiplicity of linkages and interconnections that transcend the nation-state (and by implication the societies) which make up the modern world system' (McGrew, 1992: 65). The movement of people, finance, ideas, goods, pollution, services and so on beyond the boundaries of the nation-state has supposedly exposed the inherent fragility of those boundaries, creating frenetic, voluminous networks of interdependency that criss-cross the globe. Many of the changes we are about to discuss could easily be argued to move in the explanatory orbit of globalization. The term has been incorporated into accounts of modernism and post-modernism, both optimistic (creative hybridity, global dialogue) and pessimistic (Americanism, imperialism), and is commonly argued to have political, cultural, economic and personal dimensions (Albrow, 1996; Giddens, 1999; Held, 1995; Robertson, 1992).

Why then, is this book not called 'Self and Globalization'? Globalization may often be a handy and illustrative heuristic for a multitude of inter-related changes. Furthermore, most, if not all, of the accounts summarized in subsequent chapters accept globalizing tendencies as the implicit markers of change which underpin accounts of transformations in self-identity. However, it is one of those terms where their meaning becomes assumed through popular assimilation, taken-for-granted to the point where it suggests and supports any number of claims. There is a danger of becoming blinded by the apparent descriptive power of 'globalization' as a theory of everything. Many have argued that what we call globalization is in fact the continuation of base structures of capitalism or the power of nation-states (Gilpin, 1987; Golding, 2000; Jamieson, 1991). It can also obscure the localized, differentiated and divisive ways in which multiple changes combine and are experienced. Thus the term 'social change' is preferred. That said it is informative to critically consider many of the following changes in relation to a broad process of globalization.

Technological change

> If there were no railway to overcome distances, my child would never have left his home town and I should not need the telephone in order to hear his voice.
>
> (Sigmund Freud, 2002 [1930]: 26)

Developments in communication technology are seen to be a key element in radical social upheaval, and are central to most assertions of the reality of globalization. The development of the printing press, maritime technology allowing well-tread shipping routes and the development of the mechanical clock, are amongst the innovations often claimed to be neglected technologies of communication and information in earlier historical periods. Much later, from the 1850s in the West, the telegraph network expanded rapidly to cover thousands of miles and carry millions of messages, many of them across the Atlantic between the United States and Europe, heralding an oft-forgotten era of 'globalization' (Mackay, 2002; Standage, 1990; Thrift, 1990). The steam powered rail network transformed transportation and with it our sense of distance in the same era.

As modernity developed, particularly with the expansion of industrialization and capitalism, techniques of production were revolutionized, bringing enormous interlocking changes to the nature of work, communication, public administration, surveillance, domestic life and transportation. The early- to mid-twentieth century saw rapid growth in the use of communication and information technology alongside production techniques, ushering in an era of mass-production and consumption. Key products have included the car and other motor transport, the telephone, the proliferation of radio and television reception and usage amounting to 'mass communication' (Thompson, 1995). More recent 'high-tech' developments in the late twentieth and early twenty-first centuries, though by no means accessible to all, include an increase in home computer ownership, internet and email, mass air travel, expanded use of mobile phones and portable computers (Gergen, 1991), bio-technological innovation affecting numerous aspects of life from appearance, physical and mental health and reproduction, to advanced surveillance, security and global positioning technologies. An effective means of producing and distributing goods, and of informing a mass audience of their availability, desirability and necessity are all argued to be vital components leading to a radicalization of social change currently showing no signs of flagging. There is much common ground in acknowledging the actuality of these developments, but significant differences in interpreting their social impact. Arguments abound, for example, about the extent to which technological change overcomes or maintains social inequalities, and critics of technological determinism have made a strong case for considering technology as embedded in social, cultural and political changes rather than simply driving them (e.g. Pile, 2002). Relatedly, the extent to which technologies are utilized as forces of subjection and/or reflexive self-production informs arguments made in all subsequent chapters.

The body

Technological change is not just something which happens 'out there'. Developments in technology have been central to shifts in our understanding of what it is to be human, and particularly corporeality, and the boundaries between body, nature and environment. Few would disagree that changes in technology reach into and transform our understanding of the body. In recent years, for example, body-building and fitness technologies have been developed parallel to increases in gym membership and equipment ownership. Such socio-technological developments have been argued to have a profound impact on embodied experience in early twenty-first century cultures (Dutton, 1995). The social proliferation of plastic surgery is another example of the ways in which the body has been opened up (sometimes literally) to technological change, transforming our notion of the body, and the boundaries between natural and artificial, human and non-human.

More generally, the body has taken a more central role in social theory after a history of neglect stemming back to an entrenched, masculinist, mind-body dualism in which the body tended to be viewed as the inferior, encumbering partner (Burkitt, 1991). A rejection of dualism and more 'embodied' accounts of human activity have led to an interest in the 'social body' (Crossley, 2001; Turner, 1984; Schilling, 1993): how the body is regulated, inscribed, empowered, produced by, and productive of social convention (e.g. Bourdieu, 1977; Butler, 1990; Foucault, 1979; Elias, 1978), particularly in relation to the intersections between technology, media, gender identity and embodiment (Haraway, 1997; Henwood et al., 2001; Kirkup et al., 2000; Zylinska, 2002). Theorizing the relationship between change and the body is a challenging and contested field of social theory which takes us well beyond a narrow focus on technology. Although there is not the scope in this book to encompass anything like the range of arguments in this field, theorizations of the body will be relevant to the discussions in the chapters that follow.

Time-space relations

Alongside the changes already outlined, it is commonly claimed that there is also a reconfiguration of two of the most fundamental dimensions of human existence: time and space (e.g. Castells, 1999; Giddens, 1991; Haraway, 1997; Harvey, 1989; Thompson, 1995). The way this reconfiguration is expressed varies. Giddens argues that social relations begin to *transcend* the contexts of time and space which were previously bound to locale, for example, whilst Harvey claims that 'we have been experiencing...an intense phase of time-space *compression*' (Harvey, 1989: 284; emphasis added). Despite their differences, both authors see changes in the time-space relationship allowing for a 'complex co-ordination' of social relations 'across large tracts of time-space' (Giddens, 1990: 19). Contexts for action may no longer be defined by a sense of time and space which is inseparable from the physicalities of that context. Physical presence, for example, becomes an unnecessary element in social interaction:

The advent of modernity increasingly tears space away from place by fostering relations between 'absent' others, locationally distant from any given situation of face-to-face interaction. In conditions of modernity place becomes increasingly *phantasmagoric*: that is to say, locales are thoroughly penetrated by and shaped in terms of social influences quite distant from them. (1990: 19)

Social interaction ordered by localized, relatively self-contained structures of time, space and place, is now potentially disrupted. Thus *time-space distanciation*, to use Giddens's term, further breaks the hold of tradition over social relations and the formation of identity. It is the foundation for 'the articulation of social relations across wide spans of time-space' (Giddens, 1991: 20). In this sense it is the essential cause and consequence of the other dynamics which propel modern society into a post-traditional era. The reconfiguration of time and space is central to many portrayals of social change and their impact upon subjectivity, whether couched in the terminology of psychosocial fragmentation, post-modernism or social regulation, and is a central tenet in the extended reflexivity thesis, discussed in chapter three.

Homogenization, difference and hybridity

The notion of globalization conveys what appear to be contradictory images of homogeneity, difference and hybridity. Homogenization is sometimes claimed to be an outcome of the dissolution of tradition, developments in communication and the continuation of capitalist relations. The 'timeless time...and the space of flows' (Castells, 1999: 405) opened up by such changes encourages dialogue that results in an increased sameness:

The living conditions of various nations, classes and individuals are becoming increasingly similar. In the past, different continents, cultures, ranks, trades and professions inhabited different worlds, but now they more and more live in one world. People today hear similar things, see similar things, travel back and forth between similar places for the daily grind. (Beck and Beck-Gernsheim, 2002: 174)

Other 'big' theorists, such as Bauman, also appeal to sameness as a potential form of universal humanism with a global reach, though are cautiously optimistic at best that it will be realized:

for the first time in human history everybody's self-interest and ethical principles of mutual respect and care point in the same direction and demand the same strategy. From a curse, globalization may yet turn into a blessing: 'humanity' never had a better chance. (Bauman, 2004: 88)

A different but similarly positive line of argument claims that out of a basic liberal uniformity, such as the free-exchange of information allowed by the internet, new and creative forms of difference and distinction can readily emerge (Wiley, 1999; Lupton, 2000). Building on proliferating communication and information structures, increased contact with others leads us to a kind of constant cultural summit, where differences are acknowledged, explored, and melded into innovative hybrids. Despite the apparent contrast, hopes for the increased recognition of difference rest upon similar ideals of acceptance, open communication and flexibility to the more optimistic theories of homogeneity. Such ideas are directly challenged by accounts of psychosocial fragmentation (chapter two) and cultural narcissism (chapter five), which envisage the dissolution of tradition as a disintegration of self, ripe for colonization by the forces of capital and state. Such forces, it is argued, if not involved in more explicitly divisive practices, appropriate humanism, multiculturalism and the 'acceptance of difference' as individualized commodities, further reinforcing a sense of alienation. Foucaultian analyses, discussed in chapter four, take a similarly critical approach, deconstructing what are claimed to be the fallacies of neo-liberal individualization, which rest on the optimistic proclamations of globalization. Such analyses are wary of arguing that a 'true' or core selfhood is at stake however. The extended reflexivity thesis (chapter three), on the other hand, offers qualified support for the psychological benefits inherent in the inter-relating processes of homogenization, difference and hybridity.

Transnational corporations

> The corporation's dramatic rise to dominance is one of the remarkable events of modern history.
>
> (Joel Bakan, 2004: 5)

Homogeneity is interpreted by more pessimistic commentators as an appropriation of the channels of information, products and ideas by powerful corporations and nations in new forms of imperialism (e.g. Schiller, 1976). Amongst such arguments the spread of transnational or multinational corporations (TNCs or MNCs) is commonly emphasized as a form of social change (e.g. Ritzer, 1993). Joel Bakan's recent account of corporate history and power opens with the following:

> Today, corporations govern our life. They determine what we eat, what we watch, what we wear, where we work, and what we do. We are inescapably surrounded by their culture, iconography, and ideology. And, like the church and monarchy in other times, they posture as infallible and omnipotent, glorifying themselves in imposing buildings and elaborate displays. (Bakan, 2004: 5)

Bakan's description allows us to stand back from what has undoubtedly become one of the most pervasive institutions in a relatively short historical period. In neo-liberal defences of the benefits of globalization, and in critical theories of globalization and anti-globalization, TNCs are never far from the conceptual frontline. They are seen to be integral to all the social changes discussed so far. In neo-liberal accounts, TNCs bring the liberating message of the market to every dark alley in the global network, ushering in freedom, opportunity, enterprise and democracy (e.g. Leadbeater, 2004). For critics, they impose the might of the wealthy, maintain a growing global underclass of poverty and hopelessness, and wreck the environment in an unholy pact with the modern state (e.g Klein, 2001). Either way TNCs facilitate, and are constituted by, global flows of communication, transportation, finance and labour. Thus in the constant localized, experiential reconfiguration of these interacting processes, the corporation is a forceful presence in the dynamics of social change.

The role of the corporation has warranted varied attention in accounts of social change and selfhood. For accounts of psychosocial fragmentation and cultural pathology, capitalist social relations and their institutions are seen to be primarily responsible for the ills of the age (Laing, 1967; Lasch, 1979; Marcuse, 1968). For accounts of extended reflexivity, capitalism and corporatism is subsumed under more general societal definitions, such as post-traditional, risk or network society, liquid, high or late modernity (Bauman, 2000; Beck, 1992; Castells, 1996; Giddens, 1990, 1994); some arguments have suggested that the power of contemporary formations of capitalism to stratify human relations and life chances is underplayed as a result (e.g. Bradley, 1996). In Foucaultian analyses and the more general turn to language/culture, capitalism is also in danger of being marginalized according to some critics (Rojek and Turner, 2000); the final chapter of this book is largely an attempt to reconcile suitably complex accounts of embodied, reflexive social identity formation with an appreciation of social structure substantially marked by divisions of class and gender which define the stubbornly capitalist organization of social existence.

Individualization

For Beck, Bauman and others, globalization develops hand-in-hand with *individualization* (Beck, 2004; Beck and Beck-Gernsheim, 2002; Bauman, 2001) and the term has gone on to have reasonable explanatory reach in explaining contemporary processes at work in forming self-identity (e.g. Furlong and Cartmel, 1997). Stripped of tradition, time/space, class categories and so on, the basic unit of social reproduction is now claimed to be the individual. The individualized basis for life's trajectory and all its associated opportunities and dangers set against an abstract social system of rewards and punishments is conceived, somewhat paradoxically, as the only basis for our shared reality. As with other aspects of social change, the degree of optimism invested in individualization varies amongst those who utilize it. Beck, for example, sees individualization as an important descriptive category which poses certain problems for contemporary society and those seeking to understand it, but also numerous opportunities, and asserts the need for empirical study, whereas Bauman is more ambivalent, Giddens sometimes less so (e.g. Beck, 2004; Bauman, 2004; Giddens, 1992).

The individualization thesis still recognizes socially structured inequality. However, in spite of growing inequalities between the rich and poor, class categories no longer offer a basis for solidarity. According to this thesis class is one of a number of 'zombie concepts' – like family and neighbourhood – which are way-markers of an older modernity; they should really be dead, but continue to shuffle along the sociological landscape (Beck and Beck-Gernsheim, 2002: 202–213; Beck, 2004: 11–61). The category of class helped make sense of common experiences in the past; for the working classes a sense of shared suffering and class solidarity facilitated a 'defence mechanism of social inclusion' for its members (Boyne, 2002: 121). However, detraditionalization is seen to fragment cohesive affiliations and displace the commonality of experiences which characterized identity. Giddens refers to this process as 'disembedding': 'the "lifting out" of social relations from local contexts and their rearticulation across indefinite tracts of time-space' (Giddens, 1991: 18). Vitally, re-embedding occurs on an individualized basis.

Amidst the fluidity, fragmentation and disorganization of previously binding social structures, the personal biography becomes the blueprint for making sense of one's life-course rather than broader affiliations such as class, and combines forcefully with the process of reflexivity: 'Individualization of life situations and processes thus means that biographies become *self-reflexive*; socially prescribed biography is transformed into biography that is self-produced and continues to be produced' (Beck, 1992: 135). The concept of individualization is, in a sense, an attempt to move beyond the paradigm of psychosocial fragmentation, and occupies the same analytical and political landscape as notions of extended reflexivity. As such it is a theoretical companion of the processes discussed in chapter three and referred to in the related critical discussion found there and in later chapters.

Polarization

A number of contemporary commentators see polarization as an outcome of a globalized economy balanced in favour of maintaining capital-rich economies, regions and individuals. The monopolization of capital in the hands of a few, and the deregulation of its global movement, combines with intense global competition for investment between nations and regions; coupled with a growing workforce, wage control, the erosion of union power and welfarism creates a context rife for polarization (Bauman, 1998; Bradley, 1996; Bradley *et al.*, 2000; Golding, 2000). Polarization is not just about a simplistic distinction between upper and working class, as Marx sometimes envisaged it, or even between upper and under class. Recent research suggests that inequalities cross-cut one another to produce positions of inequality. Thus Bradley claims that 'the economic changes which spring from the global restructuring of the economy have effects on all four dynamics [class, gender, age, race] of stratification. These combine to produce growing disparities between privileged and underprivileged groups' (Bradley, 1996: 210).

In terms of health and access to healthcare, working practices, educational opportunity and life expectancy, many surveys and studies support the notion of an increasing polarization in the lifestyles of populations. Research in the United Kingdom by the Smith Institute, with a sample of 16,000, studied the relationship between social background and achievement. They found that the 'opportunities gap' between those from different social backgrounds was no different for those born in 1958 and 1970, suggesting that 'today's 30-year-olds are still haunted by disadvantage and poverty at birth' (reported in *The Guardian*, July 12, 2000). In terms of 'information structures', home access to the internet may be a small example of stratification. The number of UK households with internet access has doubled in the last year to 6.5 million (25%). However, of the poorest third of the population, access varies between 3% and 6%, while for the more affluent, it reaches about 48%. There are further regional variations. One report agreed that there was a growing internet economy, suggesting parallels with Lash and Urry's information and communication structures. However, 'if you don't have access to the skills and the knowledge to thrive in that economy because of where you live, or how much money you earn, you won't be included' (Office of National Statistics report, in *The Guardian*, July 11, 2000). The economist Larry Elliot pointed out that as well as an increasing income gap between and within rich and poor countries, there is also a growing difference in life expectancy (*The Guardian*, June 29, 2000).

Accounts have detailed the lifestyles of the underpriveleged: the 'wasted lives' of refugees and impoverished migrants (Bauman, 2004); the urban slums, 'warehousing the twenty-first century's surplus humanity' (Davis, 2004: 28), total populations of which was conservatively estimated at 921 million in 2001, or a third of the global urban population (2004: 13); or the formal and informal working poor, who's working lives only serve to perpetuate their continual state of impoverishment (Ehrenreich, 2002). Others give accounts of life at the other end: the rich and powerful, increasingly hidden behind gated communities and moving through secure, defended spaces (Blakely and Snyder, 1997; Caldeira, 1996), to the point where 'some odd optical property of our highly polarized society makes the poor almost invisible to their economic superiors' (Ehrenreich, 2002: 216). Foucaultian analyses are particularly attuned to how the techniques embodied in the micropractices of everyday life – such as public surveillance, architecture, government health programmes – maintain and deepen social divisions, discussed in chapter four. How the global spread of capital, in particular, ensures a planetary consolidation of positions in the polarization of life-chances is remarkably absent from many accounts of social change and the formation of selves however, an issue considered in the final chapter.

Gender

It is commonly claimed that one of the most important transformations to have marked the last half-century is our understanding of gender, the nature of male and female identity and particularly the relations between them. As a question of selfhood, the issue of gender will be central to discussion in later chapters. As a dimension of broad social change however, it warrants a brief summary here.

Feminist theory has been central to critical social theory for over a century. It is wrong to associate feminism's achievements solely with our understanding of gender; it has been central to many if not all of the debates in the last half-century, such as the nature of social power, the usefulness of psychoanalysis as a social theory, the shift from structuralism to post-structuralism and the definition of what can be deemed political. However, feminism has been vital in unsettling social understandings of gender and the social structure they maintain and rely upon. Though papering over the fissures which increasingly define the development of feminisms, it can at least be summarized that feminism has long held 'that the social world is pervaded by gender, that men and women are socialized into distinct patterns of relating to each other, and that masculine and feminine senses of self are tied to asymmetrical relations of gender power' (Elliott, 2001: 19). There is not the space here to offer a historical overview but part of the feminist project has been to uncover the history of gender positions and the shifting gendered relations of power hidden in patriarchal histories.

But gender is being discussed here under the rubric of social change. So what has changed? That deceptively innocent question has been at least as fraught with argument, contradiction and uncertainty as any other area of supposed social transformation in the late twentieth and early twenty-first century. Many feminists assert the continuation of gender power either in long-existing or novel forms: the persistence of domestic violence and relational imbalance (Jamieson, 1998; Walby, 1990), the structuring of life chances cross-cut with other inequalities (Bradley, 1996; Skeggs, 1997, 2003) or continuing discursive and material regulation. Here the 'losers' in the polarization game appear to be gendered too (Adkins, 2002).

However some strands of post-structuralist and/or post-modern feminism see gender roles changing broadly in line with the social changes we have discussed so far. Here again a surface consensus is discernible across a number of theoretical traditions. Amidst the erosion of tradition, the collapse of established time-space configurations, changes in the workforce, cultural communication, reflexivity and individualization, gender becomes a more plastic positioning. Gender is in fact treated as a form of tradition; thus is can no longer be taken for granted, unequivocally enacted as an accepted power play.

Such claims may be expected in the broad, optimistic theorizing of a figure such as Giddens but they are also offered support from some of the proponents of the more fashionable, critical edge of feminist theory. Take Butler's post-structuralist notion of gender as a performance (Butler, 1990), for example. Gender as something we *do* is also gender as something we can *undo* and Butler has placed considerable emphasis upon the political value of disrupting traditional gender identities via a transgression and blurring of their boundaries. Butler's arguments are most readily conceived in post-traditional setting saturated by reflexivity and fluid communication structures (McNay, 1999), though she has since explicitly countered more voluntarist readings of her work (Butler, 1993). Issues of gender and gender bias thus surface in the critical account of extended reflexivity in chapter three, but are integral to the arguments made in all subsequent chapters. The extent to which social changes have been theorized in terms of gendered subjectivities, and the consequences when they are, is a prime concern.

Of course there are other changes highlighted by informed scholars, activists, journalists and so on; and there are debates still to be had over both the extent to which they are seen to facilitate a substantial qualitative break from the social order supposedly left behind (e.g. Harvey, 1989; Jamieson, 1998; Golding, 2000). There is not the space here to acknowledge arguments and approaches I am aware of but remain absent, and I can only offer apologies in advance for what is beyond that awareness. Many changes which are bound up tightly with the conceptualization of identity have purposefully been put off until they are explored in later chapters, but that is not an attempt to deny that what is missing has value.

What does all this mean for the self?

The identity configuration of a complex industrial society is likely to be fragmented and confused, and analysing it an even more speculative venture.

(Stevens, 1983: 71)

The other half of the title of this book is the 'self'. If we were concerned with how difficult it was to pin something like 'social change' down even for a moment's observation, then the self is up there with 'culture' and 'class' when it comes to evasive and problematic terms. Sociological accounts of self are vast and varied. In recent years there has been a proliferation in interest in 'identity', and its study has become an integral part of many undergraduate and postgraduate sociology and psychology courses. There has also been much time spent on attempts to differentiate between terms such as identity (and identification), self, psyche, subject, selfhood and personhood (e.g. Jenkins, 1996). The two dominant terms are self and identity. The *Penguin Dictionary of Sociology* defines identity as 'the sense of self, of personhood, of what kind of person one is'. Fine as far as it goes, but this offers no clues to the extent to which identity is a work of imagination, external imposition, or natural consequence of other components 'behind' identity. What, most pointedly, is responsible for the genesis of a sense of identity? It suggests another aspect of the self exists apart from one's identity. Perhaps that is where 'self' becomes salient (there is no separate entry for 'self' in the *Penguin* dictionary). This term might be best thought of as all the components of the individual (it is difficult not to fall back on one of the contentious terms in describing them) taken together: one's identity, the internal source of the sense of one's identity and anything else purported to be involved, such as instincts. Giddens conflates the terms into the hybrid 'self-identity', whilst defining it in a sense more akin to identity: 'the self as reflexively understood by the individual in terms of his or her biography' (Giddens, 1991: 244), whilst Jenkins defines 'self' on its own in very similar terms (Jenkins, 1996: 29–30). Jenkins prefers the term 'selfhood', as he feels its usage 'minimizes the tendency towards reification implicit in "*the* self" and emphasises the processual character of selfhood' (1996: 52).

Whilst I sympathize with Jenkins's desire to hold on to a dynamic conceptualization of self, I do not think it is necessary to adhere to one or another term; to do so itself runs the risk of reification by repetition. Amidst the confusion and conceptual overlapping, and no doubt to the chagrin of scholars of self/identity everywhere, I use the terms more or less interchangeably. This is to avoid repetition but also because the discussion of self in this book is inseparable from the social, cultural, relational, discursive fabric in which it is constituted; in this sense there are few resting places where it can become reified, whatever we call it. Differences in terminology will be discussed only when they are perceived to be salient in specific accounts.

It is perhaps worth recalling Berger and Luckmann's (1967) dialectic which allows an initial positioning between constructionism and essentialism, by viewing 'the self as a social construction, but nevertheless a centre for a degree of agency once constructed' (Butt, 2004: 125). Versions of this reframing of Marx's 'people make history but not in conditions of their own making' (paraphrased here) have gained momentum in recent frustrations with constructionism (e.g. Butler, 1997; Hekman, 2000). There are problems too with this definition, but at least it flags up my intention to hold the binaries of self/society, inner/outer, or indeed mind/body in tension, rather than accept them in a simplistic fashion. This is nothing new, certainly not in sociology, where the analyses of Goffman, Mead, Garfinkel, Simmell and countless others have again and again revealed the mutual integration of self and cultural norm or social structure.

The problem, of course, lies in the extent to which the relationship between these two entities, which only exist in relation to each other, can be adequately conceptualized to account for all manner of phenomenon, from the nature of self-experience to the possibility of social transformation. It impinges on what we can say about the nature and structure of the self and its relationship to social structures and supposed changes in both. Thus it is this problem which is thought to be more salient than the particular terminology. It is worth stating in advance though that I do not think it is feasible to eschew all assumptions of interiority in the name of constructionism and/or in fear of the sin of essentialism. Winnicott delineates in the following all that can be said for certain at this stage: 'of every individual who has reached to the state of being a unit with a limiting membrane and an outside and an inside, it can be said that there is an inner reality to that individual' (cited in Davis and Wallbridge, 1981: 33). Of course there are points of contention even here in the assertion of an 'inner'; nonetheless it is a guiding assumption which will be put to the test in the chapters to come.

Questions of general definition aside, much of this book is concerned with the more specific phenomenon of 'self-reflexivity'. The term has been popularized by Giddens, and he perceives there to be two levels of reflexivity. The first is a general 'reflexive monitoring of action' which is 'characteristic of all human action' (Giddens, 1990: 36). It is the ability to reflect on what we do, and as such is the basis of self-awareness or self-consciousness. The second form, the reflexivity of 'modern social life' extends the process 'such that thought and action are constantly refracted back upon one another' (1990: 36). Only here is reflexivity radicalized in its application to 'all aspects of human life' which 'of course includes reflection upon the nature of reflection itself'. Giddens's identity is fundamentally a social one, and the conventions and traditions in which it was once forged fall away amidst the corrosive influence of extended self-reflexivity; no aspect of our nature can remain in the shadows. The exact nature of the self-reflexive process, how it is integrated into a broader psychological substrate, and the nature and dynamics of other 'components' of that substrate is far from settled however. Much of the book's discussion is concerned with the formulation of self-reflexivity as it serves as a useful entry point into arguments over the nature of embodied psychical dynamics and their intertwining with social structures. This in no way accedes to the salience self-reflexivity is granted in the overall model of self by Giddens and others, as later critical discussion will make clear.

Self and social change

It is not difficult to imagine how some of the consequences of the changes I have outlined above have been formulated in relation to the self. Even without the benefit of a comprehensive psychological theory one might conclude that the self is likely to be troubled by the experience of uncertainty and a lack of control over events suggested here. It seems reasonable to agree with Zygmunt Bauman in asserting that the modern subject necessarily 'swims in the sea of uncertainty' (Bauman, 1993: 222). We (may) have an expanding prerogative to choose but the *basis* for such choice is increasingly problematic. Tradition loses its salience irretrievably and the self is disembedded, separating the individual from the meaningful, if relatively unquestioned, context it had in previous times been immersed in. Is the individual really disembedded from its social and cultural moorings? Does disembedding amount to new-found freedoms? How are these freedoms distributed socially? What are our options for re-embedding? What form does power take in the contemporary reconfiguration of human relations? These questions manifest at the heart of our understanding of self in relation to social change and are explored in the following chapters. It is hopefully apparent that these are not simply academic questions but potentially of profound personal and social relevance.

2

The Diminished Self

In our liquid modern times the world around us is sliced into poorly coordinated fragments while our individual lives are cut into a succession of ill-connected episodes.

(Zygmunt Bauman, 2004: 12–13)

That we are enduring a sustained period of psychosocial fragmentation is an assumption running through social theory like seaside lettering through a stick of rock. Its premise is one of the pillars of modern sociology, an abiding concern from the 'classic' approaches of Marx, Weber, Simmel, Tionnes and Durkheim, via the rise of critical theory to the contours of post-modern theory and its critical reception. This chapter will briefly survey a handful of these accounts, which are taken to be representative of this much broader tendency. Particular emphasis will be placed upon contemporary accounts which still rely heavily on a notion of psychosocial fragmentation. Though such notions will be problematized extensively in all of the chapters that follow, it is nonetheless important to first clarify the supposed nature of social and individual disintegration as it has been understood by prominent scholars.

As is often the nature with widely held beliefs, the precise logic of that fragmentation tends to be taken for granted, although the thesis is revitalized by successive generations of social theorists (Bradley, 1996: 207). The conceptualization of psychosocial fragmentation may already be apparent from some of the most common interpretations made of the changes discussed in the first chapter. At work, play and rest, in relations and in private, *Gesselschaft* formed an omnipresent context of meaning in which the individual is slotted relatively smoothly and functionally. The conduits for these meanings are the thick and firm nodes of kin and community which enmesh subjectivity in their prescriptive web from cradle to grave. Consequently each and every person can navigate a well-defined course through life in tightly-knit communities; their 'individuality' is neither more nor less than their lived experience of a long-established role.

If we attempt to predict the nature of modern societies in contrast, an account of psychosocial fragmentation is already hinted at. The modern era might be defined as *lacking* in communal bonds, extended family ties and clearly defined social groups, abandoning us to the individualized pursuit of meaning. Whereas the authority and legitimacy of tradition underpins a communal basis for meaningful identities, the dissolution of tradition and the fragmentation of social bonds *undermine* the communal foundations of 'our sense of ourselves as integrated subjects' (Hall, 1992: 275). Many accounts of psychosocial fragmentation build upon this basic interpretation, although the terminology varies. *Gesselschaft*, atomization, anomie, and neurasthenia are all familiar terms from the sociological canon accounting for social change as a turning away from organic, communal ties and towards a landscape of distinct and isolate individuals (Toennies, 1957 [1887]; Weber, 1930; Durkheim, 1897; Simmel, 1950 [1903]).

Three key assumptions can be discerned in accounts of psychosocial fragmentation. The first is that we are in a period of exceptional social change; the second is that changes are interpreted substantially in terms of loss; the third is that such loss is considered in terms of an interrelated social and psychological impact. So, for example, urbanization and industrialism created mass employment and cosmopolitanism but fostered competition and superficial association between people and a heightened sense of ennui and alienation; new technologies have allowed mobility and communication at a distance but this has in fact pushed people further and further apart in their everyday lives; face-to-face communication becomes rarer or at least rationalized and commodified, leaving the self dislocated and alone. These assumptions underpin the selection of accounts that will now be considered.

The original theorization of psychosocial fragmentation reaches back at least as far as the mid-nineteenth century, with the work of Tocqueville and Toennies (Tocqueville, 1835–1840; Toennies, 1887). Sociology took up the mantle of identifying the fragmentary impact of transformative social changes of capitalism, industrialism, urbanism and secularism upon the individual. To name but a few key concepts from that period, besides Toennies' *Germeinschaft* and *Gesselschaft* there is Durkheim's *anomie*, Marx's *alienation*, Simmel's *neurasthenia* and Weber's *rationalization*; all terms which deal extensively with the perceived negative impact of social transformations upon individuals. For all, the separation of subjectivity from a previously more integrated social fabric is seen as key in some sense. In the majority of cases, the theorists of more recent social changes and historical periods discussed in this book are best thought of as continuing this tradition. Social theory during the mid-twentieth century invigorated the psychosocial fragmentation thesis with contemporary detail and an increased urgency as modernity was perceived to be developing rapidly and destroying much in its path.

Marcuse and Laing

A vital influence upon the debate about the inter-relationship between a rapidly developing capitalist modernity and identity was the work of the Frankfurt School, particularly the writing of Herbert Marcuse. His book *One-Dimensional Man* (1964) 'is perhaps the fullest and most concrete development of these themes within the tradition of Frankfurt School Critical Theory' (Kellner, 1991: xix). Vitally, the book was an attempt to critically engage with the malaise of capitalist social relations as it was experienced in subjective awareness, revealing Marcuse's phenomenological roots and reflecting social theory's willingness to grapple issues of social and psychological interpenetration.

For Marcuse, the self is effectively repressed not by 'civilization' in Freud's general sense, but by a contingent historical configuration. It is the modern formation of capitalism and industrialism into a totalitarian society which heaps 'surplus repression' onto the masses, manipulating individual needs via mass communication, production and employment. Meanwhile individuals are encouraged to think that all is well and is generally done in the interests of all; totalitarian society disguises the continuation, and in fact heightening, of social hierarchy and domination, via an all-encompassing ideology, reducing humanity to a one-dimensional existence. Subjectivity is pummelled, reduced to an alienated and lonely existence of which we are barely aware. As Marcuse puts it, we are living in a society which reduces and/or absorbs all opposition, resulting in an 'atrophy of the mental organs', and 'the *Happy Consciousness* comes to prevail' (Marcuse, 1964: 79). There is much more to Marcuse's work of course, and he has been criticized on various points; the purpose of this brief outline is to indicate his proponency of a more general view of the nature of an increasingly global capitalist social structure and the overdetermination of subjectivity which accompanies it.

Despite their different backgrounds, professions and milieu, British psychiatrist Ronnie Laing has much in common with Marcuse. He was also influenced by phenomenological philosophy, as well as Marxism and psychoanalysis. For Laing such interest and knowledge was brewed in the stock of his practical clinical experience. He trained and worked for many years in the psychiatric profession, as a psychiatric doctor he was witness to what he saw as the crude, medieval, cruel and dehumanizing 'treatment' in the psychiatric hospitals of 1940s and 1950s Britain, including electro-shock treatment and lobotomy. He had an intimate knowledge of the language and practice of psychiatry. The outcome was the development of a radical account of mental illness in a proliferation of work during the 1960s (Laing, 1960, 1967; Laing and Esterson, 1970). What is particularly relevant for our account however, is that Laing increasingly ventured into an examination of mental health and 'normality', which, like Marcuse, he saw as an historical contingency. For Laing, the normality of contemporary existence is in fact an injurious assault on existence, a shrivelled and lonely shell compared to the human potential for awareness and identity.

Laing initially set out to discourage the scientism and objectification of mental illness in the psychiatric relationship, arguing that madness was in fact an intelligible condition if approached with genuineness, openness and commitment rather than the obfuscatory tools of psychiatric language and practice: 'how can I go straight to the patients if the psychiatric words at my disposal keep the patient at a distance from me?' (Laing, 1960: 18). Laing's work from the outset is defined by a willingness to 'get inside' or 'walk in' the world of the schizophrenic. His aim is to render his or her point of view as intelligible, within the context of his/her world. However, the context which Laing is willing to consider extends from the psychiatric discourse of his earlier work to the nexus of social relationships (1961), and eventually more general cultural, social and political frameworks in Laing's later work. The latter development is encapsulated in *The Politics of Experience and the Bird of Paradise* (1967). The book had great popular success, and it paralleled the concerns of a growing counter-culture movement at the time, as well as Laing's individual notoriety.

There is an apocalyptic air from the book's introduction onwards, where Laing paints a picture of a broken humanity, close to the brink, mired in violence; we are 'bemused and crazed creatures', every one of us murderers and prostitutes. He is concerned with our state of *alienation*. For Laing to say we are alienated means that we are separated from our natural or authentic being, split into two and living in a false state with our authentic selves, all we are capable of experiencing and thinking buried deep within, distorted and mutilated. Laing's claim is that our *normal* existence in contemporary society is one of alienation, turning the idea of madness as alienation from our sane self on its head. It is the ordinary person who is 'radically estranged' from authentic being, from what Laing calls our 'inner world' of experience: 'We are so estranged from the inner world that many are arguing that it does not exist...man is cut off from his own mind, cut off equally from his own body – a half crazed creature in a mad world' (Laing, 1967: 46–47).

He locates the root causes of the problem in many of the broader social patterns discussed in the previous chapter, which are reflected upon in a similar manner to Marcuse. Technology, capitalist relations, industrialism, the family, science and rationality all form the backdrop to mass conformity and the manipulation of individual subjectivities. Like Marcuse, Laing intimates that most of us are rarely aware how fractured we really are: 'Human beings seem to have an almost unlimited capacity to deceive themselves, and to deceive themselves into taking their own lies for truth' (1967: 61). The individual remains of a barbaric social system amount to a self-deceiving subjectivity, cut adrift from authentic relationships with one's self or others.

The most oft-cited criticism of Laing, Marcuse and the account of psychosocial fragmentation they represent is that of overdeterminism. It is argued that the individual is reduced to a passive receptacle of the prescriptions of the various guises of authority. Popular cultural forms and expression is configured as the complicit machinations of an all-powerful industry. A subsequent 'turn to culture' has attempted to recognize the ambivalent exercise of agency contained within the everyday practices of groups and individuals. Cultural practices are consequently associated with greater degrees of resistance, reparation and creativity than proponents of the psychosocial fragmentation thesis supposedly gave credit (e.g. Ang, 1985; De Certeau, 1984; Morley, 1980; Hall and Jefferson, 1978; Hebdidge, 1979). The legacy of this wave of cultural theory is felt in various theories of identity, perhaps none more so than the extended reflexivity thesis, discussed in the following chapter, but many sociological accounts of identity now incorporate a more complex understanding of agency than that found in cruder expressions of psychosocial fragmentation.

The Lonely Crowd

In the United States another treatise on psychosocial fragmentation gained popular and critical approval in the early 1960s. David Riesman's *The Lonely Crowd* (2001 [1961]) was ostensibly a less radical critique than that offered by Marcuse or Laing, less explicitly connected as it was to the leftist politics of the time, but it was similarly taken up by the counter-cultural movement as a prescient deconstruction of the social ills of the era. Riesman perfectly reflected post-war anxiety about the cultural and social upheavals already discussed, and the ascendancy of the sociological imagination as the tool to reflect upon and substantiate these anxieties. *The Lonely Crowd* sold over a million copies in the United States. It is also important for our purposes because it treated social upheavals as psychological upheavals too, in a lucid and expressive form. What's more, Riesman's arguments, alongside Marcuse's and Laing's, offer a template for how social theory has come to understand psychosocial fragmentation.

Riesman was concerned with three 'psychological types' which he saw as understandable responses to a changing social environment: tradition-directed, inner-directed and other-directed (Riesman, 2001 [1961]: 8). The tradition-directed type relies on an almost identical view of tradition as that suggested in the previous chapter. Intensive socialization embeds the individual in contexts of meaning which set firm parameters for their potential identities and reflexive awareness. All members of society learn 'to understand and appreciate patterns which have endured for centuries... the culture, in addition to its economic tasks, or as part of them, provides ritual, routine, and religion to occupy and to orient everyone' (2001 [1961]: 11). Tradition-directed types are obviously more likely and more sustainable in societies marked by encompassing traditions.

Inner-directed types emerge as traditions lose some of their salience. This happens as they come into contact with each other, extended kin networks dissolve, and a scientific rationality more generally removes some of the 'irrational' foundations of traditions. The inner-directed type relies not on external regulations so much as an internalized set of goals. These tend to be instilled via fairly intense parent-child relationships, made all the more so by their attenuation from broader family networks. The 'psychological gyroscope' which develops eventually constitutes a fairly rigid character that can nonetheless navigate in the more numerous and uncertain environments the individual is likely to confront compared to his or her forbears (2001 [1961]: 16).

Although Riesman is critical of teleological simplicity, he argues that an analysis of other-directedness is at the same time an analysis of the contemporary self. It is Riesman's analysis of the other-directed type which we will consider briefly here, as the theorization of contemporary psychosocial fragmentation is our main concern. The other-directed type is forged in the countless childhoods of what Riesman refers to as 'advanced societies'; which, writing in the 1950s, he considers to be Europe, Japan and the United States of America. The key to understanding other-directed selves is 'that their contemporaries are the source of direction for the individual' (2001 [1961]: 21). Relevant others include those not directly acquainted, and in a mass-media age the number of potentially influential others with which we make contact is in rapid ascendance. One's character is seen to shift as the temporally salient requirements of a particular constellation of others shifts. Geographic and social mobility and the marketing of 'personality' in a service economy increase the demand for a flexible self. The external context or enduring core of pre-existing beliefs which marks the tradition and inner-directed types respectively is dissolved by social requirements for the other-directed self. It is emptied of any obdurate autonomy, its only constant the continuous adherence to signals from others.

Riesman focuses most of his energy on the 'transmitters of social heritage' which are vital in shaping social character: parents, educators, peers and the mass media. With great foresight, he analyses the relationship between these transmitters to portray a social landscape which is remarkably familiar today. In advanced societies, the economic emphasis increasingly shifts from production to service. In such a climate, employees come to be differentiated not in terms of their technical skills but in terms of their individualized personal qualities: 'the product now in demand is neither a staple nor a machine; it is a personality' (2001 [1961]: 46). What is meant by personality varies from job to job; thus the required character has to be flexible and attuned to the changing demands of others.

Parents experiencing this world become uncertain of how to raise their children. The 'sharp silhouette' of the inner-directed type seems inappropriate (2001 [1961]: 47). Even if parents desire it, an inflexible, inner-directed character is un-enforceable as the actions of parents become radically destabilized by the presence in the home of a cacophony of voices thanks to the mass media. Thus the other-directed child 'faces not only the requirement that he [sic] make good but also the problem of defining what making good actually means' (2001 [1961]: 48). Erik Erikson's observations in a clinical setting some years earlier reflects Riesman's claims:

The patient of today suffers most under the problem of what he [sic] should believe in and who he should – or indeed, might – be or become [other-directed]; while the patient of early psychoanalysis suffered most under inhibitions which prevented him from being what and who he thought he knew he was [inner-directed]. (Erikson, 1950: 253)

Against a backdrop of anxious parental care and an omnipresent media, peer groups take on an important role in consolidating the other-directed self. As the influence of parents becomes less distinct, peers play a greater part in the socialization of the young. Peer groups do not operate in a social vacuum however, but in an increasingly media saturated environment. In effect, the peer group becomes a selective conduit for the influences of the media. Dependent for authenticity on public validation, personal tastes and preferences become socialized. For Riesman, how we feel and think reflects the trends of the day, as they are filtered and expressed by one's peer group: 'the proper mode of expression requires feeling out with skill and sensitivity the probable tastes of the others and then swapping mutual likes and dislikes to manoeuvre intimacy' (Riesman, 2001 [1961]: 73). The child's inner life is thus prepared for its exhaustive attunement to others from an early age. Peer group, parenting and the media are all amongst the factors which combine to create the superficial individuation of the other-directed type; a thoroughly socialized 'personality' which is: 'a mandate for manipulation and self-manipulation' (2001 [1961]: 265).

At the heart of Riesman's analysis there stands an impoverished self. It is a self reared to seek validation in the attention of others which is fundamentally alone; and it is unable to find its way back to an authentic sense with its own keenly felt impulses, reflections, preferences and commitments, caught as it is in a hall of mirrors. Community is again claimed to be both cause and salvation for the lonely other-directed self, Riesman perceiving a downward trajectory from an ideal type *Geminschaft* to a dystopian *Gesselschaft*. A superficial community of others fixes in place a society of privatized, artificial 'personalities', but 'the larger package of a neighbourhood, a society, and a way of life' is seen to be the out-of-reach vehicle for authentic feelings and aspirations (2001 [1961]: 307).

Riesman's analysis was ahead of its time. Many of the aspects of contemporary society he highlights and their impact upon subjectivity have been substantiated by more recent social theory and research which emphasizes psychosocial fragmentation in similar language (Cushman, 1995; Lasch, 1991 [1979], 1984; Mestrovic, 1997; Sennett, 1999). Still, optimistic commentators might point out that the comprehensive usurping of agency in the face of other-directedness pays scant attention to the myriad ways in which individuals and groups creatively reject and appropriate the demands of others from childhood onwards. The voices of others are not always obeyed or adhered to, and some voices tend to be more powerful than others. Points of differentiation and continuity in the power of specific and generalized others to constitute selves is also worthy of closer attention, a point which Foucault forcibly made.

There are problems too with Riesman's psychological-type differentiation if we map them on to historical time. If we accept a thorough-going account of selfhood as socially constituted, such as that found in symbolic interactionism, then all selves are to a great degree other-directed; the self relies on the direction of others to gain a sense of itself at all. The process of self awareness, Mead argues, is characterized by a development of a sense of the 'other': 'he [sic] becomes an object to himself only by taking the attitudes of other individuals towards himself within a social environment or context of experience and behaviour in which both he and they are involved' (Mead, 1934: 201). Thus the self 'is essentially a social structure, and it arises in social experience' (1934: 202). As individuals develop, the population of 'others' increases in sum, and they become assimilated into a 'generalized other':

> the self reaches its full development by organising these individual attitudes of others into the organised social or group attitudes, and by thus becoming an individual reflection of the general systematic pattern of social or group behaviour in which it and the others are all involved. (1934: 207)

No meaningful interactions, even in a society steeped in accepted traditions, nor even in one populated by the most 'inner-directed' sense of self, is possible without these social foundations. This suggests it is not possible to draw distinct lines between an era when others did *not* constitute the self. The boundaries between the different types consequently become harder to distinguish. The distinctiveness of the present fades, 'inner-directedness' appears to isolate conceptualization of the formation and maintenance of subjectivity, and 'tradition-directedness' becomes an overly-static representation of how traditions were negotiated and embodied.

Fragmenting communities

Around the same time as the publication of *The Lonely Crowd*, a sense of disappearing community was brought home vividly in the United Kingdom by Young and Wilmott's landmark study, *Family and Kinship in East London* (1957). The authors studied the patterns of community and kinship which structured the lives of residents in Bethnal Green, a cramped, working-class district in East London. They described in qualitative and quantitative detail the fabric of the community as it was spun in everyday activity. The intertwined familial bonds of married couples formed the basis for regularized contact with others in the community, particularly the overlapping lives of many mothers and daughters (Young and Wilmott, 1957: 44–61).

Family connections, in turn, provide links between individuals and other members of the community: 'when a person has relatives in the borough, as most people do, each of these relatives is a go-between with other people in the district' (1957: 104). This works partly because people remain in Bethnal Green for long periods: over half of Young and Wilmott's respondents were born there and of the remainder over half had been there for at least 15 years (1957: 104–105). The consolidations of inter-relations is compounded further by the close proximity of people. Closely packed terrace houses and local shops and services meant that people literally bumped into each other on a daily basis; people for whom, because of long residential history and far-reaching family ties, there was a good chance of mutual prior knowledge: 'The Bethnal Greener is therefore not only surrounded by his [sic] own relatives and their acquaintances, but also by his own acquaintances and their relatives' (1957: 105). Thus the potential prerequisites for conversation and the further cementing of these ties, was ever present.

Taken together, space, time of residence and kinship combined to create a complex grid of community relations constantly being reinforced. Undoubtedly there were disadvantages in this set up. Young and Wilmott were told of many feuds, and contempt for people always 'knowing your business' was expressed. On the whole, however, the residents of Bethnal Green seemed to value the embracing companionship of their community (1957: 125):

> For many people, familiarity breeds content. Bethnal Greeners are not lonely people: whenever they go for a walk in the street, for a drink in the pub, or for a row on the lake in Victoria Park, they know the faces in the crowd. (1957: 116)

Young and Wilmott highlighted many of the positive aspects of community supposedly invested in traditional societies as late as the 1950s. Their account was one of a disappearing era, however, as families were being encouraged to move out of areas like Bethnal Green into government-built estates. The study is all the more fascinating because it followed residents as they moved from Bethnal Green to the new suburban estate of Greenleigh 20 miles away, and through a series of follow-up interviews attempted to measure its impact upon a sense of community. The authors observed a steady exodus of Bethnal Green residents, and were thus privy to an early example of the phenomenon of suburbanization as it happened. The move seemed to be motivated by the promise of more space and better housing conditions generally, particularly in relation to bringing up children (1957: 124–130). They also found a sharp drop in the routine contacts with other family members. The wives interviewed had contact with close family members (parents, siblings, or parents and siblings of husband) an average of 17 times a week before leaving Bethnal Green, 3 times a week a year later in Greenleigh, and just over twice a week 2 years later.

Young and Wilmott's respondents interpreted the change negatively on the whole, particularly the women; many of the men still travelled back to Bethnal Green to work. For many women, the impersonal self-service shopping parades, few shared social spaces, the lack of adult company during the day, the presence of television at night, meant a 'sharp break with the full life they had previously shared with others' creating a sense of melancholy and loneliness (1957: 134). Young and Wilmott suggest that the loss of social life may be compensated and made tolerable over time by the gains made in the private household: more comfort and closer marital relations, though in concluding, they are more concerned that 'the tenants of tomorrow are unlikely to be bound to each other by the same ties that we observed in [Bethnal Green]' (1957: 169); and call on governments not to uproot more people if 'community spirit' is to be preserved as a 'social asset' (1957: 199).

Family and Kinship in East London is an accessible statement of the impact of specific social changes – namely the post-war shift to suburban living, with the occasional nod towards compounding factors such as the increased prevalence of electronic entertainment, the commodification of local services and the intensification of the parent-child bond – upon communal and traditional bonds in terms of social and psychological loss. The study is a detailed piece of empirical research and as such it makes few attempts to offer an overall theoretical framework beyond a general sense of a loss of social cohesion and a corresponding psychological discomfort born of isolation. At one end of the scale systemic factors facilitating and compounding the fragmentation of communities are left unexplored, at the other end the subjective impact and complexity of the changes observed are only sketched in. Nonetheless Young and Wilmott's study is an archetypal representation of how sociological research and populist concerns conceptualized psychosocial fragmentation in post-war western societies.

Contemporary settings

The studies discussed here represent only a small sample of those which have helped to build a powerful account of the relationship between self and society as one of gradual dislocation and decline. Let us now fast forward almost 50 years to the beginning of the twenty-first century. Few would doubt that since the 1950s there have been other changes afoot besides those discussed by Young and Wilmott, changes which were sketched out in the previous chapter. The interviewed inhabitants of Greenleigh may now have children with their own grown-up grandchildren. Their lives in many ways will be different from that of their grandparents; for example, in terms of the nature of their employment, household technology, forms of entertainment, how and where they travel, what they eat, how they communicate, how they vote (if at all), who they socialize with, and finally, what they make of it all in relation to a sense of self. And of course they may not live in Greenleigh at all. The broader social changes behind these differences must also be stretched beyond the changes identified by Young and Wilmott in housing policy, civic architecture and television.

So have we pieced back together our splintered self and found authenticity in good company amidst a rejuvenation of the social and cultural fabric? Or has the situation deteriorated further? Has our experience of social reality qualitatively changed at all? The nature of the answer depends on who you ask of course, but for scores of sociologists and social commentators the answer is that self-fragmentation has intensified in the light of extensive social change. Many scholars have built more complex and imaginative analyses to match an apparently more complex reality, while the defining assumption of psychosocial fragmentation and loss remains, or is heightened (e.g. Bradley, 1996; Lasch, 1991; Putnam, 2000; Sennett, 1999). A number of these analyses will now be considered.

Therapeutics

Frank Furedi's recent analysis of cultural change headlines the rise of a therapeutic sensibility (2004); an emphasis which has a distinguished history (Bellah *et al.*, 1996; Lasch, 1979; Cushman, 1997). It is claimed that the 'self' has become fetishized in therapeutic discourses, which are marked by an emphasis upon recognizing, confessing and improving one's emotional dynamics. A better career, partner, body and level of self-esteem count amongst the carrots to tempt us on the journey of self-discovery, guided by the growing therapeutic industry of professionals, handbooks, retreats and so on, towards a place of emotional well-being. Consequently, each individual's sense of autonomy and tenacity has been eroded to the point where what were once thought of as routine experiences of the life cycle are now interpreted as traumatic, and the human default condition is experienced as vulnerable, deficient, isolated. 'Therapy culture' consolidates an individual's sense of isolation by framing the solutions to problems of living in terms of external authorities which normatively regulates emotional experience in narrowly-defined ways. Furedi's focus on emotional regulation raises concerns which we will return to in chapters four and five. For now, it is the similarities between Furedi's portrayal of contemporary self-identity and those already discussed in this chapter which are of interest.

Furedi concurs with the familiar assertion that we are living through a period in which the presence of tradition is fading. As traditions come into contact with each other and become 'traditions' in inverted commas, they lose their ability to meaningfully contextualize our subjective experience in a shared social environment. Coupled with the spatial fragmentation of communities evident as a result of developments in communication, transportation, urbanization and so on, there begins 'a disengagement from a wider communal purpose...as the ties that bound them together diminish leading to social isolation' (Furedi, 2000: 86–87), and we are confronted once more with the lonely, monadic self.

Therapeutic culture steps into this psychosocial void according to Furedi, appropriating the uncertainty and anxiety of isolated selves into a trajectory of self-empowerment. Encouraging a dependence on medicalized and professionalized therapeutic disciplines maintains the vulnerability and isolation it offers salvation from. It also fragments social connections further by intervening in interpersonal processes: 'the mediation of experience by the professional has the effect of distancing people from one another, thereby fragmenting the networks of relationships still further' (2000: 101). In fact, 'the distancing of the self from other' is 'the most significant feature of therapeutic culture' (Furedi, 2004: 21). This is a process Giddens might refer to (though more positively) as the 'disembedding' of the qualities of kin and friendship relationships, and their 're-embedding' in the professionalized sphere of therapy (Giddens, 1991).

For Furedi, it is a 'distinctly feeble notion of human subjectivity' which dominant therapeutic narratives encourage individuals to occupy (Furedi, 2004: 107). It undermines the 'organic links that sustain relationships', fostering instead formalized, almost scripted inter-relations between self-estranged individuals hailed as vulnerable and monadic, thus creating further need for its prescriptions and promises. Furedi summarizes his claims thus:

> therapeutics creates a demand for itself by continually compromising the informal networks of support that people rely on to negotiate the challenges of daily life…without the insulation of a network of interpersonal relations, the individual stands exposed to the pressures of the world and experiences the condition of the self as indeed that of vulnerability. (2004: 103–105)

Thus therapeutic culture not only reflects psychosocial fragmentation along lines we are now familiar with, but intensifies it.

The wholesale surrender to a culture of victimhood, vulnerability and dependency conjured up by Furedi's polemic is interesting in that it perpetuates the passive notion of subjectivity supposedly encouraged by therapeutics. We are all rendered victims of a pervasive discourse of victimhood. But if there is more to agency than the dependency and pseudo-autonomy therapeutic culture tries to impose upon us, would it not rear its head precisely when such a culture threatens? Is the relationship between culture and identity so deterministic that 'autonomy' is always and everywhere a cultural construct? If it is then we need a more complex portrayal of the relationship between partial, embodied autonomy and cultural embeddedness. Attempts have been made in this direction, particularly regarding theoretical attempts to combine insights from psychoanalysis with feminist, post-structuralist and materialist emphasis on power and embodied subjectivity (e.g. Adkins, 2002; Burkitt, 1999; Butler, 1997; Craib, 1998; Elliott, 1999; Frosh et al., 2003; McNay, 1992). Unfortunately Furedi's analysis does not draw on any of these developments substantially, nor does it deliver the necessary complexity on its own terms.

Instead we are left with a masculinist, heroic vision of autonomy, a bounded self-reliance posited against an external social world in the indefinite past, which nonetheless appears to have been completely extinguished by the rise of a therapeutic culture. There is little evidence of its resilience in Furedi's analysis. If some form of 'pure' autonomy and self-direction *is* to remain at the heart of the conceptualization of identity then we tend towards the 'neo-modern' approaches of Beck and Giddens, who necessarily paint a more optimistic picture of the state of contemporary subjectivity. These accounts are also problematic, as we shall see in the following chapter, but in highlighting the agent's unceasing contribution to structure, they accentuate at least the potential for the autonomous expression of self-identity against a more malleable social backdrop.

In addition, Furedi sees therapeutic culture as a blanket social evil, undermining all attempts at self-direction equally. Little attention is paid to the possibility that therapeutic sensibility may be used to regulate the self-expression and development of some, empower others, and remain irrelevant to yet others. In a complex social reality it is essential to attempt to understand how even the most general processes of social change are experienced in differential and socially stratifying ways, a point which has been raised regularly in relation to other accounts of psychosocial fragmentation. There may well be both 'winners' and 'losers' in the relationship between self-identity and therapeutic culture in ways which have yet to be explored.

Yet Furedi's analysis is more than a rehash of the psychosocial fragmentation thesis. His polemical analysis of therapeutic discourse reveals not just how pervasive it can be, but also how at its heart there is often a paradoxical commodification of 'autonomy': new levels of self-understanding, self-esteem and self-direction are promised, whilst in the same moment establishing a relationship of dependence with the prescriptions of experts and advertisers. There is no doubt that many of the faces of therapeutic culture promote paradoxically prescriptive versions of autonomy, but if we acknowledge the complex relationship between culture, agency and identity more fully, this can never be the whole story.

Bowling Alone

In a study of American civil life, *Bowling Alone* (2000), the political scientist Robert Putnam has offered one of the most celebrated accounts of psychosocial fragmentation in recent years. Although exclusively focused on American society, Putnam's claims are the inheritors of arguments such as Young and Wilmott's and parallel many of Furedi's. As a general argument, it has certainly been applied to other long-industrialized nations and is increasingly considered in terms of a global rather than a national malaise (e.g. Lockard, 1997; Jones, 1998).

In fact, Putnam's account of social disintegration is the latest in a long line which stretches back beyond Young and Wilmott's study, to the work of Tocqueville, Durkheim, Weber and countless others. The novelty of his account lies primarily in his attempt to define and quantify the substance of what is lost in the process of civic disengagement as the erosion of 'social capital'. Putnam traces the concept back to a number of origins, including Bourdieu, and in his own work uses the term to refer to the webs of contact, exchange, solidarity and comfort that form between people in the course of regularized interaction – 'connections among individuals, social networks and the norms of reciprocity and trustworthiness that arise from them' (Putnam, 2000: 19) – and, according to Putnam, foster an active community and underpin a healthy participatory democracy.

For Putnam, social capital is intimately connected to political power. It serves as a vehicle for the expression of the public interest which then impacts upon government and ensures a dynamic relationship between incumbent powers and the general public (2000: 338). More than political engagement however, social capital is seen to be foundational in creating meaningful bonds between people and providing a shared vision of social reality vital for personal well-being (2000: 332–333).

Social capital is maintained in the countless associations and alliances of everyday life, both formal and informal. The key to Putnam's thesis is that, in American society at least, social capital is disappearing: 'weakened social capital is manifest in the things that have vanished almost unnoticed – neighbourhood parties and get-togethers with friends, the unreflective kindness of strangers, the shared pursuit of the public good rather than a solitary quest for private goods' (2000: 403). Although widespread, the decline is argued to be significantly generational:

> For the first two-thirds of the twentieth century a powerful tide bore Americans into ever deeper engagement in the life of their communities, but a few decades ago – silently, without warning – that tide reversed and we were overtaken by a treacherous rip current. Without at first noticing, we have been pulled apart from one another and from our communities over the last third of the century. (2000: 27)

Basically, the 1930s to 1950s generations of adults in particular were, and to some extent still are, generating decent levels of social capital. Putnam presents an impressive array of statistical indicators from voluntary group membership to petition signing to participating in bowling leagues in support of this claim (2000: 247–276). Although much of this group have maintained reasonable levels of social capital, Putnam finds a sharp dropping off of civic involvement and political activity amongst the 1960s to 1990s generations of adults. So a blanket decrease hides what for Putnam is a social problem in ascendancy.

As abundant social capital is the blood running through the veins of psychosocial well being, the consequences of this creeping malaise are far-reaching: 'social connectedness matters to our lives in the most profound way' (2000: 326). As one reviewer suggests: 'this deep, steady civic decline would seem to have dire consequences not only for political institutions but for the general state of health and happiness, education, family welfare, safety, culture, and economic prosperity' (Boggs, 2001: 282). In allegiance with the theoretical positions discussed in this chapter, Putnam also suggests that a deleterious fragmentation of self-identity and associated existential anxiety and isolation is a vital 'dire consequence' within a general threat to health. Not only does a lack of social ties significantly increase your chances of becoming seriously ill or dying, it also accompanies a decrease in mental health (Putnam, 2000: 331).

The isolation and privatism of contemporary cultural life is concisely captured in Putnam's dominant titular metaphor and front page illustration – the contemporary American 'bowls alone' rather than in community leagues. His claims amount to a contemporary restatement of a long-standing conceptual correlation between a general decline in psychological health, which he understands in terms of 'sadness, loneliness, low-self-esteem', and a decline in the quality and quantity of social connections. Where there is correlation Putnam also finds cause. At the personal level as much as the social, 'we are paying a significant price for a quarter century's disengagement from each other' (2000: 335).

With a decline in social capital established as the major source of a crisis in self-identity, Putnam turns his attention to the causes of that decline, and they are numerous. Time and money pressures, such as having to work longer hours, two-career families, and 'economic distress' has a 'modest' role in declining social connectedness (2000: 203). Echoing Young and Wilmott, suburbanization and urbanization are associated with privatism and something akin to Goffman's 'civil indifference' respectively. Both thus contribute to the downturn in social capital but again, only a 'small fraction' of it (2000: 215). As Young and Wilmott hinted at back in the 1950s, television and other domestic electronic entertainments on the other hand have become 'ringleaders' in the crime of civic disengagement; particularly as their ascendancy coincides most closely with its historical and generational specifics (2000: 246). However, despite the apparent power of television, Putnam attributes 'much of the decline in civic engagement' to one singular cause: successive generational decline: 'to the replacement of an unusually civic generation by several generations (their children and their grandchildren) that are less embedded in community life' (2000: 275).

It seems peculiar that generational change is given causal primacy by Putnam. It amounts to a circular attempt to explain a gradual dropping-off in social capital by pointing to a generational dropping-off of social capital. The key question of *why* later generations are not as capable or as willing to civically engage remains unanswered. Within the discussion of generational drop-off, Putnam suggests that the Second World War and its after effects may have been a key catalyst for high levels of social capital. The spirit of solidarity, volunteerism and comradery during the war equated to an 'extraordinary burst of civic activity' (2000: 268) which proved foundational for a 'massive postwar civic renaissance' (2000: 270). In fact then, the main causal factor is not generational change, but the impact of a world war. Important though it may have been during that period, it has little positive explanatory power for explaining a long-term *decline* in civic engagement. It seems to claim that heightened social capital was a historical 'blip', or possibly the absurd suggestion that world wars are the basis for civic engagement and cohesion (unless aggressive American foreign policy at the time of writing reflects a desire for a cohesive populous).

One critic has argued that Putnam fails to capture vital aspects of social structure because of a conceptual misunderstanding of the link between social capital and political power (Boggs, 2001). Putnam elides what he sees as well-springs of social capital – rotary clubs, bowling leagues etc. – with progressive and participatory political activity; there appears to be an objective and critical relationship between social capital and political structures. Boggs argues that social groups can in fact sit quite comfortably within conservative political systems, and that 'both the functions and trajectory of community groups will always depend on the cultural or ideological environment – not only internally but externally, as part of the hegemonic system of ideas and beliefs' (2001: 285). Whatever the level and nature of social capital, it cannot be assumed that it simply converts into 'viable political modes of engagement' (2001: 287); there is no easy correspondence, so a more differentiated understanding of social capital than Putnam's is required.

Boggs argues that there has in fact been a growth in many forms of social capital but at the same time a decline in political activity. The latter is the result of an eroding public sphere *a là* Habermas. To meaningfully be informed, consider issues, disseminate information, congregate and debate democratically in spaces which have a meaningful and reciprocal impact upon social structures of power is becoming less and less possible. Some of the causes for this parallel are located by Putnam in relation to social capital, but he misses one factor bigger than the rest: 'the massive growth of corporate power…It is within this historical context that increasing depoliticization, above all the severe decline in citizenship and local decision-making must be situated' (2001: 288–289).

The problem for Boggs is that modern forms of social capital, encouraged and compounded by a corporatized economy and political system, lead relating individuals away from political public sphere activity. It seems an obvious point but Putnam's persuasive logic can blind the reader to his marginalization of social systemic power as he pursues narrow causal models and grants social capital unmerited conceptual primacy (2001: 94). Boggs concludes that: 'until the corporate stranglehold over American social and political life is decisively broken, none of Putnam's outmoded, tepid prescriptions – and no rejuvenation of bowling leagues, choir ensembles, and reading groups – will make a dent in the process of civic disengagement' (2001: 96).

Another problem with Putnam's work is that it offers very little detail on the supposed existential anxiety created by a decline in social capital beyond broad markers such as occasional references to depression. There is thus little evidence to suggest that anyone cares or is affected by the supposed decline in concrete negative ways. Putnam seems to imply that people increasingly accept their social and psychic isolation with passivity, simply responding to social determinants and automatically living out their individualized, disconnected lives as programmed. As with so many accounts of psychosocial fragmentation, a convincing account of agency is absent in Putnam's account. There is no sense of individuals struggling with the existential ramifications of a supposed decline in social capital, challenging its demise or reinventing it in novel interpersonal settings. Thus there is a lack of detail in terms of psychological as well as social systemic complexity.

In sum, for Putnam, the declension of social capital is a conceptual tool which is used to make contemporary sense of the perceived problem of psychosocial fragmentation. In the United States his ideas have proved influential, and his crusade to reinvent civic life, encouraging group membership and similar such gestures (Putnam, 2000: 405–410; www. bowlingalone.com) has garnered widespread sympathy and exposure. Although his work has little to say about the finer detail of the impact of declining social capital upon self-identity, it is a powerful popular statement which consolidates a now familiar discourse of selfhood as adrift, isolated and alienated amidst generalized social breakdown.

In light of Putnam's critical reception, which to my mind is largely deserved, we are encouraged to search for contemporary accounts of the changing social landscape which pay closer attention to the systemic processes explored in the previous chapter and hinted at in the criticisms raised here. Later on we will consider analyses which in doing so paint a very different picture of the plight of subjectivity, but for now, we will remain with accounts of psychosocial fragmentation and loss. There are plenty of contemporary accounts which draw similar conclusions to Putnam, even if their explanatory logic is different, offering more thorough accounts of systemic change and/or the personal, existential dimension of declensionism. New forms of communication, global corporate culture, short-term employment and changing gender roles are just some of the factors claimed by some late-modernists and post-modernists to underpin complex social change which makes the experience and presentation of self a continuous process of shifting and readjustment in response to the array of contexts and stimuli that confront us.

Corroded character

Sennett's recent concern is with the 'corrosion of character', which amounts to another contemporary take on the psychosocial fragmentation thesis (1998), but has been a concern of Sennett's throughout his career (Sennett and Cobb, 1972; Sennett, 1977). 'Character' refers to the experience of self which is established over a long period, forged in relations with others. It develops in the inter-relationship between mutual commitments, responsibilities and 'connections to the world' more generally and inner-emotional experiences, sentiments, and desires (Sennett, 1999: 10). 'Character' is more or less equivalent to the term 'identity', which acknowledges the social dimension of selfhood, though may be an attempt to acknowledge more explicitly a psychoanalytic understanding of inner dynamism. As with all of the accounts discussed so far in this chapter, Sennett portrays a social world in decline, fracturing and fragmenting our experience of our own selves as it deteriorates. Reiterating a familiar metaphor, the social world sets the 'emotional, inner life adrift' (1998: 21).

Unlike Putnam, Sennett locates the origin of psychosocial fragmentation in a single systemic cause: the temporal dimensions of contemporary capitalism: 'The conditions of time in the new capitalism have created a new conflict between character and experience, the experience of disjointed time threatening the ability of people to form their characters into sustained narratives' (1998: 31). Capitalist relations demand a new framework for the organization and experience of time for its workers, and its impacts are far reaching; for Sennett it is a 'key dimension of social change' (1998: 22), as was claimed in chapter one. Whilst Sennett's analysis agrees with much of the account of time offered there, his account is more centred on 'working time', and he brings his own terminology and insights which help broaden our grasp of psychosocial fragmentation in relation to systemic shifts in the ordering of time.

Sennett brings these changes to light via the juxtaposition of two personal narratives, conveying concrete experiences, though representative of the experience of many (1998: 11, 31). The first story is that of Enrico, who Sennett originally interviewed for an earlier study (Sennett and Cobb, 1972). A Greek immigrant, he spent his life working in a busy bakery, and dwelt comfortably enough in a male expatriate community where he commanded respect for sticking out his job and providing for his family, and his home life, where identity was affirmed in living out family dynamics, and respect allotted by maintaining the anonymity and privatism necessary for a smooth-running suburbia. Enrico's working life was embedded in what Sennett calls 'linear time': predictable from one day to the next, and from one year to the next, his income protected by union membership and his social and economic standing marked by steady, cumulative achievements (Sennett, 1998: 15–16). Enrico's secure career, if relatively lowly and physically draining, provided him with a substantial degree of ontological security by generating a coherent, consistent network of meanings; a narrative within which he could make sense of himself and his relations. In Sennett's words he 'carved out a clear story for himself' and 'felt he became the author of his life' (1998: 16).

Enrico's story sharply contrasts with that of his son, Rico. His tale is conveyed as a personal representation of the consequences of flexible capitalism's ordering of time, which have, according to Sennett, heralded transformative changes in character within a generation. Thus, before we consider Rico's story it is worth filling in a little more detail of Sennett's critical account of flexibility. The dynamics of the market place and the impatience of capital have created a change in institutional structure encapsulated in the widespread demand for 'flexibility'. Flexibility has become a favoured term in defining and defending contemporary capitalist social relations, which Sennett views as the latest attempt to obscure the oppressive nature of the social system whilst also encapsulating a number of developments (1998: 9). It collects together a number of important changes in the way paid work is organized, and more importantly, experienced, which in turn has implications for the nature of contemporary identity.

One of the most substantial aspects of change is the widespread periodization of employment:

> The traditional career progressing step by step through the corridors of one or two institutions is withering, so is the deployment of a single set of skills through the course of a working life. Today, a young American with at least two years of college can expect to change jobs at least eleven times in the course of working, and change his or her skill base at least three times during those forty years of labour (1998: 22).

Short-term contracts are increasingly the norm, exemplified by the rise in employment agencies. One of few growth industries, these agencies specialize in providing a contingent workforce adaptable to the requirements of post-Fordist corporations, which are geared towards flexible production and mobile capital (Harvey, 1989). They help create a permanent pool of casualized labour, particularly amongst the lowest strata of employees or 'neo-proletariat' (Gorz, 1982), with few rights and little security.

Taken together, these changes in the nature of work reach beyond the sphere of employment and employee identity, altering the general fabric of self-identity or character, as Sennett attempts to indicate with the story of Rico, Enrico's son. Rico is a successful business consultant. He is married to a similarly successful accountant and they have two young children. They have moved numerous times, both geographically and in the nature of their employment. On the surface they appear to be paragons of flexibility: open to change, willing to redirect, uproot and adapt in order to succeed in a flexible regime. However, Sennett claims that both 'fear they are on the edge of losing control over their lives'; a fear which reflects a more general malaise (Sennett, 1998: 19). Their anxiety is the concrete outcome of the changes just discussed.

Rico's relations at work tend to be the fleeting, instrumental ties of short-termism. Although mutual trust and a sense of commitment, loyalty and shared goals are vital for social well-being they get little chance to develop amidst the relations demanded by flexible capitalism: 'Detachment and superficial cooperativeness are better armour for dealing with current realities than behaviour based on values of loyalty and service' (1998: 25). Outside of work, a sense of genuine community, built on reciprocal bonds of trust, is displaced in the geographical mobility which has marked Rico's working life: 'Rico has had literally too little time in each of the places he's lived to experience community' (1998: 143). The lack of personal meaning and uncertainty engendered contributes to the generalized fear of losing control Rico has, consolidated further by his concerns for his family. Putnam's arguments sail closely to Sennett's, emphasizing as it does the importance of informal social bonds, as did Young and Wilmott's before it. Whereas Putnam attributes the deterioration of social relations to the civic community more generally however, and Young and Wilmott look to suburbanization, Sennett pinpoints contemporary capitalism and the realm of work.

Rico is, says Sennett, fully aware that the qualities needed to get by at work are not the same as those he wants to pass on to his children. Flexibility amounts to a lack of commitment and an exhaustive adaptability. Rico finds that entreating his children to value self-sacrifice, mutual responsibility and commitment – qualities he knows make 'good character' – ring hollow when they are not founded on concrete examples in the world of work. Here we can easily imagine a Riesman-esque scenario of parenting besieged by 'other-directedness'. Parental socialization is halting and uncertain, as the type of person one should be matters less than the ability to adapt to the demands of others. Rico's awareness of this dilemma does not provide a solution to it, in fact it appears to heighten his anxiety about losing control. One response is the 'static assertion' of one or another character typology, but Sennett argues that this is impossible to sustain when there is a lack of coherent and continuous narrative to structure such an assertion (1998: 30).

For Lash and Urry, the losers in the flexibility game are those at the margins of society, working, if at all, for less than subsistence wages, and living in slums, producing the goods and services for the 'winners' in the global economy (Lash and Urry, 1994). For Sennett however, the dividing line comes at a different point, as the negative effects of the new capitalism appear more pervasive. Rico, for example, displays all the trappings of success, but he still belongs to what appear to be a majority whose sense of self has become subject to the fissures of psychosocial fragmentation.

According to Sennett then, for the majority the instability, uncertainty and anxiety of the flexible regime spills over into social relations and the everyday maintenance of a sense of self, bringing ontological fragmentation and insecurity for Rico and countless others like him. To experience one's self – as Enrico did – in terms of a continuous narrative developing along the fixed grooves of linear time becomes not only impossible but undesirable against a backdrop of flexible capitalism. Attempting to adhere to a constancy of self becomes 'dysfunctional' (Sennett, 1998: 24), an unwelcome load. In the words of Zygmunt Bauman:

> A cohesive, firmly riveted and solidly constructed identity would be a burden, a constraint, a limitation on the freedom to choose. It would portend an incapacity to unlock the door when the next opportunity knocks...it would be a recipe for inflexibility...a condition that it is almost unanimously recommended to be wary of and scrupulously avoided. (Bauman, 2004: 53)

Flexibility is so often demanded of us that it becomes a normative requirement, at the same time making a coherent sense of self increasingly unlikely: 'How can a human being develop a narrative of identity and life history in a society composed of episodes and fragments...short-term capitalism threatens to corrode his character, particularly those qualities of character which bind human beings to one another and furnishes each with a sense of sustainable self' (Sennett, 1998: 27). Thus Sennett reiterates the rhetorical question so often posed by proponents of the psychosocial fragmentation.

Sennett locates the source of declension in the dynamics of contemporary capitalism and its regulation of time; subsequently his analysis has a number of strengths. Firstly, Sennett recognizes how central work is to our sense of self even if its impact is often disavowed and/or perceived as negative. In the clamour to acknowledge post-Fordist processes of consumption in the differentiation of identities, the continuing salience of 'work', however loosely we define it, is often lost. Secondly, he attempts to connect the experience of work and work-derived identity up to broader psychosocial changes, such as changes in community and family life, though he does so less comprehensively. Finally, in thinking through the impact of social changes upon subjectivity, Sennett draws broadly on psychoanalytical insight to portray the individual as an active, engaged meaning-maker differentially enmeshed in contexts of power and control. Sennett's narrative creates characters who are conscious, flawed subjects struggling with their experiences of the world, thus the excesses of voluntarism and determinism common in sociological analyses of selfhood are minimized.

That said, Sennett does pass over other dimensions of social change rather too briefly. Room needs to be made in any contemporary account of identity to *assess* claims that as patterns of work have changed, other social configurations have come to impact upon the constitution of self, involving factors such as consumption, technology, forms of communication, gender relations (e.g. Woodward, 1997: 2). There *may* be a case for the claim that, rather than floating aimlessly in a world of weak and shifting work identities, people have found harbours in these more varied and predominant aspects of social existence. Other research has led to claims that people's self-investments at work are much more creative and meaningful than Sennett suggests, and not just in 'highly-skilled' professions (Bolton and Boyd, 2003). There is a danger in oversimplifying the complex webs of social and personal meaning when we take the realm of work in relation to capitalism as a template, and generalize upwards from there to questions of self-identity.

Sennett's work also lacks global focus. The consequences of flexible capitalism stretch well beyond the anxieties of those in richer nations being dealt short-term contracts, lacking communal bonds and suffering from self doubt. Once combined with the other social changes outlined in chapter one, problems are not containable to the working lives of the rich and the 'making-do' of wealthier nations. Global slums, disease, territorial wars and mass migration are just some of the systemic factors intimately bound up with global capitalism and are having an enormous impact on people's personal well-being and sense of self across the globe in complex, differential ways, qualitatively distinct from those conceptualized by Sennett (Bauman, 2004; Bradley, 1996; Brah, 1996; Davies, 2004; Ehrenreich, 2001; Haraway, 1997; Klein, 2000). In Sennett's worldview, those *most* adversely affected by flexible capitalism are rarely centre stage.

Sennett actually spends very little time discussing the social-subjective dimensions of how one comes to 'feel at home' in the context of flexible capitalism. It begs the question of why those apparently succeeding in a flexible regime are not plagued by the doubts which gnaw at Rico's sense of self. What makes Bill Gates impervious at this level? It may be, paradoxically, that championing of flexibility becomes a viable 'static assertion' in the cultural, social and economic contexts of the elite, if not in Rico's world; it can add up to a coherent narrative for those able to confidently embrace it, and this seems to be what Sennett implies. It is the 'ordinary' person who cannot sustain a meaningful narrative of selfhood in the context of all-encompassing flexibility: 'the flexibility they celebrate does not give, it cannot give, any guidance for the conduct of ordinary life' (Sennett, 1998: 147). By under-theorizing such a possibility once it is introduced, however select those it applies to, there is a danger that his prognosis of a 'corrosion of character' appears overplayed by comparison. That is, if escaping to a secure ontological plateau simply takes capital and the confidence to embrace risk, the psychosocial complexity of the decline of the 'ordinary' self is rendered somewhat superfluous.

Sennett's 'rather gloomy portrait of the self' meets its antithesis in some strands of recent social theory (Elliott, 2001: 132). A number of accounts drawing from paradigms as diverse as modernism, feminism and postmodernism, far from decrying adaptable and flexible self-identities, or noting their restricted application, see a potentially liberating vision of selfhood emerging from the shackles of predictable, prescriptive cultural narratives Sennett appears keen to defend (Gergen, 1991; Giddens, 1991; Lupton, 2000). We shall turn our attention to these perspectives in the next chapter, but they also inform some aspects of a final critique of accounts of psychosocial fragmentation, which will close this chapter.

New communities

Fundamental to most if not all of the analyses discussed so far is the assumption that there is a *decline* in meaningful communal activity which amounts to a significant social change. In earlier accounts like Young and Wilmott's, communal bonds were thought to be bound up in the everyday life of its members who shared physical space over a reasonably long period of time. In comparison, successive generations are seen to be increasingly mobile and private. They are shifting homes, jobs and area, consuming leisure in small family units, relating to others via the abstract systems of an impersonal and indifferent late or post-modernity. This is more or less the story of psychosocial fragmentation as it has been presented here. However a more recent tendency in sociology, and particularly cultural studies, has attempted to 'stretch the notion of community' (Jordan, 2002: 244). It has been argued that contemporary subjects may in fact be perfectly capable of generating a sense of community and thus psychosocial cohesion, but in specifically contemporary guises (Boggs, 2000; Savage et al., 2005; Phillips and Western, 2005).

Boggs highlights some of the different forms new communities can take: 'civil rights, anti-war, women's, environmental, community and gay rights' – have mobilized socially transformative communities. But there are other phenomena beyond the larger social movements too: 'thousands of self-help and new-age groups, religious movements, and community organizations...resource centres, clinics, bookstores, periodicals, public interest groups, tenants associations and so forth' (Boggs, 2001: 285–286).

These examples seem to be contemporary examples of age-old networks: people meeting and sharing ideas and concerns in specific places. In addition, Jordan claims that contemporary forms of community often unravel the coordinates of shared space over routinized time once foundational to community (Jordan, 2002).

An example is the 'rave' phenomenon of the late 1980s and early 1990s. Rave culture revolved around large gatherings of people, often in the open air, ostensibly to dance to music. There were numerous other components to rave culture however. Drugs were an essential ingredient, and the ascendancy of rave was paralleled by the availability of ecstasy, a drug renowned for generating states of euphoria, empathy and heightened sensitivity to music and movement. Amphetamines, cannabis and LSD were also prevalent. In addition raves were illegal for a time in the UK. This meant that a culture also grew around organizing and attending raves built around the emerging technologies of mobile phones and involving secrecy, subterfuge and no small degree of creativity and commitment on the part of organizers and would-be revellers. Although dance music moved into clubs and issues of dealing, policing and risk complicated the culture as it developed, the basic components remained in place. The music, the drugs, the effort, the presence of other likeminded individuals, all intertwined with its own symbols and myths to create rave culture (Jordan, 2002: 247; Garratt, 1998; Reynolds, 1998).

Jordan claims that rave culture is a perfect example of a contemporary community. He draws on numerous accounts of the time to argue that raves created and recreated pleasures which came to be routine. Out of the 'collective delirium' produced by thousands dancing together, and the shared moments queuing, travelling, etc. emerged 'routine, home-like and habitual activities', however extraordinary and hedonistic these routines appeared. The experience of being at a rave is a particular sense of community, but one which can be experienced at any rave. Thus, a raver who parties one night in London and the next in Bristol states that they were both in the 'same place', or rather 'that the place that trance took me was the same' (cited in Jordan, 2002: 248). For Jordan, rave culture indicates how physical space can become separate from shared communal 'place' in generation of a sense of community with others: 'rave creates the same "place" across numerous spaces'.

Bethnal Green inhabitants relied upon geographical proximity for their sense of community and well-being, as an absence sorely missed by the Greenleigh suburbanites. In contemporary settings, new networks of community are argued to emerge which transcend those parameters, allowing communities to 'live nowhere' but still generate and maintain meaningful identities for those participating (Jordan, 2002: 249). Some argue that computer-mediated communication further collapses the boundaries of time and space to create new kinds of communities. The internet, email, chat rooms, gaming, blogging, podcasting and a plethora of related activities can provide individuals with the means to relate to others in novel ways. Communities are formed and dissolved around shared concerns, likes and dislikes. In such a space physical appearance and ability can matter little, and traditional identity markers like class and gender can be temporarily discarded; identities are instead defined by the communities of interest the self becomes involved in (Tsang, 2000). In other uses, internet communication can be utilized to strengthen 'traditional' communal ties, such as national identity for globally dispersed diaspora (Miller and Slater, 2000).

Whilst Jordan's research strongly suggests that new communities are capable of being formed which can negotiate the parameters of recent social change, claims made by those who advocate new communities as harbours for a new era of flexible identities are more susceptible to criticism. In an argument reminiscent of Marcuse, for example, Golding suggests that the idea of a self being able to construct itself freely amidst the shifting communities of cyberspace is a fallacy which obscures a number of important continuities between modernity and post-modernity (Golding, 2000; Jameson, 1984; Harvey, 1989). Amongst other criticisms, Golding suggests that the symbolic resources for creating identities are controlled by a corporate culture industry rather than operating as a free-floating system for whoever passes by; material inequalities still determine access to the technology to access the 'space' of new communities. We are thus reminded of Boggs's assertion that the growing corporate power further entrenches material divisions; there is continuity in the social differentiation and division of resourced identities despite changes in technology and communication.

Critical overview

Does the quote which opens this chapter adequately capture the predominant subjective experience of the inhabitants of contemporary global society? Or more broadly, does the notion of psychosocial fragmentation reflect the reality of cultural and social changes and their impact upon the self? Many of those accounts discussed would probably answer with a qualified 'yes'. However, critics have suggested that it is a partial or distorted portrayal of social change, selfhood, and their inter-relationship. Problems have been raised with specific theories of psychosocial fragmentation in the process of discussing them. The remainder of this chapter will rehearse three broad criticisms which draw together some of the specific criticisms raised and apply to the thesis of psychosocial fragmentation more generally. The first concerns issues of agency; the second argues for a more positive interpretation of fragmentation; the third emphasizes processes of social regulation and power. These criticisms will form the basis of the alternative visions of self and social change explored in the chapters to come.

The first argument suggests that the idea of psychosocial fragmentation does not do justice to the human powers of agency and creativity which continue to maintain a reasonably consistent sense of self; this point was raised in relation to the work of Marcuse, Furedi, Putnam and Sennett. In fact it is commonly argued that recent social changes have 'opened up' the once unquestioningly self-constitutive scripts of myth, tradition, and social role to human intervention. A consequence of tinkering with these scripts, or even abandoning them all together, is said to lead to identities which are, at least potentially, more choice-based and self-reflexive. Relationships with others are freed from previous boundaries which traditions maintained, including those of time and space. Once formed, alliances may be cancellable but their fluidity is more suited to a mobile, individualized identity. The self is more flexible maybe, but the author's voice is more clearly asserted and indelible, rather than fragmented, alone, and disillusioned. Accounts of psychosocial fragmentation are thus claimed to be overdeterminist in that they place too much emphasis on the flow of constitutive power from society to self. This general critical tendency and alternative formulation is most visible in the work of Anthony Giddens and Ulrich Beck (Giddens, 1991, 1992, 1994, 1999; Beck, 1992, 1994; Beck and Beck-Gernshien,1995, 2002), and will be explored in the next chapter.

A second criticism stems from more radical post-modern accounts additionally bringing into question the above critique. It is suggested that once all the layers of culture and tradition are peeled away there is no authentic self, no heroic author at the core, prepared to embark on a pioneering journey of self-mastery. Rather than denying that processes of fragmentation are occurring, or qualifying them in relation to new forms of autonomy, this version of post-modernism accepts the premise of psychosocial fragmentation, but celebrates it. The bounded, rational self is seen to be a product of Enlightenment and modernist Reason, a powerful discursive fallacy which has long produced us as selves but is now under threat. The alternative is a self which is allowed to cast off the traditional restraints of social structure, and instead acknowledge the relational, dialogic constitution of self, encourage multi-voiced selves and engender a much more dynamic, playful and situated sense of identity more generally (Gergen, 1991; Hermans and Kempen, 1993; Rowan and Cooper, 1999).

Various post-modernist accounts celebrate the appearance of what has been termed a 'plural self' (Rowan and Cooper, 1999). A *pluralized* notion of selfhood is one in which the fissures and contradictions highlighted by the psychosocial fragmentation thesis are acknowledged but not dismissed as degenerative. Instead 'the multi-voicedness of the self is expressed in the supposition that there is a multiplicity of positions or voices, each associated with their particular system of valuations [and] set of feelings' (Hermans, 1999: 113). Hermans's account draws on Bakhtin's notion of the self as a simultaneous polyphony of voices in constant dialogue. 'A multiplicity of personal...meanings emerge' in which 'self-discrepancies and self-contradictions between voices are seen as intrinsic to a healthy functioning of the self and as contributing to its innovation' (1999: 128). For him it is a healthy self which recognizes the multiplicity of voices which contribute to our identity and allows them to be heard. Psychosocial fragmentation, sweeping away traditions and bringing us into contact with other ways of seeing, allows more selves to come to the fore. Interpreted as positive post-modernism, it creates more opportunities for new voices to develop, and for them to be recognized. In this sense Hermans's normative view of selfhood is quintessentially post-modern, revealing a much more positive outcome of the process of fragmentation. Against this view, some stress the need for continuity in sense of identity (Chandler *et al.*, 2003; Glass, 1993; Hekman, 2000). Such critiques do not necessarily reassert the psychosocial fragmentation thesis, but do temper more fervent advocates of post-modern fluidity with thornier issues of the apparent need for ontological continuity and the difficulty of theorizing interiority out of the equation (Butler, 1997).

A third critical tendency has stressed continuity in experiences of self and its relation to society rather than radical fragmentation and decline. This argument has been raised in relation to Riesman's work and to claims made about new communities, but it applies to all the perspectives considered so far. The importance of continuity can be emphasized in different ways. From one perspective, the self has always been constituted in historically contingent power relations, and still is today, even if the specific configurations of those power relations have changed. Thus social systems of control still constitute the self in complex ways rather than fading into the background and casting a vulnerably exposed self into the random currents of psychosocial fragmentation. After a considered analysis of contemporary forms of social stratification, for example, Bradley acknowledges that identities are complex hybrids reflecting personal history and cross-cutting demands of social categorizations which vary in their power to confine or facilitate agency (Bradley, 1996). However, she is also wary of defining current processes of fragmentation as a radical departure from the past. Bradley argues that the underlying dynamics of capitalist social relations tend towards fragmentation and dislocation, and have been with us for a long time: 'people have always been subject to processes of economic differentiation together with differences of ethnicity, gender and age. The potential for fracturing of identities has long existed' (1996: 212).

A Foucaultian approach to the nature of identity also suggests that the networks of relationships between self and other are still being actively fostered in contemporary societies, and are historically contingent. Such an approach tends to take discourse as its focal point rather than communal bonds. However, discourses are mediated by social relations and such an emphasis has allowed for many detailed accounts of how contemporary identities are regulated and determined rather than fragmenting. What is seen to be continuous here is the discursive regulation of identity rather than the specific elements of an established social structure. An emphasis upon Foucaultian approaches to regulated identity will be considered in chapter four.

Overall the portrayal of self as fragmented and de-centred should now be familiar. Such a self is seen to arise in response to social changes which have made previously accepted categories of belonging problematic, whilst also rendering the processes of reciprocity and shared meaning upon which they were founded more difficult to achieve than ever. The critical limits of the psychosocial fragmentation thesis, as explored by proponents of extended reflexivity in the formation of contemporary identities, forms the basis for the next chapter.

3

The Reflexive Self

The old rules about what we are allowed, or supposed to do and be at each life stage have been torn up. To a large degree, we make our own futures now, which is both a new freedom and a new pressure.

(Editorial comment, *Psychologies* magazine, November 2005)

Since the early 1990s there has been a proliferation of interest in the concept of reflexivity as a dimension of contemporary identity. Originally a grammatical term, in the context of identity it refers to the act of an individual subject directing awareness towards itself; reflecting upon its own practices, preferences and even the process of reflection itself. The publication of Anthony Giddens's *Modernity and Self-Identity* (1991) played a key part in generating interest for the term.[1] Giddens here set out a comprehensive vision of an emerging process of identity – the reflexive project of selfhood – in response to a number of radical social changes. Reflexivity *per se* is not peculiar to a post-traditional society; it has always formed an integral part of the self and social relations in Giddens's formulation – 'nothing is more central to, and distinctive of, human life than the reflexive monitoring of behaviour, which is expected by all "competent" members of society of others' (Giddens, 1976: 114). However, Giddens argues that a different sense of reflexivity can be attributed to late-modern, or to use his more recent term, post-traditional, societies:

Thought and action are constantly refracted back upon one another...The reflexivity of modern social life consists in the fact that social practices are constantly examined and reformed in the light of incoming information about those very practices, thus constitutively altering their character...We are abroad in a world which is thoroughly constituted through reflexively applied knowledge, but where at the same time we can never be sure that any given element of that knowledge will not be revised. (Giddens, 1990: 38–39)

Giddens has not been alone in indexing a supposed increase of reflexivity in the everyday task of being a self; recent social theory is punctuated with similar claims made with varying degrees of optimism (Castells, 1997; Gergen, 1991; Heelas *et al.*, 1996; Lash, 1994; MacDonald, 1999). Beck's analysis of risk society is closely allied with extended reflexivity; it is reflexivity which generates an 'awareness of risk *as* risk: the knowledge gaps in risks cannot be converted into certainties by religious or magical knowledge' (Giddens, 1990: 125; Beck, 1992; Beck *et al.*, 1994). Related disciplines and approaches, such as ego-psychology, resource mobilization theory, rational choice theory, and 'preference theory' similarly place a reflexive and calculating individual at the heart of their social analysis (Breen and Goldthorpe, 1997; Carling, 1992; Coleman, 1973, 1990; Emerson, 1972; Elster, 1986; Goldthorpe, 1998; Hakim, 2004). Post-modernism too, often places an extended reflexivity at the heart of that condition. Indeed for Bauman,

> postmodernity, perhaps more than anything else, is a state of mind. More precisely, a state of those minds who have the habit (or is it the compulsion?) to reflect upon themselves, to search their own contents and report what they found. (Bauman, 2001: 117)

We might even go as far as to state that Giddens's work reflects a general tendency in social theory that emphasizes emerging or established reflexive capabilities in the context of social change (Adams, 2006; Adkins, 2003; McNay, 1999; Sweetman, 2003). This tendency I have elsewhere referred to as the *extended reflexivity thesis* (Adams, 2003), which is also reflected in more populist understandings of identity, exemplified in the opening quote of this chapter.

Traditional societies

Post-traditional settings are, predictably, contrasted with the closed identities provided by tradition. Kenneth Gergen's discussion of the relationship between tradition and identity neatly reflects Giddens's vision of traditional society as spatially, relationally and normatively enveloping identities:

> In the traditional community, where relationships were reliable, continuous, and face-to-face, a firm sense of self was favoured. One's sense of identity was broadly and continuously supported. Further there was strong agreement on patterns of 'right' and 'wrong' behaviour. One could simply…be, for there was little question of being otherwise. (Gergen, 1991: 147)

As well as space, *time* is seen to be experienced in a prescriptive way in traditional societies. Both time and space are 'contextually implicated in the nature of lived activities' (Giddens, 1990: 105). Echoing Giddens, Thompson argues that traditional communities were structured by a 'task-oriented' grasp of the passing of time. To illustrate this concept, he cites the example of a crofting and fishing community:

> whose framework of marketing and administration is minimal, and in which the day's tasks (which might vary from fishing to farming, building, mending of nets, thatching, making a cradle or a coffin) seem to disclose themselves, by the logic of need, before the crofter's eyes. (Thompson, 1993: 357)

The particulars of the community's interaction with their immediate physical environment decide the structure of their day. In sum the habits and customs generated by kinship relations, work patterns, the local community, and religious cosmologies of tradition offer relatively prescribed narratives of identity in more traditional settings (Giddens, 1990: 102; Gergen, 1991).

Giddens, Beck, Bauman and others suggest that modernity was itself complicitly reliant on tradition for its perpetuation for the bulk of its historical development:

> For most of its history, modernity has rebuilt tradition as it has dissolved it. Within Western societies the persistence and recreation of tradition was central to the legitimation of power...For tradition placed in stasis some core aspects of social life – not least the family and sexual identity – which were left largely untouched so far as 'radicalizing' Enlightenment was concerned...Most important, the continuing influence of tradition within modernity remained obscure so long as 'modern' meant 'Western'. (Giddens, 1994: 56)

The prevalence and power of Enlightenment thinking problematized the premise of tradition, and removed the boundaries which had previously contained traditional discourses of knowledge. Traditional forms, or rather *certain* traditional forms were questioned and undermined by reason's exclusive claim to objectivity and 'truth'. However, the doubt intrinsic to rational enquiry was not turned upon its origins, nor the emerging institutions of modernity. As Giddens notes here, the contradiction of a supposed affinity with truth and certainty based upon the systematic application of doubt, was hidden, paradoxically enough, in the escalation of science itself to the status of tradition:

> For a long while, the tensions inherent in such a situation were masked by the distinctive status which science, understood in a specific way, enjoyed in modern societies – plus a more or less unquestioned dominance that the West held over the rest of the world. (Giddens, 1994: 86–87)

The 'traditions' of modernity provided relatively stable guidelines for social interaction and options for identity formation, as traditions had done in previous epochs. More specifically, 'tradition placed in stasis some core aspects of social life – not least the family and sexual identity – which were left largely untouched so far as "radicalizing Enlightenment" was concerned' (Giddens, 1994: 56). Bauman similarly argues that for a long time, national and class identifications provided the necessary 'picture on the box' from which the jigsaw of identity could be constructed (Bauman, 2004: 48–49), facilitating a sense of 'social inclusion' (Boyne, 2002: 121).

In summary, traditional communities were maintained by established beliefs and rituals, channelled via powerful elites, tightly-bound by the localized experience of time/space, all-in-all providing 'a relatively fixed horizon of action' (Giddens, 1994: 76). Bauman, Beck, Gergen and Giddens, amongst some of the most influential social theorists in the last 20 years, all produce accounts of tradition which parallel the one outlined here. A similar portrayal, against which contemporary society is contrasted, is prevalent in numerous accounts of social change (Lasch, 1979, 1984; Lash and Friedman, 1992: 4–5; Heelas *et al.*, 1996: 4–5; Sennett, 1999). Even in theory which does not explicitly discuss 'traditional society', it is often the implied other-half of a binary which accentuates fluidity and flexibility in modern settings.

Contemporary societies

> We have landed in a fully and truly foreign country…An unknown, unexplored, unmapped land – we have not been here before, we have not heard of it before. All cultures we know of, at all times, tried, with mixed success, to bridge the gap between the brevity of mortal life and the eternity of the universe. Each culture offered a formula for the alchemist's feat: a reforging of base, fragile and transient substances into precious metals which could resist erosion, be everlasting. We are perhaps the first generation to enter life and live it without such a formula.
>
> (Bauman, 2004: 75)

Bauman continues Giddens's theme of finding ourselves 'abroad' to develop a sense of how to confront the present in the foundational logic of the extended reflexivity thesis. All cultures of the past provided a 'formula' to convert the chaos of an infinite universe into a meaningful constellation by which to navigate conscious, finite human lives. In Giddens's terminology, the 'formulaic truths' integral to the cultures of the past provided the necessary answers for existential questions – 'queries about basic dimensions of existence' (Giddens, 1991: 242) – which in turn allowed us to 'go on' in everyday life with a sense of purpose.

In stark contrast the present is imagined as a radically discontinuous break from the past; it is, in Bauman's words, 'fully and truly foreign', 'unknown', 'unexplored', unheard of. The present is also universalized; 'we' appears to be imagined as homogeneous at least in as far as the shift in our experience of self/culture. What 'we' face at this marked historical disjuncture is a kind of cultural disenfranchisement of the present. Bauman suggests that whereas formulas have varied throughout history, the defining feature of recent social change is that it forces us to live without any formula at all. The existential scaffolding of cultural narratives is removed, exposed for its relativity and arbitrariness. Consequently the processes of self-identity can no longer feast on tried and tested prescriptions; they are stripped to their foundations, nakedly exposed to a transparently contingent world.

How have we reached this post-traditional present? The dissolution of cultural scripts and the extension of self-reflexivity is argued to be the outcome of the convergence and interpenetration of the type of social changes discussed here and in the first chapter, and the post-war period serves as a loose marker of the cumulative effects of such changes

(Giddens, 1994: 57; Beck and Beck-Gernsheim, 2002: 8). Rapidly expanding networks of finance, employment, media, communication and travel create a regularized, criss-crossing, global flow in the traffic of human activity which confounds the previous confines of time and space. Consequently the cohesive affiliations and commonality of experiences which once characterized identity are displaced and dissolved. Giddens refers to this process as 'disembedding': 'the 'lifting out' of social relations from local contexts and their rearticulation across indefinite tracts of time-space' (Giddens, 1991: 18).

Social relations become rearticulated against a backdrop of increasingly impersonal 'abstract systems' (Giddens, 1991). Transactions and exchanges occur in a 'place' emptied of localized parameters. Even interaction which is still localized is shot through with broader globalized dynamics; there is a 'fostering [of] relations between "absent" others, location-ally distant from any given situation of face-to-face interaction... place becomes increasingly *phantasmagoric*: that is to say, locales are thoroughly penetrated by and shaped in terms of social influences quite distant from them' (Giddens, 1990: 19). The procedures, services, goods and activities generated in our relations with social institutions are reconfigured in terms of abstract, globalized symbolic meanings and expertise, which is then re-presented to the individual as an element to be chosen in the reflexive project of their own individualized identity.

In the quote that begins this section, the narrative ends here; but it is the next step that completes the logic of the extended reflexivity thesis. Self-identity, once exposed to a world stripped of pre-given meanings, is faced with no other option but to rely on their own decisions, preferences and inclinations in the everyday business of constructing themselves. Individuals are released from rigid, prescribed social positions such as gender roles and have to 'build up a life of their own', ordering their own biographies (Beck and Beck-Gernsheim, 1995: 6). They must still draw on the resources of the social world to generate a meaningful sense of self, but this is a chronically reflexive process. The self is thus constructed and maintained from a series of reflexive choices, 'individuals must innovate rules in a bricolage of their own identities' (Lash, 1999: 3). The individual as an active agent is implicated in their own sense of self to an unprecedented degree. The self 'becomes a reflexive project' (Giddens, 1991: 32), involving 'the strategic adoption of lifestyle options' related to a planned 'trajectory', all geared to maintaining a meaningful biographical narrative (1991: 243–244). In fact, 'life-plans are the substantial content of the reflexively organized trajectory of the self' (1991: 85). In Ulrich Beck's words, 'biographies become *self-reflexive*; socially prescribed biography is transformed into biography that is self-produced and continues to be produced' (Beck, 1992: 135). Social theorists whose work otherwise differs in many ways converge in an emphasis upon extended reflexivity: 'identity is in the process of being redefined as a pure reflexive capacity' (Melucci, 1996: 36); '[there is] an increasingly significant reflexive subjectivity'

(Lash and Urry, 1994: 3); 'people have to turn to their own resources to decide what they value, to organize their priorities and to make sense of their lives' (Heelas, 1996: 5).

In this context, one's self-awareness is no longer so severely conditioned by one's specific cultural and historical settings. Self awareness becomes, in a sense, 'pure', standing outside of tradition and reflexively selecting beliefs and practices – a lifestyle – which contribute to a self-identity. Without the support of traditional criteria for how to act, what to do and what to be, the self faces new opportunities, new dilemmas. Maintaining a meaningful self-identity is not easy when all knowledge is corrigible. All spheres of life, work, leisure, relationships, diet, health, etc. become ordered into a series of choices to be made from impersonal expert knowledge systems. However, choice alone provides little of the automatic, normative and embedding authority – a formula – upon which the self once relied. To re-embed ourselves depends upon our own abilities to construct a personally-meaningful narrative over time.

Vitally, re-embedding occurs on an *individualized* basis (Beck, 2004; Bauman, 2001); the term individualization is a companion concept to that of extended self-reflexivity. In the space opened up between distant social institutions and the self, the personal biography becomes the blueprint for making sense of one's life-course rather than broader affiliations such as class, and combines forcefully with the process of reflexivity: 'Individualization of life situations and processes thus means that biographies become *self-reflexive*; socially prescribed biography is transformed into biography that is self-produced and continues to be produced' (Beck, 1992: 135). Chronic doubt can become an existential condition, and thus the modern self is faced with a 'dangerous adventure', which is 'both liberating and disturbing' (Giddens, 1994: 59, 87). There is a risky ambivalence to the modern project of individualized selfhood: 'Th[e] project is fraught with new possibilities and dangers, as traditional road maps for the development of personal identity crumble in the face of the juggernaut of late modernity' (Tucker, 1998: 207).

The dynamic opening up of time and space combined with the erosion of tradition creates a level of inter-relatedness which allows for flows of influence to emanate *outwards* from individualized choice, which impact upon global institutions and perpetually reconfigures them:

> The disembedding mechanisms intrude into the heart of self-identity; but they do not 'empty out' the self any more than they simply remove prior supports on which self-identity was based. Rather, they allow the self (in principle) to achieve much greater mastery over the social relations and social contexts reflexively incorporated into the forging of self-identity than was previously possible. (Giddens, 1992: 148–149)

Profound social changes have to be understood dialectically in relation to power and self-identity, incorporating both the loss and regaining of power.

Giddens acknowledges, for example, that reflexivity can facilitate uncertainty, which can lead in extreme cases to pathological states such as paranoia, obsessive compulsion, addiction or 'paralysis of the will' (Giddens, 1990: 196). In this sense, reflexivity could be seen as a loss of power. In addition, the way globalization empties localized experience of their grounding constituents is a loss in an immediate sense: 'With the expansion of abstract systems…the conditions of daily life become transformed and recombined across much larger space-time tracts; such disembedding processes are processes of loss' (Giddens, 1991: 138). On the other hand, reflexivity plays a key role in transforming self-identity by allowing new forms of mastery over the circumstances of one's life, which are at least potentially highly satisfying. It is a world where 'social bonds have effectively to be *made*, rather than inherited from the past – on the personal and more collective levels this is a fraught and difficult enterprise, but one also that holds out the promise of great rewards' (Giddens, 1994: 107).

On balance, Giddens seems to suggest that these opportunities outweigh any losses – 'the capability of adopting freely chosen lifestyles' is 'a fundamental benefit generated by a post-traditional social order' (Giddens, 1992: 231). Positive dimensions of social change thus reach into individual experience: as all social bonds reach new levels of reciprocity, the individual is implicated in a radically reflexive, empowering and appropriating relationship with social structure. But the positive potential of reflexivity extends beyond the confines of the individual self to include 'a diversity of opportunities for individuals to search out others of like interests and form associations with them'; and 'more chance for the cultivation of a diversity of interests in pursuits in general' (1992: 174); the democratization of intimate relationships in 'the transformation of intimacy' (1992), and even a more democratic global society – 'a cosmopolitan conversation of humankind' (Giddens, 1994: 100).

In sum, the traditions, rituals and rules of culture which once shaped the contours of subjectivity have lost their salience irretrievably. The self has become 'disembedded', separating the individual from the meaningful, if relatively unquestioned, context it had in previous times been immersed in. Consequently the self faces both the liberation and the burden of autonomous self-construction: 'The self today is for everyone a reflexive project – a more or less continuous interrogation of past, present and future' (Giddens, 1992: 30). Such accounts clearly go beyond the vision of contemporary society deriving from theories of alienation and psychosocial fragmentation established in the previous chapter and are often critical of what is perceived to be the totalizing determinism of such accounts. There is a sense of ambivalence, an attempt to counterpoise the loss of tradition with the possibility of a 'positive appropriation of life' (Giddens, 1994: 207). The overall impression is of an autonomous self emerging in a setting conducive to minimal interference from troublesome social and cultural structures. The individual is no longer painting by numbers, so to speak, but is creating their own work of art.

The extended reflexivity thesis: critical appraisal

Although versions of the extended reflexivity thesis imbue self-reflexivity with various degrees of optimism, the radical 'disembedding' and 'individualization' of the self, indicated respectively by Giddens and Beck, which heralds the extension of reflexivity into all realms of experience, is a staple portrayal. However, such an analysis of contemporary selfhood and its social context has come under a great deal of criticism, a substantial body of which is warranted. The following section will discuss some of the ways in which reflexivity serves only as a partial explanation of the processes involved in the concrete experience of selfhood in contemporary settings. The key proposition to be considered is whether or not the recent social changes discussed here really do allow more people, more of the time, the power to transform their selves, via heightened reflexive self-awareness, and what the specific social distribution and availability of this 'power' is, if it does exist. 'Transformations' are not considered here in a grand or final sense, but in terms of an increased ability to alter the course of one's life, the nature of one's self, the experiences they have, and the unfettered setting of priorities and goals.

Weak social structure

One major criticism stems from the common accusation that the extended reflexivity thesis employs an excessively weak concept of social structure which gives 'short shrift to the structural and cultural factors still at work in fashioning the self' (Tucker, 1998: 208; Bendle, 2002; Hay et al., 1997; Mestrovic, 1998; O'Brien, 1999). A tenet of the extended reflexivity thesis, to reiterate, is that new levels of relatedness mean that the modern individual also has a chance to affect the broader social system:

> The day-to-day activities of an individual today are globally consequential. My decision to purchase a particular item of clothing, for example, or a specific type of foodstuff, has manifold implications...[an] extraordinary, and still accelerating, connectedness between everyday decisions and global outcomes. (Giddens, 1994: 57–58)

As all social bonds reach new levels of reciprocity, the individual is implicated in a radically reflexive relationship with social structure. However, little attempt is made to differentiate between experiences of people in diverse, structurally positioned settings. Consequent theorizations of self-identity fail to account for the socially differentiated restraints on agency and/or reflexivity which either persist in contemporary societies, or are novel to them (Tucker, 1998; Craib, 1992; Mestrovic, 1998; Lash, 1994). In other words, the extended reflexivity thesis is an excessively uniform analysis which marginalizes differentiations between experiences of people in diverse contemporary situations maintained by powerful social structures, such as class and gender (Lash, 1994; Adkins, 2002). Others have voiced a broader suspicion of social theory envisioning a situation 'where agency is set free from structure' (Lash, 1994: 119), and assert the necessity of a more sophisticated account of degrees of reflexivity, freedom and constraint in relation to changing, but not disappearing social structures (Craib, 1992; Lash, 1994; Jamieson, 1999, 1998). Consequently, the extended reflexivity thesis *universalizes* individual experience somewhat, and instates an *undifferentiated* version of social structure. It succumbs, as McNay pithily states, to a 'fetishization of the indeterminacy of social structures' (McNay, 1999: 105). This critique will be further substantiated in the final chapter.

Empirical support

Empirical research to assess the role of extended reflexivity in contemporary identity formations as a response to social change has been remarkable mainly for its absence according to one study (Phillips and Western, 2005: 163). This general paucity may mean that no firm conclusions can be made from research that has been carried out, but there is perhaps more to consider than Phillips and Western suggest. Some have offered qualified support for the claim that self-reflexivity is an organizing principle of identities in relation to specific areas such as reincarnation or emotional work (Bolton and Boyd, 2003; Walter, 2001). Other studies have tended to support theoretical critiques of extended reflexivity on the point that social structure still underpins identities in differential ways (Brannen and Nilsen, 2005; Frost, 2005; O'Connor, 2006). Continuity in the ways identities are formed in relation to markers of social structure (class, gender, ethnicity, etc.) and new ways of marking these structures are at least as important as the breaks and discontinuities, apparently wrought by social change, emphasized by the extended reflexivity thesis and some post-modern accounts (Gill *et al.*, 2005; Jagger, 2001; Jamieson, 1998; Kelly and Kenway, 2001; Plumridge and Thomson, 2003; Thomson *et al.*, 2002). In a similar vein Phillips and Western's detailed study of sources of identification concluded that the evidence they collected 'does not suggest that the contemporary period is one in which social identity processes are distinctively different from earlier times' (Phillips and Western, 2005: 183; see also Scott and Scott, 2001). The majority of empirical work thus appears to offer support for the critique developed in this chapter.

There is a related, and often implicit, criticism of the extended reflexivity thesis in the recent expansion of research on social stratification drawing on a Bourdieuvian perspective (e.g. Devine *et al.*, 2005; Mitchell and Green, 2002; Skeggs, 1997). Whilst distinct differences in identity formation are sometimes indicated in these studies, the continuing importance of social structure is seen to persist, if in novel ways. Emphasizing the role of habitus and embodiment as they do, whilst refocusing on ethnographic research and studies of locales, offers the possibility of a comprehensive qualification of the notion that there is a widespread 'disembedding' of identities from social structure. This work is discussed in more detail in chapter six.

Our critique of reflexivity has so far drawn strength from the feminist insight that the normative idealization of a reflexive self is a disembedded and disembodied 'masculinist' positioning of subjectivity (McNay, 1999). If in a sense we have tried to re-embed reflexivity in the critical points now made, those remaining are loosely concerned with its re-embodiment.

Relational, non-reflexive and embodied subjectivity

Social theory is replete with attempts to conceptualize the ways in which fundamentally embodied and routinely non-reflexive aspects of subjectivity co-exist with self-reflexive practices. Bourdieu's 'doxa' and 'habitus' (1977, 1990b, 1998), Goffman's 'Umwelt' (1971) and Schultz's 'natural attitude' (1962, 1964) are examples of such an attempt. However, McNay discerns 'a tendency in certain theories of identity transformations to construe identity as a process of symbolic identification without considering its mediation in embodied practice' (McNay, 1999: 19). The theories she has in mind include those of extended reflexivity. Bendle is worried that the same theories 'give little recognition to the constraining significance of internal psychological conflict and ambivalence' (Bendle, 2002: 13). Clearly there is a danger in underestimating habitual, unconscious, ambiguous, and emotional dimensions in a selfhood increasingly governed by a ratiocinating, rationalizing reflexivity. Giddens's own work actually makes space for the processes of an 'unconscious' and 'practical consciousness', often overlooked by critics, providing it with a defence against some of the stronger accusations of excessive cognitivism, rationalism and voluntarism.

The realm of the unconscious is of primary importance for the development of self-identity in Giddens's work at least, as it is here where relationships of 'basic trust' are initiated. Although cognitive understandings of the self and social worlds are essential in providing 'faith' in the world, they do not facilitate a meaningful existence in themselves. What is needed initially is an emotional attachment to the world and relevant others – which tends to remain unconscious and unquestioned: 'Cognitive frames of meaning will not generate that faith without a corresponding level of underlying emotional commitment – whose origins…are largely unconscious' (Giddens, 1991: 38).[2] Practical consciousness tends to be what Giddens's refers to as 'non-conscious'. It is learnt knowledge which has become second nature or taken-for-granted, but is nonetheless potentially available to reflexivity. Practical consciousness keeps us the right side of chaos by 'bracketing out' an array of fears, concerns and questions which would otherwise dog our every movement. Furthermore, by removing them from routine discursive contemplation, we experience what we *do* do, what is 'bracketed in', as the normal and reasonable way of doing things – as the 'natural attitude'.

I think Giddens's conceptualization of both the unconscious and practical consciousness is seriously flawed on a number of counts, but there is not the space here to go into these criticisms in detail. The main point to be raised for the purposes of this discussion is that in order to incorporate them into a model of self in which reflexivity plays a pervasive and ascendant role, they are both shorn of important elements. As McNay suggests then, despite Giddens's theoretical sophistication, problems persist in conceptualizing an adequately embodied version of self-reflexivity. Elements of his topographic model appear to be imagined as distinct identities, operating independently but civilly within a functioning self; little is said of the intangibility of their boundaries, or their inter-relationship.

Problems with psychological dimensions supposedly co-existing with reflexivity help reveal the poverty of the conceptualization of self at the heart of the extended reflexivity thesis. Giddens's version of the unconscious, in particular, often appears self-contained and carefully partitioned from reflexive awareness. In this overly-mechanistic portrayal there is little acknowledgement of the conflictual or contradictory tendencies, irrationalities, inconsistencies and obfuscations apparent in psychoanalytic literature. An excessively 'tidy' portrayal of unconscious mechanisms is presented, lacking complexity and ambivalence with regard to its relationship to the thoughts and actions of the self in everyday life. It 'is grounded in a very strong positivistic ego psychology' (Lash and Urry, 1994: 38), according to which all seems to fall under the spell of the defining characteristics of reflexivity, leaving an overall picture of an ordered, voluntarist and predictable psyche. All the influences upon the 'choices' one makes in the reflexive project of selfhood appear to be easily acknowledged or safely tucked away, operating the machinery of the self-system behind the scenes, and are thus irrelevant.

It is possible to interpret a lack of elaboration concerning the complexities of the unconscious as a tendentious device (conscious or otherwise!) in the context of the neo-modern theorization of self-identity, as Thrift has argued. He refers to an overall 'absence of absence in Giddens's presence': 'That is, Giddens's impoverished notion of the unconscious. It is, in fact, difficult to work out whether Giddens has a theory of the unconscious or whether it is simply a supplement which enables him to privilege practical consciousness and knowledge' (Thrift, 1996: 55). More charitably perhaps, Craib argues that there is an inevitable and unavoidable problem in attempting to incorporate unconscious activity into a rational theory of action:

> If sociology is to give an account of agency...there is a sense in which it cannot allow concepts, such as the unconscious, which suggest that human beings routinely work in irrational, un-routine ways...Giddens seems to do this with ease, but then to deny its effect. (Craib, 1992: 142)

A watered-down or 'neat' version of the unconscious allows Giddens and others to maintain an important part of the psyche, while avoiding potential compromises in his attempts to reformulate and extend the scope of reflexive agency in modern settings. To allow the unconscious to exist, Giddens has to subdue it to these principles of orderliness and voluntarism, a task which puts him not just at loggerheads with classical psychoanalysis, but also much of contemporary feminist, post-structuralist and psychoanalytically-oriented social theory: 'What they positively value as the heterogeneous play of an unconscious structured by "complexity" and "difference", he sees as a threat to ontological security' (Lash and Urry, 1994: 42). These theories more readily acknowledge the chaos which the unconscious brings with it, and place it at the heart of human experience, including experience of self (Elliott, 2004). But for the extended reflexivity thesis, the 'ego is the hero of the battle against ontological security' (Lash and Urry, 1994: 42), and in becoming so it structures the unconscious along similar rationalistic, ordered lines.

It is worth noting that the development of ego-psychology, largely in the United States, has been subjected to sustained critique on exactly the same point – a purportedly exaggerated emphasis upon the autonomy of the ego leading to voluntarism and rationalism in the theorization of the self (Bendle, 2002; Brubaker and Cooper, 2000; Lacan, 1977; Thrift, 1996). One suspects that if the unconscious revealed its true colours in Giddens's battle, it would more than blunt the range and power of reflexive awareness. Once the concept of the unconscious *is* accepted as part of the psyche, allocating it a tidy corner and keeping it there is a difficult task. If such an emphasis poses a contradiction which is not easy to overcome, the extended reflexivity thesis resolves the problem by largely ignoring it.

By contrast, according to the Freudian model, unconscious processes impact substantially on the more 'rational' and accessible aspects of consciousness; 'there is always emotional and irrational seepage that eludes the enunciation of such a rational position' (Hey, 2005: 863). By definition, this impact cannot be easily understood by the reflexive awareness it affects. As one psychoanalytic theorist astutely puts it, the self-aware subject 'arrives on the scene rather late in the day. By the time we are capable of a meaningful interpretation of our existence...we have already been constituted via the ego's [unconscious] negotiation with the environment' (Bollas, 1987: 8). Thus the basic rudiments of a psychoanalytic perspective can be used to question the theorization of reflexive awareness as a clear and distinct realm from the unconscious, with a relatively simplistic interrelationship. Consequently, claims about the scope of reflexive awareness may need to be revised.

A related assertion is that the fundamental *corporeality* of human subjectivity is another fly in the ointment of a reflexive project of selfhood. Following a 'turn' to the body, once a neglected aspect of sociology and psychology (Burkitt, 1999: 1), it is now an established critical point that being a body combines with intersubjectivity to both allow and place limitations on the reflexive construction of identity through choice in complex ways (Burkitt, 1991, 1999; Crossley, 2001; Jenkins, 1996; Turner, 1984,

1992). Such a critique does not bemoan the shackles of the body; it tends towards an integrationist account in which our reflexive choices are necessarily embodied, as evident in Charlesworth's eloquent summary of his phenomenological perspective: 'my sense of the world and my sense of the body cohere because it is an inextricable mix, that I have learnt, through involved intimacy with others, the sense of both through each other' (Charlesworth, 2000: 17). The worlds that bodies come into shape and inscribe the practices and preferences of that body from the moment of birth (perhaps earlier), and the body here includes the bases of consciousness and thought.

'Internal' dimensions of embodiment incorporate unconscious activity just discussed but other phenomenon too. It might include the emotional dimension of subjectivity; which ought, according to some at least, be a crucial concern of critical social theory (Elliott, 2004: 66); and which has complex relationships with self-reflexivity. It is not the case, for example, that reflexive processes of self-awareness can simply 'translate' emotion into an appropriately transparent language which we can then cognize and incorporate into a reflexive project. Again psychodynamic theory offers a cautionary tale against such a reading. The reflexive process is itself imbued with the embodied and intersubjective ambiguities of affect which are not laid bare by a turning of one aspect of the self back upon its self.

To ignore or marginalize perplexing conceptualizations of emotional life is to do an injustice to the complexity of the self and the dynamics of the reflexive and non-reflexive, leaving us with 'a very shallow picture of the human being indeed' (Craib, 1992: 177; Cohen, 1989). The converse of the decentring of emotional experience is argued to be the exaggeration of the extent to which contemporary agency is logical, autonomous and masterful: a weakness of the extended reflexivity thesis already established in related critiques of voluntarism. Mestrovic's polemic critique often reminds us of this point in relation to Giddens's work:

> The result is a portrait of the agent based on oversimplified wishful thinking, a caricature based on modernist ideology in which the agent is reflexive, able to monitor his/her actions, skilled, and knowledgeable at all times... Giddens's agent is all mind and no heart...ultimately a rationalist, a modernist caricature of what it means to be human. (Mestrovic, 1998: 78–80)

Some authors, such as Thrift (1996) and Alexander (1996), drawing broadly on psychoanalytic insight, argue that non-rational events form the basis of any rational processes, and thus have a pervasive influence. Thought is experientially *fused* with what we might call the non-rational, in this instance emotion. The way in which we think about our own self, others and the world around us, is inseparable from our emotional experience; furthermore, as Burkitt asserts, it is inseparable from intersubjective experience: 'if emotions are expressive of anything, it is of the relations and interdependencies that they are an integral part of, and in this sense emotions are essentially communicative: they are expressions occurring between people and registered on the body, rather than expressions of something contained inside a single person' (Burkitt, 1991: 113). What we separate out as concepts – the body, emotion, mind – are in fact contemporaneously woven into the process of intersubjective experience. Thought is often irrational, fantastical and surreal, shaped as it is by a chaotic collage of interexperience. Thus the hope for a blossoming reflexivity to oversee the processes of subjectivity is argued to be a vain one.

Reflexivity as culturally relative

A third and related critical point is that the extended reflexivity thesis fails to recognize that reflexivity is itself a discourse embedded in the cultural and historical norms of modernity rather than transcending them (Adams, 2003). In other words, the complex narrative of a perspicuous post-cultural, post-traditional and post-conventional process of self-understanding and constitution is itself a convention, a dynamic artefact of a particular cultural, historical and political framework – namely modernity (Alexander, 1996, 1999; Mestrovic, 1998). Alexander asserts that reflexivity, in whatever historical period, 'can be understood only within the context of cultural tradition, not outside of it' (Alexander, 1996: 136). Mestrovic similarly accuses Giddens in particular of being 'unaware that the meaning of reflexivity, agency and dialogue vary across cultures'. The specific connotations of what we understand 'reflexivity' to be is inevitably conditioned by the cultural symbols already available to us. More specifically, dominant understandings of reflexivity, and their take-up in self-understandings, are argued to be shaped by a 'neo-modernist' and 'masculinist' normative take on culture, which valorizes rationality, teleology, voluntarism and instrumentalism.

In what more specific sense is the concept of reflexivity 'neo-modern'? The use of a traditional/post-traditional dichotomy is said to revive earlier theories of modernization in its representation of different cultures and subjectivites; the model 'rests upon the same *simpliste* set of binary oppositions as did earlier modernization theory in its most banal form' (Alexander, 1995: 44). Giddens, Beck, etc. argue that tradition once structured and determined our lives in relative ignorance. Thus, retrospectively in terms of western culture, we were once naive cultural dupes. More 'traditional' cultures which still persist today may also be perceived as more naive than the predominately post-traditional West (or 'global' society). 'Traditional' societies were once similarly conceptualized in anthropology, geographical distance from Europe equating to regressive temporal distance in a 'denial of covalescence' (Fabian, 1983: 26; Argyrou, 2003). In post-traditional society reflexivity has released the subject from such deterministic constraints, allowing her/him to construct their identity and environment with new-found freedom. Similarly, theories of modernization suggested that rationally-ordered capitalist economies were the pinnacle of civilization, as they successfully swept away the weight of tradition, which held back 'development' if adhered to.

Once Alexander makes the comparison with the traditional/post-traditional model, connections with modernization theory are clearly apparent. They provide, according to Alexander, a 'historically arbitrary, Western centred, and theoretically tendentious approach to tradition' (Alexander, 1995: 45); all accusations which could equally be made in relation to early modernization theories. Alexander's criticism may seem a little exaggerated in light of some of the complexities of the extended reflexivity thesis. Undoubtedly though, it contains at least the seed of a valuable critique. It makes possible a consideration of what is 'othered' by normative accounts of reflexive subjectivity, and asks us to consider other ways of being 'reflexive' within other cultures and traditions, as well as in the West's history. In addition it suggests how contemporary notions of reflexivity are susceptible to reproducing the taken-for-granted assumptions which underpin the hegemonic culture and traditions of western, late-modern society rather than liberating us from them.

Considering one example from a discussion between Giddens and Christopher Pierson, this susceptibility is subtly apparent: 'The truth of tradition is given by the codes of practice which it enshrines. This is the crux of the differences between traditional ways of doing things and those based upon rational or scientific enquiry' (Giddens and Pierson, 1998: 128). It could be argued that 'scientific enquiry' is itself a 'code of practice', involving rituals and traditions which provide their own 'truth', an established critical claim (e.g. Adorno and Horkheimer, 1997 [1947]). There is a danger in ignoring the wealth of philosophical and social theory which has *relativized* the position of science, rationality and Enlightenment theory as messengers of truth (e.g. Latour, 1993; Wynne, 1996). Beck is more wary of scientific wisdom, but the cultural origins of reflexivity extend beyond 'science'. In overlooking the cultural origins of the concept and value of self-reflexivity more generally, there is a danger that we might fail to recognize 'reflexive thinking' as a related, conceptual product of western modernity, not a universally accepted cognitive function. To use Giddens's terminology, he is assuming that reflexivity 'disembeds' the individual from traditions. What he and others neglect to contemplate is that the concept of reflexivity, rationality, and other Enlightenment terms, are themselves ways of 'embedding' the individual in a particular cultural framework:

> one could argue that modernists are embedded in their own provincial cosmopolitanisms despite the outward appearance of globalization. Westerners gaze at the developing world through the eyes of their Enlightenment-based spectacles, thereby remaining *provincial* and *ethnocentric*...Modernism is a specific belief system which leads modernists to their own distinctive forms of irrationality. (Mestrovic, 1998: 155)

These 'provincial cosmopolitanisms' might include an unquestionable faith in the separateness of self and surroundings; a teleology of self-mastery;

a grasping of a meaningful life as a rationally-induced future-oriented project; a disjunctive relationship between language and reality which progressive reason can overcome, or in a view of the individual as a bounded, cognitive isolate or 'monad' (Burkitt, 1991). Or consider Mestrovic's own list of the 'cults' of modernity: 'the cult of mechanization, the cult of conspicuous consumption, the cult of science [and] the cult of being "nice" among others...each of these phenomena exerts tremendous constraint on the knowledgeable and skilled agent to conform' (Mestrovic, 1998: 150). Reflexivity, as a primary and extended attribute of contemporary society and self, draws on all of these beliefs, which in turn impinge upon the contemporary agent's knowledgeability.

The extended reflexivity thesis clearly has a normative dimension; reflexivity is championed, though somewhat ambivalently, as capable of transcending tradition, amongst other issues. The faith in continued progress, in the gradual 'uncovering' of the reality behind previous cultural formations via rational faculties is a re-engagement with modernist principles, a form of 'neo-modernism' (Szerszynski, 1996: 112; Mestrovic, 1998). The self, in its neo-modernist guise, stands outside of culture in an illusory disconnectedness. Similar claims are routinely made in philosophy:

> The demands we make for philosophical explanations come, seem to come, from a position in which we are, as it were, looking down onto the relation between ourselves and some reality, some kind of fact or real possibility...the characteristic form of the illusion is precisely of philosophy as an area of inquiry, in the sense in which we are familiar with it. (Diamond, cited in Thrift, 1996: 35)

Diamond implies that privileged positions from which we view our relationship with the world (including ourselves) are a fallacy, an 'illusion'. They are part and parcel of the discourse which forms our understanding of everyday life, and which we can never step outside. As Castoriadis succinctly claims here:

> There exists no place, no point of view outside of history and society, or 'logically prior' to them, where one could be placed in order to construct a theory of them – a place from which to inspect them, contemplate them, affirm the determined necessity of their being – thus, constitute them, reflect upon them or reflect them in their totality. (Castoriadis, 1987: 3)

In the parallel realm of the sociology of identity, it could be argued that this is exactly the role assigned to reflexivity by those heralding its radical extension.

The reconceptualization of reflexivity, in both analytical and normative terms, is a possible avenue for the further development and application of the criticisms raised here. Three examples will be briefly considered now. Nicholas Mouzelis's attempt to consider alternative types of reflexivity, accounts of subjectivity which place the relation to the other at the centre of accounts of reflexivity, and a psychoanalytically-informed ethnographic study, all reconceptualize reflexivity in ways which potentially accommodate the criticisms raised here.

Apophatic reflexivity

Nicholas Mouzelis claims that Giddens's notion of reflexivity is 'western-specific', leading to a narrowness of definition. Giddens develops an 'over-activistic' understanding of reflexivity, which excessively emphasizes and lauds an ordering, instrumental, chronically monitoring and revising approach to self-identity (Mouzelis, 1999: 85–86). Mouzelis argues that this is a severe limitation of possible forms of reflexive response to post-traditional settings. It is a conceptualization rooted in western traditions which have celebrated activistic aspects of self-experience and self-development.

Mouzelis refers to Giddens's reflexivity as 'cataphatic', which has an 'exact opposite', labelled 'apophatic' by Mouzelis.[3] In general terms, cataphatic reflexivity emphasizes the role of cognition, and the application of rational thinking, in the affirmation of identity. Apophatic reflexivity, on the other hand, stresses that rational thinking should be minimized, used to keep the mind 'empty' for a non-rational, supposedly more authentic, experience of self-identity. Apophatic discourses, Mouzelis argues, can offer an important insight into other understandings of reflexivity, and thus reveal aspects of self-identity which Giddens neglects: '[Giddens's] theory of reflexivity over-emphasises the activistic, purposive, instrumental aspects of intra-active, self-self relationships, and under-emphasises their apophatic, non-instrumental, non-activistic aspects' (1999: 95). Apophatic reflexivity originates in religious attempts to attain spiritual purity; it 'aims at cleaning out the material and spiritual self so that the believer becomes an "empty vessel" ready to receive divine illumination' (1999: 86). However, Mouzelis is more interested in secular accounts of apophaticism.[4] He draws from the work of the anti-religious spiritual philosopher Krishnamurti to provide an example of a secular, apophatic, discourse of reflexivity.

Krishnamurti's supposedly apophatic perspective demands that individuals give up on almost all forms of rational thinking in ordering their existence meaningfully. Furthermore: 'Beliefs, divine revelations, sacred texts, as well as rationalistically derived moral codes, are not only quite irrelevant in the search for a spiritual, meaningful existence today, but they actually constitute serious obstacles to such a search' (Mouzelis, 1999: 88). Krishnamurti's belief is that genuine self-awareness comes about only when rationalized schemes and projects for the self are abandoned; 'when ratiocination, planning and cognitively constructed means-end schemata are peripheralised' (1999: 88). He argues that 'the fundamental understanding of oneself does not come through knowledge or through the cultivation of experiences' (Krishnamurti, 1970: 25). To exist authentically, one has to explore one's own self through 'silent and continuous gazing inwards' (Mouzelis, 1999: 89). From this state, 'a tranquility that is not a product of the mind, a tranquility that is neither imagined nor cultivated' is possible (Krishnamurti, 1970: 28).

Mouzelis argues that Giddens's and Krishnamurti's approaches to self-identity both amount to forms of reflexivity, and both operate, to various degrees 'whatever the type of communication one has with one's self' (Mouzelis, 1999: 90). They are both potential and actual elements of reflexive self-identity in post-traditional settings, and 'the theorisation of both is absolutely necessary in order to make sense of the complex ways in which subjects face the "empty space" of growing choices created by detraditionalization' (1999: 95). I have not sought to explore Krishnamurti's perspective in any detail here, nor indeed Mouzelis's. What Mouzelis's analysis indicates is that alternative formulations of reflexivity are possible. In this instance, goal-oriented thought processes take a back seat to a more contemplative and tranquil awareness of self.

Adorno is similarly critical of dominant formulations of emancipation, which, he argues, focus upon 'the conception of unfettered activity, of uninterrupted procreation, chubby insatiability, of freedom as frantic bustle' (Adorno, 1951: 156). Adorno anticipates Mouzelis's apophatic reflexivity when he imagines a world where 'lying on water and looking peacefully at the sky, being, nothing else, without any further definition and fulfilment, might take the place of process, act, satisfaction' (1951: 157). Apophatic reflexivity is just one way of considering reflexivity differently; it does not attempt to do justice to the entirety of critical points levelled at the term. In pursuing these alternatives, a more complex and representative understanding of reflexivity and self-identity may be generated. At the same time, alternative discourses may further illustrate and problematize the one-sidedness of the extended reflexivity thesis.

Reflexivity and the other

Developments in psychology, social psychology and sociology have emphasized the role of the other in a relational conceptualization of the dynamics of self-identity which can be used to problematize the notion of extended reflexivity further (e.g. Hermans, 1999, 2002; Hermans and Kempen, 1993). George Mead's work is an example of social psychology more akin to the view that the fundamentals of subjectivity are in fact firmly embedded in its social and cultural context. Although still 'greatly undervalued and widely misunderstood' (Burkitt, 1991: 25), his account of the how the self is formed and maintained is persuasive and Burkitt is one of a number of critical advocates (e.g. Atkinson and Housley, 2003; Dennis and Martin, 2005; Plummer, 2000). Mead's is a thoroughly relational account of the origins and maintenance of the processes of self-reflexivity. This process, Mead argues, is characterized by a development of a sense of the self from the viewpoint of the 'other': 'he [sic] becomes an object to himself only by taking the attitudes of other individuals towards himself within a social environment or context of experience and behaviour in which both he and they are involved' (Mead, 1934: 201).

Mead argues that in concrete social groups, humans modify their gestural responses based on the stimulating signals of others with the intention of creating further stimuli. All human activity is inevitably caught up in this web of reciprocity for Mead. To be able to transform that environment in appropriate and meaningful ways means developing a sense of one's position in relation to significant others, and later, the group as a whole. What is required is the ability to perceive one's self from the 'outside' as it were, as an object in the environment, though which can only emerge, of course, from the subject in question. This requirement is the basis for the turning back upon one's self – the reflexivity – of self-consciousness; gaining an appreciation of the nature of one's own conduct 'involves the individual being thrown into an attitude of self-reflection' (Burkitt, 1991: 33). Mead argues that this moment of reflexivity is always already social; the point of objectification is located, not 'in' the self or the other, but in the relating dynamic, the taking up of the attitude of the other towards one's self.

Thus the self 'is essentially a social structure, and it arises in social experience' (Mead, 1934: 202). It is only through taking the view of the other that we 'become aware of ourselves as objects' and thus how 'we come to see, assess, judge self, and create identities' (Charon, 1995: 151). As individuals develop, the population of 'others' increases in sum, and they become assimilated into a 'generalized other':

> the self reaches its full development by organising these individual attitudes of others into the organised social or group attitudes, and by thus becoming an individual reflection of the general systematic pattern of social or group behaviour in which it and the others are all involved. (Mead, 1934: 207)

No meaningful interactions, nor even the most intimate sense of self, is possible, without these social foundations. Mead makes this clear in an eloquent summary:

> unless the individual has thus become an object to himself he would not be self-conscious or have a self at all. Apart from his social interaction with other individuals, he would not be able to relate the private or 'subjective' contents of his experience to himself and he could not become aware of himself as such, that is, as an individual, a person, merely by means or in terms of these contents of his experience; for in order to become aware of himself as such, he must, to repeat, become an object to himself, or enter his own experience as an object, and only by social means – only by taking the attitude of others towards himself – is he able to become an object to himself. (1934: 246)

Mead here repeats his central assertion, that the nascent self is indebted to its social environment for its development. Even the most 'internal' or 'subjective' experiences stem from the ability to be aware of one's self as an object. And this awareness is possible only by locating one's view towards one's self from an externally anchored position – 'by taking the attitudes of others toward himself'. From this position the self as a meaningful, interacting object emerges, yet remains inextricably social.

Mediated in innumerable forms, this process is what makes up the practice of 'culture'; from family traditions handed down generation to generation, to expected conduct on a busy walkway, to the institutionalized rituals of a sociological conference and so on. Following Mead, all these activities, and of course countless others, are forms of interaction which require an objectification of self according to pre-given meanings. Thus culture is undeniably implicated in the ability to be reflexive at all, and in the nature of that reflexivity. In a Meadian analysis then, the process of self-reflexivity, even at its most 'private', is bound to mirror cultural norms to some degree (Burkitt, 1991: 40). The value of his analysis lies in its rendering of the foundational processes of self-reflexivity comprehensively as a relational and discursive process. It allows us to reassert the critical point established earlier, that self-reflexivity needs to be conceptualized as culturally-situated, and examined for the specifics of that situatedness, rather than detached from social or cultural relations in a simplistic manner.

For our purposes it provides enough of a canvas upon which to sketch a possible conceptualization of a culturally situated, relationally-oriented reflexive awareness, which poses certain problems for the theorization of an extended reflexivity. Mead's theory makes a complex case for reflexivity being reducible, in the first instance, to interaction, and by extension, to the specific cultural frameworks which contextualize and give meanings to self-experience. The point from which reflexivity emanates is here understood to be an echo of the accrued voices of others. This implies that there is no organizing principle within the self which is fully aware of itself and all its influences. Mead's ideas can be used to deny the existence of a mundanely accessible space 'outside' culture and see the very notion of a reflexive and disembedded self as one possible construction (however hegemonic), which constructs and reflects our experience in certain ways.

The self is not stripped of cultural meaning and 'exposed' to a bleached and malleable terrain. Notions of reflexivity, and in fact any form of self-consciousness are all a product of culture in this sense. The individual cannot stand aside from their social and cultural origins and use them, transparently, as a variety of options with which to resource an individualized reflexive self-identity. The concept of a reflexive project of selfhood is as much a product of social and cultural interactions as any other; it does not transcend them. In fact the construction of the self as an empowered, liberated agent is itself the unreflexive product of a neo-liberal inheritance of cultural legacy – western modernity. A reconceptualization of reflexivity along these lines suggests it might have a regulative role in the constitution of modern subjectivity at least as much as a liberating one; Foucaultian analyses of the thorough-going social and discursive regulation of self-reflexivity in this sense reiterate Mead's insight; this suggestion will be considered further in the following chapter. It also suggests that reflexivity can be understood as a multi-dimensional phenomenon, existing in different ways depending on the social and cultural positions of those wielding it, or conceptualizing it.

However, others have argued that Mead's theory, whilst acknowledging the social origins of selfhood, fails to accommodate a detailed analysis of the complexities of modern forms of social organization, or to consider the impact of social or psychic conflict upon the establishment of self-identity (Burkitt, 1991: 50–53; Elliott, 2001), and these are valid criticisms. A Meadian notion of selfhood can also appear to be an excessively cognitive or functional model of the interactive processes at the heart of selfhood. Although the self-other boundary is effectively complicated, the 'internalization' of symbolic interaction appears to be a fairly transparent and rationalistic process once revealed. Thus a Meadian analysis may not overcome criticisms made of the extended reflexivity thesis in terms of an under-appreciation of the experiential reality of embodiment, emotion, psychical conflict, particularly in comparison to psychoanalysis, 'a language that stresses the ungovernableness of identity, emotion and the "self" ' (Hey, 2005: 863).

In a field generally indebted to Klein, Winnicot, and Fairburn amongst others, broad developments of object-relations perspectives in psychoanalysis offer another interesting reinterpretation of the nature of self-reflexivity, which could go some way to appeasing a Meadian and a psychodynamic approach (e.g. Laplanche, 1999; Bollas, 1987; Butler, 1997; Layton, 1998). Like symbolic interactionism, object-relations theory defines a core subject as 'constituted through discourse and relational experience...rather than an absolute universal substance' (Hekman, 2000: 301). Winnicott once claimed, for example, that 'there is no such thing as a baby – meaning that if you set out to describe a baby, you will find you are describing a baby and someone' (cited in Davis and Wallbridge, 1981: 34). Even in the healthy adult, 'independence is never absolute', and the individual and the environment remain 'interdependent' (Winnicott, 1965: 59). Indeed object-relations theory has much in common with the post-modern theorization of the subject on this point.

However, unlike post-modernism, or Lacanian psychoanalysis, object relations still assumes the creation of a core of subjecthood, one that 'emerges from relational forces in the subject's early years' and that 'is a necessity for healthy subjectivity' (Hekman, 2000: 301). Becoming an object to one's self and that object, or objects, having continuity over time is thought to be essential; not 'finding a way to exist as oneself' is argued to be a painful experience (Winnicott, 1971: 117).

Of importance for our purposes is that in some applications of this object-relations perspective, the Meadian process of subjectivization remains relational, but is rendered more uncertain, less transparent. It thus offers the promise of a more relational conceptualization of subjectivity found in Meadian psychology without the traces of cognitivism already problematized in the extended reflexivity thesis. For example Phillips argues that behind Laplanche's sophisticated conceptualization of the 'enigmatic signifier' lies a 'mercifully simple and compelling idea' (Phillips, 2002: 202), and it is Phillips's interpretation of Laplanche that forms the basis for my thinking here. The terms refers to a particular body of 'messages' transmitted by the parents to the infant; not just verbal messages but also 'gestural, olfactory, tonal and so on' (2002: 202). As the child develops, and even from birth, they can 'translate' some of these messages and absorb them readily, but many remain 'enigmatic'. They are enigmatic on two accounts: firstly because the child cannot make sense of them because of his or her yet-nascent ability to understand those messages; secondly because the parents do not understand them, nor are they aware of them, because they are unconscious. This means every child incorporates a substantial 'residue' which 'constitutes an unconscious of foreign bodies' (2002: 202). Laplanche builds a complex account of cathexis, fantasy and sexuality upon this claim, but the basic insight is more straightforwardly plausible: 'that parents convey far more than they intend, and that children take in, in whatever form, far more than the parents or the children suspect' (2003: 203).

It is in this sense that the unconscious, for Laplanche, is not another version of self, a more primal or authentic one, but 'the repressed residue of the other person' (Laplanche, cited in Phillips, 2002: 202); returning us, in a sense, to Freud's notion of ego-identity being forged in the melancholic introjection of lost others, initially the mother's body (Freud, 1914, 1923) – 'a structured sedimentation of lost objects; objects incorporated into the tissue of subjectivity itself' (Elliott, 2000: 136). As Phillips states it, Laplanche's reading is of a more generalized integration of the other: 'what is inescapable in the genesis and development of every person is the presence inside them – the psychic forcefield, the aura, the atmosphere, the messages – of another person' (Philips, 2003: 203). He goes on to discuss the potential of psychoanalysis for translating some of these messages in adult life via therapy, or at least accepting their un-translatableness. For our purposes, Laplanche's decentring of the self via his relational concept of the unconscious has some important parallels with Meadian notions of self. The self is still constructed relationally, but the point of emergence for the reflexive voice is always obscured by the ambiguous and uncertain 'messages' of significant others, rather than internalized as a transparent and instantaneous process of becoming both subject and object.

Christopher Bollas utilizes a similarly foundational understanding of the other:

> the concept of the self should refer to the positions or points of view from which and through which we sense, feel, observe and reflect on distinct and separate experiences in our being. One crucial point of view comes through the other who experiences us. (Bollas, 1987: 9–10).

Bollas's psychodynamic perspective on the centrality of other to self-understandings is remarkably sympathetic to a Meadian reading, though perhaps the latter would claim it is *the* 'crucial point of view' rather than one of them. Like Winnicott, Bollas identifies the importance of the 'first object' – the breast, but also the associated physicality of care provided by carers – as a 'transformational object'. Bollas portrays the pre-representational grasp of the other as a 'recurrent experience of being' (1987: 14); thus it is inseparable from the subjective experience of self and the m/other (or we might say significant care-giver). The first object 'is experienced as a process of trans-formation' (1987: 14); be it from hungry to full, cold to warm, discomforted to comfortable. The other is not perceived as a separate object, but as a trans-formative element of the nascent self.

Bollas claims that the pursuit of 'symbolic equivalents' to the transfor-mational object is in fact central to the identifications we make in adult life (1987: 17); 'in the persons' search for an object (a person, place, event, ide-ology) that promises to transform the self' (1987: 14). An overly-general claim perhaps, stemming from the mundane but indisputable insight that 'persons and things resonate with more sense than we normally cognize' (Charlesworth, 2000: 18); but when Bollas suggests that there are traces of the transformational object in aesthetic experience, 'when a person feels uncannily embraced by an object', it registers as a powerful symbolization of its pervasiveness (Bollas, 1987: 8).

Interestingly, the argument applies when the self is taken to be the object of transformation too: 'we may imagine the self as the transforma-tional facilitator, and we may invest ourselves with capacities to alter the environment' (1987: 17). Although Bollas comments that taking the self as an object in this way may be perceived on later reflection as 'impossible' and 'embarrassing', it is in fact a basic premise of the extended reflexivity thesis. The self is imagined as turning back upon itself in the process of transforming itself as it sees fit via its amalgam for choices. The reflexive project of selfhood, whether we agree with Bollas that it is an impossible fantasy or not, is here part of a more broadly reimagined self-self rela-tionship which is thoroughly infiltrated by self-other relationships, but perhaps in a more conflictual, contradictory and ambiguous way than a Meadian analysis allows. Our relation to the other is in fact built upon our initial instantiation in the transformational grasp of the other. In a sense the search for the transformational object is a symbiotic desire, paradoxi-cally aimed at a reparation of the fault lines of the separate self whilst attempting to forge the separateness of the self. A contemporary interpre-tation of this position explicitly holds in tension the paradoxical dynamic of the manifestation of self:

> The desire to persist in one's own being requires submitting to a world of others that is fundamentally not one's own (a submission that does not take place at a later date, but which frames and makes possible the desire to be). Only by persisting in alterity does one persist in one's own being. (Butler, 1997: 28)

Furthermore, this dimension of our experience is fundamentally uncon-scious according to Bollas, which again takes us away from the parameters of a Meadian analysis whilst continuing to emphasize the relational underpinnings of self-reflexivity. It is initiated before the development of thought or language and its drawing power remains lodged there; 'the experience of the object precedes the knowing of it' (Bollas, 1987: 39). This non-cognitive experience of being held and transformed is a vital aspect of the developing subject. As a form of 'object-seeking that recurrently enacts a pre-verbal ego memory' (1987: 16) it is based on a rapport with another object which, to reiterate, *depends* for its power on a non-discursive economy of affect: 'in our induction by the object we are suddenly captured in an embrace that is an experience of being rather than mind, rooted in the total involvement of the self rather than objectified via representational or abstract thought' (1987: 32). Bollas argues that the existential recollection of the intersubjectivity of the first object-relations live on in an 'aesthetic of care' we direct towards ourselves. The nature of the adult psyche depends largely on the internalization of the primary caregiver's initial aesthetic of care: 'character is an aesthetic of being, as we have internalized the structure of our existence, the phenomenological reality of the maternal aesthetic' (1987: 35). The 'aesthetic mode' in adult life is a key aspect of well-being, epitomized in 'an experience of reverie or rapport which does not stimulate the self into thought' and in fact shares a great deal with Mouzelis's 'apophatic reflexivity' discussed above.

Experiential ambiguity considered in relational terms, or what Bollas refers to as the realm of the 'unthought known' is an area of increasing interest in social theory, developed in numerous directions (Bauman, 2004; Bjerrum Nielsen, 1999; Butt and Langdridge, 2003; Craib, 1998; Hekman, 2000; Schofield, 2003). What I find fascinating here in sum are the twofold implications of Bollas's arguments and other object-relations accounts, under-explored though they are here, for the version of the self portrayed in the extended reflexivity thesis. Firstly, it is not that the other is merely important to the construction and maintenance of a self, but that both are rendered fundamental to their co-construction in a theoretically coherent way which does not jettison the complexities of unconscious, ambiguous, affective and social location dimensions.[5] This suggests, as a Meadian analysis does, that the cultural contingencies of contemporary reflexivity are worthy of attention, but also that cultural and social discourses do not appropriate self-reflexivity in a straightforward manner but mediate and are mediated through complex inter- and intra-psychic dynamics. Secondly, non-reflexive, cognitively and discursively ambiguous phenomenon are seen to be of central importance to the foundations and maintenance of self-reflexivity, thus problematizing the normative ascendancy of reflexive capabilities in their ability to master and transform the self. What is at stake is not just a possible *in*ability to reflect on all of our experience, but an *ability* to act meaningfully and creatively in the world, and in relation to our own selves, based not only on cognition and reflexivity but on ambiguity, relatedness and uncertainty. It suggests that the self is not adequately defined as a transparent medium through which either an internal cognitive reflexivity or an external regulatory discursive grid is refracted.

Object-relational psychoanalysis is an area that can be drawn on productively in the intersections between social theory and subjectivity, as it has been by feminist accounts (Chodorow, 1978; Flax, 1990; Hekman, 2000; Sprengnether, 1990). Object-relations interpretations throw up a well-spring of reference points in other areas relevant to this book that are difficult to contain in any coherent fashion. The emphasis upon symbiosis as a paradoxical partner of individuation in the development of self leads to a consideration of Lasch's understanding of the cultural pathology of narcissism and critical feminist responses; the role of objects in the transformation of self also raises interesting questions about the nature of consumer capitalism and the place of commodification (see chapter five); an aesthetics of care developed via object-relations either raises problems for, or adds a further dimension to, the later Foucault's emphasis upon an ideal of the care of the self and associated accusations of individualism (see chapter four); it potentially compliments post-Foucaultian analyses of agency whilst offering a grounding to their problematically 'groundless' accounts (Hekman, 2000; see chapter four); and as briefly discussed here, it offers a possible extension of Meadian analyses of the self-society inter-relationship. There is not the space to develop object-relations theory in anything like the complexity it deserves here however, and we shall now move on to a different, if related, interpretation of the reflexive project of selfhood in psychoanalytic terms.

The reflexive project and the ego-ideal

Widick's bold attempt to develop Bourdieu's analysis more firmly in the direction of psychoanalysis is another useful resource for alternative conceptualizations of self-reflexive processes which draws explicitly on inter-subjective dynamics (Widick, 2003). Bourdieu's work is discussed in more detail in chapter six, so to avoid any repetition discussion here will be restricted to Widick's interpretation of it. He argues that Bourdieu's formulations are under-theorized in terms of an understanding of the pleasures and investments people make in the embodied configuration of habitus. Despite brief forays into psychoanalytic language, he claims that Bourdieu relies on a reductive cognitive-behaviourist model. Indeed Bourdieu points to the need to:

> analyse the genesis of investment in a field of social relations, thus constituted as an object of interest and preoccupation, in which the child is increasingly implicated and which constitutes the paradigm and also the principle of investment in the social game…This exchange, involving the whole person of the two partners, especially the child of course, but also the parents, is highly charged with affectivity. The child incorporates the social in the forms of affects, socially coloured and qualified. (Bourdieu, cited in Widick, 2003: 692)

Bourdieu seems to implicate that the child becomes an object to itself via the primacy of libidinally-charged object-relations; these are the foundations of habitus and the foundations of any later self-reflexivity. However,

Widick argues that Bourdieu retreats from, and never returns to, a more psychoanalytic reading of habitus. More importantly for our purposes, it leads him to develop Bourdieu in the direction of psychoanalytic language in ways which have a direct bearing on an alternative conceptualization of self-reflexivity capable, perhaps, of accommodating the critical qualifications made so far. What Widick wants to do, in a sense, is answer the question, posed here by Blackman, of 'why subjects invest in particular discourses and narratives rather than others in their dialogue with their own bodily experiences (which are never separate from and prior to the social)' (Blackman, 2005: 202).

Widick develops his analysis via a study of floor trading at the Pacific Stock Exchange. His ethnographic observations reveal that trading consists of a 'highly schematized and totally standardized set of actions' (Widick, 2003: 698). To succeed means to allow the logic of this activity to become ingrained in the body; trading is an 'intense bodily practice...alive with a physical and psychological intersubjectivity' (2003: 699). In this setting, self-reflexivity becomes a hindrance, a loss of momentum in the enactment of the *illuso*, and self-knowledge demands the ability to suspend moments of reflexivity; it is perhaps akin to Mouzelis's 'cataphatic reflexivity'; a self-reflexivity greater than the cognitive-linguistic conventions of thought. In fact, in interviews with traders, there is discernible a reflexive lionization of the habitus of trading:

> if you know what the right thing to do is, if your judgement is so good that you can do that, it makes you seem like some sort of mystical, like, 'Oh he's tied in, he's like this Buddhist'...this guy's in synch. (cited in Widick, 2003: 700).

So far so Bourdieuvian: it is the 'necessity of mastering the idiom' which 'drives the naturalization process' towards the state of habitus (2003: 703). The discourses of 'possessive, utilitarianism individualism' are literally embodied, for becoming a trader means 'experiencing the market in these bodily terms' (2003: 703–706). But for Widick, Bourdieu's concepts do not address all aspects of the trader's experience.

A lack is argued to become apparent in attempting to account for the texts and talk which accompany the practice of trading. Widick finds there a veneration of personal qualities which coalesce in the mythical status of the SuperTrader (2003: 704). The SuperTrader epitomizes the idealized repertoire of a trader's personal characseristics: aggressive competitiveness, calculativeness, a self-conscious 'frontiersman' ethos, fantasies of autonomy through economic accumulation, emotional discipline and profound self-knowledge (2003: 704–709). And the SuperTrader is omnipresent: 'a fantasy figure that moves through this discursive space, often unnamed but sometimes explicitly, guiding the traders in their self-understanding...a common reference point against which to judge their success or their failure, and to grow toward and to mature' (2003: 709).

Making a shift into psychoanalytical language, the SuperTrader amounts to an 'ego-ideal for the trader identity' (2003: 709). For Freud the ego-ideal was the grown-up, potentially non-pathological heir of primary narcissism

(Freud, 1914, 1922, 1927).[6] Following the realization of separation from other 'objects', initially the mother (Chasseguet-Smirgel, 1975), the ego attempts to internalize it and other desired objects, but vitally, as part of the self; 'to be their own ideal once more' (Freud, 1914: 95). In other words, the ego-ideal represents the internalization of primary object-relations into the self-structure as a split-off element of the ego; a part of the self which is driven by the command 'you ought to be like this' (Widick, 2003: 709), via a sequence of sought-out substitutes. According to Widick, 'for the traders this long line of substitutes ultimately encounters the elevated, culture-laden figure of the SuperTrader' (2003: 710). He, and it is always a he, is exemplified as what one 'ought to be', and is realized in highly gendered habitual performances. What motivates individual subjects is the original (and ultimately futile) narcissistic charge behind the ego-ideal; a desire for completeness, and a defence against its 'always threatening structural disunity' (2003: 712) potentially involving both repression and sublimation of instinctual drives (Frosh, 1991: 82).[7]

The nature and function of the ego-ideal is much-debated in psychoanalytic literature and there is not the space to enter into a discussion here. Of greatest importance for this discussion is the fact that Widick generalizes his point to argue that the operation of habitus, via the fantasy figure of the SuperTrader in this instance, has 'dynamic unconscious dimensions' which are nonetheless inseparable from a 'meaning- and value-laden imaginary order' (Widdick, 2003: 713). The 'identificatory logic' which invigorates the bodily inscription of habitus:

> cannot be subordinated to a cognitive logic of repetition, inculcation, routinized learning, schematized habit, environmental trigger and conditioned response; it must instead be explored in the affective, cathective, imaginary terms of a psychoanalysis tuned to the image that the SuperTrader presents to the up-and-coming trader. (2003: 711)

Leading Widick's discussion in the direction of the concerns of this chapter, it is possible to see numerous correlations between the SuperTrader and the reflexive project of selfhood. They are by no means equivalent but their sameness is anyway a secondary consideration. More importantly it is possible to re-imagine the reflexive project of selfhood *itself* as an ego-ideal developed in response to pervasive social changes; it is an idealized figure, culturally well resourced and scripted, yet contingent on the particular historical configuration of post-traditional societies.

This point is supported by drawing further parallels between the extended reflexivity thesis and ego-psychology. Briefly discussed earlier, ego-psychology alters the balance of the psychoanalytical model of the self by recasting the functions of the ego. In sum, contrary to psychoanalytic emphasis upon the difficulties faced by the beleaguered ego in its dynamic relationship with id, it maintains that the former: 'could become autonomous and equivalent to the id in determination of behaviour…possessed a degree of freedom from psychic conflict that made rational adaptation to the environment possible…[and had the] capacity freely to adapt to internal and external challenges' (Bendle, 2002: 12).

The qualities newly associated with the ego are remarkably similar to those demanded of it in the self-actualization and mastery central to the reflexive project of selfhood. In fact Lash and Urry claim that Giddens's notion of the self in particular 'is grounded in a very strong positivistic ego psychology' (Lash and Urry, 1994: 38). If these points of similarity may be accepted, more salient still is Bendle's reiteration of the psycho-analytic retort to ego-psychology's therapeutic aims; that if 'the goal of therapy therefore became the attainment of a strong, healthy, well-adapted ego' it did so only by 'ignoring the psychoanalytical insight that such an ideal view of the ego is in effect *a form of narcissism*' (Bendle, 2002: 12; emphasis added). Consequently, the concept of the self at the heart of the extended reflexivity thesis is recast as a narcissistic distortion.

If the ego-ideal *per se* is a form of narcissism, as Freud originally claimed, and the reflexive project of selfhood is a particularly narcissisti-cally charged ego-ideal, then it follows that the reflexive self is itself a form of nariccissism. The critiques of Bendle and Widick, although with very different purposes in mind, offer mutual support for a psychoana-lytic notion of the reflexive project of selfhood as a culturally venerated ego-ideal rather than an accurate portrayal of the reality of self-identity as it is experienced. Thus Bendle claims that the reflexive self and the soci-ology behind it 'could even be seen as a projection of fantasies about the nature of the world and the self that are taken as realities' (2002: 13).

The appeal of the reflexive project as an ego-ideal will depend on social positioning, a point not lost on Freud's own formulation of the ego-ideal: 'Each individual is a component part of numerous groups, he [sic] is bound by ties of identification in many directions, and he has built up his ego ideal upon the most various models' (Freud, 1922: 78). Perhaps it reflects the preoccupations of a metropolitan, comfortably-off cultural elite, but is here detached from claims about the *actual* mastery of the self; instead it is rendered a psycho-socio-cultural symptom of its functioning. Although only roughly approximated here, reflexive project as ego-ideal usefully submerges the former within the ambiguous and dynamic language of psychoanalysis, which goes some way towards accommodat-ing the criticisms raised in this chapter. The reflexive self is recast in a socially located realm of the imaginary, a partly unconscious object-relation, contradictory, complex and irrational. The more specific implica-tions of self-reflexivity re-imagined as narcissism will be considered in greater depth in chapter five.

Inside out

The 'internal' ambiguities of affective, unconscious, habitual and inter-subjective experience thus pose a serious challenge to the supposed efficacy of reflexive capabilities in post-traditional societies. For any inte-grationist account of social embodiment worth its salt of course, the inter-nal and external distinction falls somewhere between a regrettable fallacy and a necessary illusion (Winnicot, 1974). 'Inner' and 'internal' are held within inverted commas not only because even the most intimate aspects of self are foundationally interpersonal. It is additionally because the dynamics discussed here also play a key role in the reproduction of socially structured differentiation of life chances. The *particular* positioning of bodies in a social structure delimits and engenders particular activities and forms of awareness as Foucault and Bourdieu's work has suggested in complex detail.

Issues of embodiment, unconsciousness, affect and habituation in relation to reflexivity are not merely questions of psychological structure. The assertion that self-reflexivity cohabits in the realm of the psyche, and is thus a partial process, is at the same time a critique of the more sociological ramifications of the extended reflexivity thesis. For the conditions and consequences of these routinely non-reflexive aspects of experience contribute substantially to social differentiation, the structuring of life chances, subsequent identity positions and the parameters of self-reflexivity. Here the embeddedness of the self in the external and its embodiment and internality interrelate. Such logic brings us close to Bourdieu's conceptualization of social structure and a broadly phenomenological worldview. For therein:

> The initial 'world' through which we come to self-knowledge is one of taken-for-granted, non-cognitive attitudes to objects and other persons, manifest in forms of behaviour, or comportment, that 'teach' purely practically, the grounds of an affective-attitude; that operates like an attitude to existence and which is the body's style of being. These styles of being constitute distinct social groups at the deepest level of being. (Charlesworth, 2000: 17)

And they continue to do so not in spite of, but alongside and via contemporary forms of subjectivity including discourses of self-reflexivity. This important thread of continuity between the psychological and the social, 'internal' and 'external' will be taken up in the chapters that follow.

Conclusion

Basically stated, the vaunting of rational capacities inherent in a notion of heightened reflexivity ignores the centrality of emotional, unconscious, irrational, relational and ambiguous dynamics and exaggerates the salience of individuation, predictability and routine in the play of self-experience. The critical discussion in this chapter supports, in sum, Hey's assertion that 'dominant social explanations within the discursive field of reflexive modernization theory...inadvertently obscure how the production of social change is secured as a *locational, emotional and relational* problematic (Hey, 2005: 857). The end-result is an established critical claim that the extended reflexivity thesis relies on an excessively voluntarist notion of individual agency, free to make transparent self-choices in the absence of 'inner' complexity.

Even if it could be agreed that a more expansive definition of the reflexive process could be found, and that reflexivity is an increasingly predominant aspect of self-identity, it remains imperative that analyses of this growth need to be understood further by examining the *distribution* of reflexivity. This has to be done by considering the patterns of, for example, work and leisure generated by new information and communication structures, and the gradients and polarities that exist within these structures in terms of opportunities for resourcing a meaningful and reflexive self-identity; a move towards an acknowledgement of more 'outer' complexity in other words. The issue here is not simply one of whether or not there is an increased reflexive relationship to one's self-identity detectable in only certain groups within a global society. It is equally important to examine the opportunities individuals have to transform reflexive awareness into an opening out of choices for an effective and autonomous self-identity, focusing on the ways in which opportunity, or the lack of opportunity gravitates towards particular social groups, and the extent to which such transformation is normatively expected and/or desired. We will return to the relationship between reflexivity and social stratification in chapter six.

Another dimension to a possible revised concept of reflexivity that has been the concern of this chapter also concerns 'outer' complexity: the continuing importance social and cultural practices have in shaping self-identity. While Giddens acknowledges that the reflexive project of the self is a product of contemporary cultural and social changes, these elements are not integrated. The patterns for one's self-development, and the specific discursive nature of self-awareness have not in any final sense become transparent, that is, open to 'pure' reflexive ordering. The self is still constructed according to established patterns, set by the cultural norms, traditions and sanctions in which one's self-development takes place (Adams, 2003). Giddens may be correct that, as a result of numerous social changes, reflexive awareness has allowed for the relativization of a whole body of cultural patterns which may have once been experienced as taken-for-granted stocks of knowledge. Consequently identity may indeed be a more chronically reflexive process. Nonetheless cultural understandings of gender, sexuality, relationships, work, leisure, consumption, communication and so on are still loaded with assumptions and practices that persist, are difficult to change and even distinguish in everyday experience, and undoubtedly impact upon self-identity.

Furthermore, the notion of the reflexive self is itself a product of its time. Giddens has been labelled a 'neo-modernist' (Alexander, 1996) or the 'last modernist' (Mestrovic, 1999) because his understanding of self identity is seen to reaffirm the normative cultural motifs of the modernist project. He is 'wedded ambiguously to...modernist narratives...Giddens's underlying aim seems to be to rescue the Enlightenment project by softening and taming it' (Mestrovic, 1999: 169) and the same can be said of the extended reflexivity thesis more generally. The notion of a reflexive project of selfhood is thus itself permeated by cultural factors, factors which underpin concepts such as 'reflexivity' and so precondition the ability of 'reflexivity' to see through cultural forms and expose identity to some kind of transparent self-awareness. Theories concerned with processes of regulation from a Foucaultian perspective extend this concern, often portraying the 'reflexive project of the self' as a discursive formation which regulates and polices self-awareness rather than liberating it. It is Foucault's work which will form the basis of the next chapter.

Notes to the text

1 Giddens is undoubtedly the intellectual flag-waver for the concept of reflexivity, and although other theorists will be drawn upon, his work will be the main focus of the summary that follows.

2 It could be argued that the very nature of the unconscious involves a certain amount of conceptual ambiguity. Still, such ambiguity is not apparent in Giddens's formulation, where the unconscious is a distinct, accountable and separate aspect of the psyche.

3 'In the Greek, *cataphaticos* entails the notion of affirmation, and is the opposite of *apophaticos*' (Mouzelis, 1999: 96).

4 For an account of the connections between a number of social psychological theories of self-identity and Eastern religions, see Claxton (ed.), 1986. Of particular relevance is Claxton's chapter on 'The Psychology of No-Self' (51–70), where he talks about 'becoming disillusioned' as a positive, rather than negative, process within Buddhism, involving a surmounting of the illusions of a rationalized self (51). Buddhist practice, Claxton argues, aims to overcome the 'choosing, deciding, intending, willing' domination of the psyche (1984: 57), and acknowledge 'a deeper, more organismic, more whollistic, more tacit level of processing' (1984: 61). Claxton's discussion of Buddhism thus has certain parallels with Mouzelis's analysis of certain forms of secular spiritualism.

5 As Phillips suggests however (2002: 224), we should be wary of 'fetishizing' the other as a normative phial for all that is 'real' and vital in the constitution of psychical worlds; self and other are best thought of as mutually constitutive.

6 The ego-ideal was interchangeable with the super-ego in much of Freud's work, and viewed as an outcome of the oedipal complex (1923: 26). Following uncertainty in Freud's own later revisions of his own metapsychology (see following note), and a shift in some psychoanalytical and feminist schools towards pre-oedipal relationships, super-ego and ego-ideal are conceived of as separate processes. Though by no means universally agreed upon, the latter is generally aligned with the primary narcissism of the maternal bond, the former with the oedipal complex (e.g. Barrett and McIntosh, 1982; Benjamin, 1978; Chasseguet-Smirgel, 1985a; Frosh, 1991; Widick, 2001).

7 In later discussions of the ego-ideal, Freud seems to imply a more object-relational reading of development than his drive theory implies (Frosh, 1991: 80–2); individual development is based upon early relations with others, which shape the later construction of an ego-ideal and super-ego.

4

The Regulated Self

If accounts of post-traditional societies and reflexive selves can seem excessively celebratory, what is the alternative? Critical discussion in the previous chapter suggested that conceptualizing self-identity in relation to social change needs to acknowledge how self-reflexive projects are embedded in social, cultural and corporeal contexts. Other theoretical models have paid closer attention to the ways in which fundamental processes of self-awareness and identification are socially structured and constructed. A key figure behind such models is Michel Foucault. His legacy is extensive and has been developed, researched, questioned and debated to a remarkable degree, particularly in relation to feminism. Needless to say it is beyond the means of this chapter to keep abreast with the many nuances of these conversations. The intention is rather to convey a sense of how Foucault and some who have developed his work grasp the socially determined or *regulated* nature of contemporary selves. Far from emphasizing indeterminate social structures, Foucault and Foucaultian analyses have indexed how a particular sense of self is reliant upon the intersection of historically contingent relations of power. Such an understanding will create a counterpoint to the reflexive self of the previous chapter.

Discourse, regulation and the self

Foucault introduced or invigorated a number of concepts which have been taken up and interpreted and applied in various ways by others, such as government and governmentality, body and bio-power, technologies and techniques of self, discourse and discursive practices. A number of these will be covered in the course of this discussion but is by no means an attempt to convey the extent or impact of Foucaultian terminology, much less an assertion of definitive meanings.

One of the most important of Foucault's terms for contemporary social theory is 'discourse': 'the social rules, practices and forms of knowledge that govern what is knowable, sayable and doable in any given context' (Redman, 2002: 69).[1] The study of discourse in the details of its form, content and practice, tries to answer questions such as the following:

What is it possible to speak of?...Which utterances are destined to disappear without a trace?...Which are marked down as reusable, and to what ends?...Which are repressed and censored?...Which utterances does everyone recognize as valid, or debatable, or definitely invalid?...What individuals, what groups or classes have access to a particular kind of discourse?...How is struggle for control of discourses conducted between classes, nations, linguistic, cultural or ethnic collectivities? (Foucault, 1991a: 59–60)

Foucault saw himself as a kind of philosophical archaeologist (Foucault, 1976: 131–138; 1991a: 59). His work often attempted to sift through the layers of discourse, the sediments that have formed throughout history to govern what came to be understood as the 'truth' about contentious subjective experiences. He was interested in how different related discourses join together to form powerful, historically contingent rules and procedures – 'regimes of truth' (Foucault, 1980b) – and how they come to be taken up by people, by societies, and effectively *produced* as tangible realities and a basis for personal conduct and self-understandings.

Foucault argued that we are effectively *compelled* to take up and embody dominant discourses, to situate one's self in relation to that specific framework of language and associated practices, within a context of nominal freedom and agency (Foucault, 1982: 221). Thus what we come to understand as 'normal' in our experience of self is in fact the result of the subject's initiation by dominant discourses. In other words, 'subjection consists precisely in this fundamental dependency on a discourse we never chose but that, paradoxically, initiates and sustains our agency' (Butler, 1997: 2). The history of the self is not the history of the feats and quirks of human agency turned upon itself, but the way in which its options for expression and conduct have been regulated, calculated and produced by the policed discourses of powerful institutions.

Approaches inspired by Foucault have yielded much of their worth to a critical sociology, helping to push the discipline to new levels of creativity in how it understands the self and particularly the self-society relationship. Key to Foucaultian approaches is the displacement of the notion of 'a unitary subject, consistent and transparent to itself' (Dean, 2002: 232). Such displacement is a consequence of Foucault's understanding of the relationship between subjectivity and discourses:

There are not on the one hand inert discourses, which are already more than half dead, and on the other hand an all powerful subject which manipulates them, overturns them, renews them...discoursing subjects form a part of the discursive field – they have their place within it...Discourse is not a place into which the subjectivity irrupts; it is a space of differentiated subject-positions and subject functions. (Foucault, 1991: 58)

The relationship is consistently evoked by Foucault in relation to specific discursive formations, though he is at pains to stress the productive and corporeal aspects of this relationship. In *Discipline and Punish* (1977), for example, Foucault follows a shift in object-focus of the techniques of discipline and punishment. Whereas in the past torture and imprisonment, for example, was focused squarely on punishing the corporal body (e.g. the practice of 'quartering' those found guilty of treason), punitive power has increasingly displaced the body, through a series of minor changes, and evoked instead non-corporal qualities of the subject – liberty, choice, rehabilitation – which coalesce into the human 'soul'. The technologies of the soul are 'educationalists, psychologists and psychiatrists' (Focault, 1977: 29; today we might add psychotherapists, reality and confessional television producers, industrial relations experts, corporate managers and welfare officers amongst others).

This does not mean the 'soul' is merely an 'illusion' or 'ideological effect'. There are no pre-existing, fully-formed selves which come to be duped by interlocking discourses into taking up one subject position rather than a more 'natural' one. They have a historical reality borne 'out of methods of punishment, supervision and constraint' (Foucault, 1977: 29). The 'soul' as a specific form of subjectivity is forcibly conjured and then constantly invoked and made concrete via the complex web of discourses (psychiatric, medical, penal, etc.) entwined with 'non-discursive' practices such as corporal and public punishments and rewards – 'the micro-physics of power' (1977: 26). But it is worth reiterating the vital point that this logic does not lead, for Foucault, to the conclusion that the 'soul' or any other discursively located technology of self is an imposition upon an already existing authentic body. The person we are 'invited to free' is always 'already, in himself [sic] the effect of a subjection much more profound than himself' (1977: 30). Thus the self does not come to discourses as pre-formed; there is no external vantage point from which discourses can simply be wielded, manipulated, nor an immutable consciousness which can be manipulated.

Governmentality

So far we have emphasized some elements of Foucault's general theory of how selves come to be produced but what does he, and those who have developed his work, have to say about social change and how it has impacted upon subjectivity? A great deal, in fact. Much of Foucault's work is historical, and he was particularly attuned to the identification of change and discontinuity. However, his method of study is an articulation of the 'polymorphous interweaving of correlations' which constitute 'ensembles of discourses' to get a sense of a historical period (Foucault, 1991: 58, 55), rather than an attempt to uncover epochal stages, or grand narratives emerging and dissolving. Thus there is no hope of conveying Foucault's understanding of the countless microscopic social changes which together have formed, or are forming, our modern era. That said, in terms of the concerns of this book, Foucault's concept of governmentality in contemporary societies is worth developing further, particularly as it translates into what he refers to as technologies of self. Governmentality refers at its most general to 'the conduct of conduct', any 'form of activity aiming to shape, guide or affect the conduct of some person or persons' at all levels from self to interpersonal to institution to sovereignty (Gordon, 1991: 2–3). Although the specific term was developed in Foucault's later work, its concerns also encompass his earlier conceptualization of discipline and power/knowledge.

Foucault notes how in the seventeenth and eighteenth century the disciplinary practices of what Goffman would call total institutions (barracks, monasteries, asylums) were becoming 'general formulas of domination' (Foucault, 1977: 137). They were being taken up to produce certain types of bodies in more and more social locations such as schools, hospitals and workplaces.

> What was then being formed was a policy of coercions that act upon the body, a calculated manipulation of its elements, its gestures, its behaviour. The human body was entering a machinery of power that explores it, breaks it down, and rearranges it...Thus discipline produces subjected and practiced bodies. (1977: 135–147)

The shift in disciplinary techniques is perhaps clearest in the treatment of marginal populations, who during this period were increasingly 'sorted' into different specialist institutions (workhouse, asylum, prison) and subject to programmes of individualized regulation and reform rather than simply being confined (Foucault, 1965; 1977).

Increasingly every dimension of social life and psychic reality is mapped, made visible, subject to administration by the expert and tutelary systems made up of doctors, psychiatrists, teachers, social workers, and so on (Donzelot, 1979; Dean, 1999; Rose, 1990, 1996a; Armstrong, 2004). Of particular importance is the shift towards 'liberal regulation' and self-surveillance and Foucault uses a simple but powerful metaphor to illustrate it: Jeremy Bentham's 'panopticon' (Foucault, 1977: 195–228). The panopticon was originally Bentham's design for a prison, whereby a central tower is surrounded by a circular building. This outer-building is broken up into individual cells, each walled on the outside and on both internal sides, with a barred front looking towards the central tower. The tower is windowed all around. The overall impression is a little like a bicycle wheel: the tower the central hub, the cells the wheel rim, the spokes the lines of vision between the guard, who stands in the tower, and the prisoners. The panopticon radically alters the nature of imprisonment for Foucault, for while the medieval dungeon removed the prisoner from sight and light, the panopticon makes him/her constantly visible (1977: 200). The panopticon is much more effective than previous forms of discipline which simply aimed to confine masses and remove individuals, due to Foucault's understanding of the mechanisms of power.

The power of the panopticon lies in singular exposure of every prisoner. In the back-lit cells 'each actor is alone, perfectly individualized and constantly visible', and, as Foucault concisely asserts, 'visibility is a trap' (1977: 200). Each prisoner is invisible to their neighbours, minimizing the potential for plotting and disorder. Vitally, from the vantage point of the tower the supervisor can also be invisible to the prisoner (shrouded in darkness, hidden by venetian blinds or two-way mirrors), whilst potentially observing their every gesture. The invisibility of authority is key to the power relations of the panopticon. Power becomes 'visible and unverifiable', and is thus instilled as a state of consciousness in the prisoner, a sense of permanent visibility, whether the supervisor is in the tower or not (1977: 201). To paraphrase Foucault, the architecture of the panopticon thus equates to the perfect state of power: where its actual exercise is unnecessary (1977: 201). Consequently the phenomenon of *self-surveillance* emerges, as Foucault indicates here in damningly eloquent fashion:

> He [sic] who is subjected to a field of visibility, and who knows it, assumes responsibility for the constraints of power; he makes them play spontaneously upon himself; he inscribes in himself the power relation in which he simultaneously plays both roles; he becomes the principle of his own subjection. (1977: 201–202)

Although fascinating as a history of forms of discipline, Foucault's key contribution for our purposes is his generalization of the disciplinary coordinates of the panopticon in the concept of 'panopticism'. Foucault takes the architecture of the panopticon as a metaphor for the regulation of selves in modern societies more generally. We have already mentioned Foucault's argument that the panopticon can be applied to other institutions, whereby rather than prisoners, 'a madman [sic], a patient, a condemned man, a worker or a schoolboy' (1977: 200) might be housed. More broadly still, it is a 'generalisable model of functioning; a way of defining power relations in the everyday life of men [sic]' (1977: 205); it has 'spread throughout the whole social body' (1977: 207).

It achieves a state of generalization as the 'disciplines' – schooling, policing, industry and employment, welfare, religion, medicine, the armed forces – that were homogenously contained or conjoined by cruder forms of earlier disciplinary techniques both expanded their reach via technological and administrative power, and *disaggregated* or 'de-institutionalized' into diffuse social and private spaces such as home visits and welfare offices: 'in the case of the indigent, the moralization and normalization of large sections of the poor could occur in their homes and other social spaces, by such means as philanthropic social work' (Dean, 2002: 245). The reach of disciplines stretched beyond firm boundaries: schools learn to discipline parents through their children (Foucault, 1977: 211); employment norms discipline school children (Cremin, 2005); the therapist disciplines the community (Furedi, 2004); and the family becomes the site of convergence for them all – 'the privileged locus of emergence for the disciplinary question of the normal and the abnormal' (Foucault, 1977: 215). Coercive containment of large numbers is no longer (always) necessary to keep people 'in check'. Foucault's Orwellian description of the state centralization of policing provides a good illustration of a creeping panopticism more generally: 'a faceless gaze that transformed the whole social body into a field of perception: thousands of eyes posted everywhere, mobile attentions ever on the alert' (1977: 214).

Key here is the sense of constant visibility, characteristic of the panopticon, generated at a societal level. The consequences for the free individual become equivalent to those of the prisoner; the power of regulation becomes worked by the self upon the self in a pervasive state of self-surveillance, monitoring, amending, modifying. The visible element of the social disciplinary-mechanism of panopticism does not simply contain and restrict individuals; it is more concerned with creating more *useful* and *productive* individuals (Foucault, 1991b). Self-surveillance and self-regulation does not repress or truncate the self so much as it ensures one which is purposive and productive in particular ways. Foucault argues that this form of subtle coercion is an almost inevitable by-product of the appliance of instrumental rationality to the emergence of mass-capitalist societies. Such societies are simply not possible 'without the growth of an apparatus of production capable of both sustaining them and using them' (Foucault, 1977: 221). Carefully disciplined, 'docility and utility' maximized (1977: 220), mass populations and mass societies become mutually reinforcing. Thus, while the panopticon may at first appear to be an architectural oddity, its principles are seen to be extended and 'through it, a whole type of society emerges' (1977: 214).

Recent accounts follow Foucault's assertion of the ascendancy of 'panopticism' in suggesting that discursive regulation has shifted in emphasis. Explicitly external, authoritarian forms of control and allied discourses have waned as surveillance techniques have become central in the exercise of power/knowledge. Put simply, the power of surveillance 'works by making individuals visible such that they can be corrected when they step out of line and such that, aware of this surveillance, they come increasingly to police their own conduct' (Crossley, 2005: 225). A more subtle form of self-government has become the pervasive framework for guiding personal conduct, to the point where: 'today many individuals can be governed through their own capacities for self-regulation' (Dean, 2002: 246).

As well as reaching 'inwards' towards self-governance, regulatory discourses have apparently radiated outwards towards an increasing number of social institutions: the policing of families (Donzelot, 1979); at work (Du Gay, 1996; Tracy, 2000) in medicine (Armstrong, 2004); schools (Cremin, 2003, 2005; Walkerdine, 1998; Reay and William, 1999); unemployment offices (Theodore and Peck, 1999); the local community (Rose, 2000); crime control (Stenson, 2000); the practice of psychology (Burman, 1994; Rose, 1990; Sampson, 1981) the mass media (Blackman and Walkerdine, 2001), even television soaps (Ravenhill, 2005). Contemporary 'geographies of regulation' are thus argued to colonize many aspects of individual lives:

> Think about the lifestyle of the individual, and consider the range of services and expertise concerned with shaping our choices and conduct around such

things as: reproduction and genetic risk...schools and appropriate residential neighbourhoods; vocational guidance; sex and relationships; maintaining a healthy lifestyle, diet, exercise; performance in the workplace; stress and mental health; and insuring against the risks of crime, unemployment and poverty in old age. The list is practically limitless, but it indicates the way in which the regulation and normalization of the self occurs through a myriad of different agencies...and authorities...using many different techniques. (Dean, 2002: 249)

Following Foucault, the 'subjectifying practices' (Rose, 1996b: 241) found in Dean's list are not simply imposed upon individuals but work through choices and desires which constantly confront and construct the individual – 'a whole series of little machines for fabricating and holding in place the psychological self' (1996b: 241). In this sense the government of selves relies on 'the active agency and participation of those who are governed' (Dean, 2002: 249). These new spaces of regulation work in complex ways. They are often quasi-therapeutic (how do *you* feel your job is going?); apparently there to assist the self in reaching its potential as much as to regulate it. Liberal forms of regulation emphasize and engage the active, autonomous individual as a citizen or consumer.

Mentioned in Dean's list is a key area to have felt the 'Foucault effect' of a desire to understand 'processes of subjectification and normalization of the self' (Elliott, 2001: 101): the study of work and work identity. Research in this area will now be considered in an attempt to ascertain how a Foucaultian perspective might help make sense of the relationship between self and social change.

Regulating the self at work

Although modern organizations produce engine parts, meals, telecommunication services, government information, or whatever, they also contribute to the production of people.

(Jenkins, 1996: 155–156)

Whereas the personal identities and emotional nuances of employees in large organizations may have been deemed irrelevant or taken-for-granted by management in the past, the culturalization of the work place, combined with technological innovations and the continuing priorities of capitalist organization, has meant that today, many workers are provided with endless training 'opportunities' and subjected to novel surveillance techniques. Perhaps unsurprisingly then, the study of work has turned to Foucault to help make sense of such changes. Rather than seeing the impact upon selves of changes in the cultures of work environments in terms of loss and psychosocial fragmentation, the dominant interpretation considered in chapter two, a Foucaultian perspective focuses on how particular self-understandings get produced by discursive formations; the production of an alternative copy rather than the reduction of an authentic original.

A basic Foucaultian position might argue that exposed to high levels of individualized visibility, employees become self-monitoring and instil neo-liberal governmentalities of autonomy, personal responsibility, choice and self-realization. Individuals thus come to conduct themselves in ways which coalesce with the goals and demands of state and/or corporate power. Studies in the sociology of work have variously supported and contested this Foucaultian assertion. To some of these we will now turn in order to get a clearer sense of the possible application of his philosophical claims to an account of self and social change.

It is well known that in the United Kingdom and other long-industrialized nations, an increasing majority of the population work in the service sector. 'Service' covers a broad spectrum of employment horizontally, and vertically in terms of status and pay. One of the fastest growing occupations is the computer telephonist or call centre worker: 'Today call centre operations have become the norm in retailing, telecoms, the entertainment industry, utilities and the travel trade' (Datamonitor, cited in Taylor *et al.*, 2002: 134). In fact, 'there are more computer telephonists than employees in vehicle production, steel and coal put together' (Fernie and Metcalf, 1998: 2). Unlike the latter forms of employment, call centre work is more likely to employ females, part-time workers and not be unionized. At least one large-scale study has also suggested that it is an occupation defined by high levels of surveillance and regulation: 'the possibilities for monitoring behaviour and measuring output are amazing to behold – the "tyranny of the assembly line" is but a Sunday school picnic compared with the control that management can exercise in computer telephony' (1998: 2).

The call centre employees studied by Fernie and Metcalf dealt with incoming calls. Calls were fed through each line automatically; as one call finished, another was put through – 'an unstoppable telephonic conveyor belt' (1998: 8); unless administration time was requested, which has to be 'clocked' in and out via the employee's computer. Any other 'idle' time not answering calls is also monitored. Calls themselves can be listened in on and/or recorded by supervisors. Via interconnected computers employees are under a state of continual potential surveillance. In addition supervisors can, in real time, quickly view information on individual employees and teams such as how many calls are waiting, the duration of the current call, outcomes of past calls, and whether pre-programmed schedules are being met (1998: 8). Combine such measures with the spatial division of employees into partitioned areas with a monitor, desk and little else and the comparison of call centres to battery farms seems quite apt (Arkin, 1997). A more fitting analogy for the authors of the study in question however, is Bentham's Panopticon – call centres are the 'archetypal organization' to represent Foucault's application of it. Thanks to the computer screen, 'the agents are constantly visible and the supervisor's power has indeed been rendered perfect' – to the point where its actual use is unnecessary (Fernie and Metcalf, 1998: 8–9).

Since Fernie and Metcalf's study, academic interest in call centre work has grown substantially (e.g. Callaghan and Thompson, 2001, 2002; Frenkel *et al.*, 1998; Lankshear, 2001; Taylor and Bain, 1999) and their 'electronic panopticon' perspective extended and challenged (Gandy, 1993; Reeve, 1998; Bain and Taylor, 2000). Subsequent studies have found that surveillance techniques, management control and the experience of employees varies depending on a number of important variables, such as: 'size, industrial sector, market conditions, complexity and call cycle times, the nature of operations (inbound, outbound), the precise manner of technological integration, the effectiveness of representative organizations, and management styles, priorities and human resource practices' (Taylor *et al.*, 2002: 134; Batt and Moynihan, 2004; Kinnie *et al.*, 2000). Secondly, research has also indicated that employee resistance is also widespread (Taylor and Bain, 2003; Flemming and Sewell, 2002) – a point that will be taken up more generally later in this chapter. In acknowledging complexity in the sector, it is claimed that the 'depiction of the call centre as a regime of all-encompassing electronic surveillance' was to some extent 'mistaken' (Taylor *et al.*, 2002: 134). Although a justifiable claim in the face of workplace variations, descriptions of the call centre experience, even in papers ostensibly critical of Fernie and Metcalf, seem to offer partial support at least for Foucault's more complex view of panopticism as a diffuse, generalizable social function implicit in techniques of subjectification. Thus despite the above assertion, Taylor *et al.*'s case studies of various call centre scenarios indicate the widespread practice of observation and control of the minutiae of employee's conduct:

> [there is a] *systematic* attempt to extend monitoring from more straightforward quantitative measurements into the very heart of the customer interface. Not only are operators assessed on their conformity to prescribed call conventions ('opening' and 'closure') but also on the structure and style of their speech ('pace', 'pitch', 'emphasis', 'inflection', 'construction', 'control'). This is not the end of the matter for criteria which make judgements on attitude, manner and behaviour ('rapport', 'listening skills', etc.) are applied as well as those which indicate operators' success in interesting customers in a particular service ('product knowledge'), dealing with queries ('problem solving') or assessing customers' potential value to the business ('profiling'). The sheer range of criteria aimed at modifying and improving the operators' performance in customer encounters is quite staggering. (2002: 145; emphasis added).

The attempt to colonize personal, relational conduct at a 'systematic' level does seem to reflect Foucault's understanding of panopticism, not literally embodied (though the call centre often comes close) but rather as a more broadly defined form of 'liberal' government. This is the sense that every word and gesture which makes up one's overall conduct can be broken down, disaggregated, analyzed, monitored, regulated and rewarded, by the managerial gaze, to the point where there is a kind of internal vigilance, a constant self-surveillance, an absorption of externally imposed goals: 'a gaze which each individual under its weight will end by interiorizing' (Foucault, 1980: 155). Such visibility renders the actual exercise of managerial power over the individual unnecessary – 'to the point that he [sic] is his own overseer, each individual thus exercising this surveillance over, and against, himself' (1980: 155) – or at least remarkably increases its reach and efficiency. Required levels and inflections of 'enthusiasm', 'helpfulness' and 'tone' (Taylor et al., 2002: 137) thus become autogenous. Though not explicitly drawing on Foucault, more recent work, including Taylor and Bain's, perhaps more readily acknowledges his emphasis upon governmentality; for despite heterogeneity, 'production-line call centres proliferate' (Bain et al., 2002: 184) and 'evidence of extensive control mechanisms is compelling' (Taylor and Bain, 2004: 264; Thompson et al., 2004).[2]

The entrepreneur of the self

In accounts of the contemporary demands organizations make on its employees, a key discursive formation related to those so far discussed is argued to coalesce around the concept of 'enterprise'. A more detailed extension of Foucault's understanding of how self-identities come to be formed in the way they do is found in the discourses and forms of government which are argued to have formed around this concept (Cameron, 2000; Du Gay, 1996, 1997, 2004; Gordon, 1987, 1991; Keat and Abercrombie, 1991; Miller and Rose, 1990). Long established as a model for business, 'enterprise' was initially defined in opposition to the perceived lumbering, inefficient and archaic organizational principles of bureaucracy (Du Gay, 2004), and as a necessary response to combined social changes including the globalization of labour markets, short-term and temporary contract culture, and a shift from manufacturing to service industries in the West. It was also fuelled by a growing belief that the culture of organizations is central to how work and productivity is managed (Du Gay, 1997: 286).

Culture is here understood as the 'norms, values and beliefs' within an organization which can be utilized as a managerial technique to encourage employees to identify with their work and the goals of the organization, to which countless management consultancy firms and texts now attest (1997: 286). In terms of panopticism, it is about rendering the individual's motivations, aspirations and relational conduct with regards to work more visible – a 'glass cage' of subjective transparency rather than an iron cage of rationality (Gabriel, 2001, cited in Hughes, 2005: 615). Organizational practices geared towards visibility include electronic surveillance front and back stage, 'transparency reviews', 'reflective practice', group training and regular monitored self-evaluations. In the broadest sense it is the managerial acknowledgement that self-presentation and the self-reflexive process can also be 'managed' to fit the goals of the company tied to some notion of self-development and self-actualization.

Studying numerous training programmes in some detail leads Cameron to assert that:

> Essentially trainees are encouraged to do more consciously what they would do normally without reflection, and given a metalanguage with which to reflect on common behaviours…They are told to think consciously about gaze, posture, gesture and so on rather than doing what comes naturally, but at the same time warned that the resulting behaviour should not display any evidence of self-consciousness. (Cameron, 2000: 69–70)

In such encouragements attempts are being made to make self-conduct visible, and reconstruct it along the lines of the company, with what in this instance appear to be paradoxical and perplexing consequences for the self-reflexive subject position of the employee.[3] The specific forms of conduct expected of an enterprising self are 'a set of attributes, values and behaviours – such as resourcefulness, self-discipline, openness to risk and change' (2000: 7); 'autonomy, responsibility and the freedom/obligation of individuals to actively make choices for themselves' (Du Gay, 2004: 41); and a therapeutic sensibility of self-realization, quality of life and self-fulfilment (Miller and Rose, 1990).[4] It is the way in which the discourse of enterprise is claimed to construct identity that reveals the influence of Foucault; in answering the question 'how precisely and practically is the self-directing service worker "made up" ' (Du Gay, 1997: 315)?

Du Gay's research into the retailing industry has attempted to indicate the 'extensive' use of 'enterprising technologies of regulation' (Du Gay, 1996: 139). One aspect of such technology is the primacy of an ethic of customer service: satisfying the 'customer' is valorized as a shared goal of employer and employee alike. It is the central drive behind the conduct of the enterprising employee; enhanced by workshops, training programmes and general policy which encourages creative identification with an imaginary customer; the regular visits announced or unannounced of expert 'mystery shoppers' and an attempt to turn work relations into customer relations, turning 'employees into each other's customers' (1996: 140). At the UK retail chain WHSmith, for example, store managers were assessed on a number of points by their own 'customers' – staff under their supervision. From the start, staff conduct is rendered permanently visible via the gaze of the customer, whilst they are recast as autonomous individuals, handed the responsibility of supervising their own supervision. Following poor feedback in terms of listening skills and staff involvement, some store managers were retrained to meet the new requirement for 'empowering facilitators of staff', thus 'governing in an enterprising manner' (1996: 140).

In a different retail company floor staff were assessed on 'manner of approach, attitude/rapport, efficiency and farewell' by a consultancy firm posing as mystery shoppers over a number of weeks. Each staff member was observed and measured four times by four separate anonymous 'customers' in terms of detailed criteria relating to the above. The use of 'mystery shoppers' in this intensive sense, but also as a more general threat, is an illustrative instance of how a permanent sense of visibility works as a government of conduct primarily by instilling self-monitoring and self-regulation. In this exercise the results were collated and fed back to staff individually. 'Winners' with the highest scores were treated to gift vouchers, certificates and a champagne reception whilst the losers are invited to work upon themselves via further training in the spirit of entrepreneurship (1996: 140–141).

Another firm embarked on a major shift in its recruitment and training policy away from specific technical skills required for retail work towards being able to identify and encourage enterprising selves: self-motivated, proactive, adaptable and able to take on new skills. One such skill was encouraged in training in transactional analysis (TA), a theory of human interaction appropriated by management consultants to provide staff with the skills to conduct relationships with customers, employers, and other employees. Training techniques such as TA are couched in the terminology of enterprise and autonomy: 'It's very much an empowering thing that way. If they have a customer who goes away still arguing then they've failed. The challenge is to turn the customer around' (training manager, cited in Du Gay, 1996: 142). In this way, relational conduct is governed, made visible, and at the same time becomes the personal responsibility of the self-monitoring employee. Cameron's study of training materials also found that TA cropped up regularly. She notes that the tendency to see conflict as a technical problem and make staff responsible for resolving it depends upon being instructed into a particular discourse of what was to be 'expected of a mature, responsible, well-balanced person' which 'fits particularly well with the goals and values of the enterprising organisation' (Cameron, 2000: 69).

In another employment study Tracy interviewed some of the 700 staff members on a transatlantic cruise ship accommodating 1,600 paying guests (Tracy, 2000). Interested in the nature of employee experience, Tracy takes a Foucaultian approach to the emotional labour which is expected of the staff in their roles as hosts, entertainers and activities co-ordinators: 'service orientation now evident on cruise ships and in most Western tourist arenas is not inherently normal or natural but is historically contingent' and that 'the expectation of emotion labour has heightened' (2000: 106). A discourse of service expectation aimed at regulating the behaviour of the ship's employees along the lines of emotional labour is epitomized in the 'company credo'. The credo is placed on crew bathroom and cabin doors, bedroom headboards and on wallet cards which it is compulsory to carry at all times:

The credo included mandates such as "We never say no," "We smile, we are on stage," "We are ambassadors of our cruise ship when at work and at play," and "We use proper telephone etiquette…and answer with a smile in our voice…""We must always speak English," and "Always greet passengers; say hello ma'am, good morning sir," and "We always say please and thank you." (2000: 107)

These are directives which undoubtedly involve a certain presentation of one's self and the manipulation of one's emotions. Despite their constant presence in off-stage areas, such measures could be seen to encourage self-regulation and self-monitoring in social contexts where direct supervision is not possible, and thus an interiorization of normative conduct. A further element of employee supervision was the use of passenger 'comment cards'. These allowed passengers to provide supervisors with detailed feedback on individual employee members in terms relating to the service credo. Supervisors in turn used these forms as both a quantitative (scores) and qualitative (comments) basis for evaluating, disciplining and promoting staff, in similar ways to those found by Du Gay in the retailing industry. As staff were 'on-stage' in uniforms and name badges for up to 15 hours a day, this amounted to a high degree of scrutiny, channelled through the gaze of the customer rather than the management: 'the watchful eyes of passengers and peers unobtrusively created for cruise staff a state of permanent visibility and a virtually incontestable system of control' (2000: 209). The use of comment cards in this way reinforces the company credo in terms of panopticism. The 'trap' of permanent visibility further facilitates self-surveillance and aligns self-construction with organizational demands.

A further supervisory technique was an invitation to staff to enter suggestions for improving the service they provide into a monthly draw. The 'best' suggestion was announced and implemented, the employee responsible rewarded with a prize from the management. Tracy gives the example of one suggestion: the insertion of mirrors in staff elevators so appearance can be checked just before going on-stage (2000: 209). The draw is a further example of the 'handing back' of autonomy to enterprising workers, an autonomy carefully delineated to assist in their own supervision and engender the habit of self-monitoring.

What we end up with, or at least what is hoped for from a management point of view, is a concurrence of the needs of employers and the perceived needs of employees; the 'harmonizing' of individual and organizational goals as one management theorist put it (Bagshaw, cited in Hughes, 2005: 610). Donzelot's study in governmentality at work made a similar point some time ago (Donselot, 1991 [1980]) in a discussion of the establishment of the *formation permanente* (continual training) in 1970s France. In what appears to be a precursor to the 'flexible regime' of Sennett's view of 1990s capitalist relations (Sennett, 1999), the institution of *formation permanente* was ostensibly aimed at encouraging individual willingness to change, adapt, be flexible in the face of social and technological changes in the workplace. It was framed more generally though as an invitation to autonomy; 'to make every person capable of becoming an agent of change' in the words of one government official (Schwartz, cited in Donzelot, 1991 [1980]: 273). For Donzelot, the *formation permanente* is part of a mode of discipline, 'mobilizing' the psychological subject in a particular way. This is more, he says, than simply the imposition of a repressive discourse: 'Actually at issue is…a transformation, a point of coalescence of the position of the subject and the order of social relations of production. It does not signify the mechanical subordination of one to the other, but rather the act of placing both terms on one and the same footing of truth' (Donzelot, 1991 [1980]). Subjectivity is thus constituted in the social re-imagining of employment relations along the lines of 'enterprise'. Miller and Rose couch the 'fit' between self-identity and the normative discourse of enterprise in similar terms:

> The rapproachment of the self-actualization of the worker with the competitive advancement of the company enables an alignment between the technologies of work and technologies of subjectivity. For the entrepreneurial self, work is no longer necessarily a constraint upon the freedom of the individual to fulfil his or her potential through strivings for autonomy, creativity and responsibility. Work is an essential element in the path to self-realization...The government of work now passes through the psychological strivings of each and every individual for fulfilment. (Miller and Rose, 1990: 29)

In Foucaultian terminology, enterprise is established over a number of sites to become a powerful discursive formation. It becomes a way of governing individuals, a technology tied to various forms of productive discipline (employment contracts and incentives, training handbooks, policy initiatives, recruitment specifications, etc.). These procedures are utilized by individuals. In doing so they become technologies or techniques of self, worked upon the self to produce a certain subject-position. Thus a certain point from which the subject makes sense of him/herself, others, and their environment is established in relation to a discursive formation, and bound by it; but it does so by engaging and mobilizing the productive powers – desire, habit, thought – of the individual.

What is fundamental here is the claim that the most foundational processes of self-identity become constructed through the discourse of enterprise: 'The corporate identity becomes individualised through a reflective process in which the needs of the company are emphasised within individual thought as a means for achieving career success' (Cremin, 2003: 118).[5] The same point was made some time ago by Goffman, though he took a little more time, as did Foucault, to accentuate the choices and investments made by the individual in their normative regulation:

> In organizations patterned after a bureaucratic model...personnel come to define their career line in terms of a sequence of legitimate expectations and to base their self-conceptions on the assumption that in due course they will be what the institution allows persons to become. (Goffman, 1952: 455)

Goffman softens the air of insidious determinism often apparent in accounts of the control of employee subjectivity, while perfectly highlighting the thorough-going interpenetration of agency, self-conceptualization and institutional norms central to a Foucaultian account of identity, employment and changes in the structure and process of governmentality.

Beyond work

Although the discourse of enterprise originates in the world of work, more general claims are made about its pervasive social role as a technology of self. 'Enterprise' has not only embraced the conduct of business and government but become a generalizable model for conduct; a powerful discursive formation:

> No longer does 'enterprise' refer simply to the creation of a independent business venture or to the characteristic habits of model entrepreneurs or (successful) persons in business for themselves, rather it refers to the ways in which economic, political, social and personal vitality is considered best achieved by the generalization of a particular conception of the enterprise form to all forms of conduct…to the conduct of government and its agencies and to the conduct of individuals. (Du Gay, 2004: 38–39)

'Enterprising' conduct is expected in more and more social contexts, to the point where 'it is becoming harder to say when one is working. Activities at work become preparation for turning the family into a family enterprise that absorbs all leisure; family and leisure activities become preconditions of employability' (Sabel, cited in Du Gay, 1996: 182–183). 'Government through the family' has long been recognized as playing an important part in the normative construction of selves, as it is here where all the expert systems of modernity readily converge (Foucault, 1977: 215–216; Donzelot, 1979; Hirst, 1981), so it is perhaps not surprising that it is seen as a site in which the entrepreneurial self is regulated. Besides the family, study in other areas such as schools, welfare schemes, curriculum vitae, the consulting room, social work interview, radio phone-in and television confessional are seen to be implicit in constructing and compelling subject-positions akin to the enterprising self (Rose, 1996b; Cremin, 2003, 2005; Skeggs, 2003, 2002; Woodward, 2002). Dean sums up the contradictory nature of these disciplining discourses nicely: 'the regulation of the self is thus simultaneously about *facilitating* selves and *forcing* them to do certain things, about governing through freedom and punishing what is viewed as the failure to exercise that freedom or be active enough' (Dean, 2002: 251).

To take an example from British educational practices, it is now a national requirement in the United Kingdom that school leavers (15–16 year olds) have a complete Record of Achievment (ROA), much like a CV (Cremin, 2005). They are aimed at the abstracted gaze of 'the employer', regardless of the particular pupil's destination, and this knowledge is expected to form the basis for which activities and personal characteristics are selected for ROAs, which are worked on throughout a pupil's final year. The ROAs focus on punctuality, appearance, conformity to college rules, cooperation with staff, attitude to work, out-of-school interests, sociability, employable qualities, achievements, ambitions and important experiences. The tutor guidelines and detailed records amount, according to Cremin, to the framing of student 'subjectivities in relation to employees' in terms of the 'enterprising self-governance', described above (Cremin, 2005: 316–317). Echoing Donzelot, Miller and Rose, Cremin sees a convergence of processes of self-understanding and the normative discourse of selfhood propagated by particular interests: 'as codes governing behaviour are self-reflexively configured to current structural demands, the qualities that companies outline as requisite to getting and sustaining a job, become the de facto benchmarks of a successfully socialized (and instrumentalized) personality' (2005: 331).

The broader impact of neo-liberal enterprising discourses upon selves remain speculative in Cremin's study as there is no engagement made with the affective impact of students putting themselves through the ROAs, or their subjective awareness.[6] Nonetheless it helps illustrate what Gordon, Rose and others have argued to be the broader reach of 'enterprise' as a discursive formation, beyond the confines of paid employment, suggesting it may be an increasingly important technology of selfhood in contemporary societies. Thus the qualities of the enterprising self at work have become generalizable qualities of selfhood, key technologies of the self not just at work but in the 'conduct of conduct' more generally (Rose, 1996; Dean, 1999; Schram, 1995). 'The 'entrepreneur' as a category of 'person', rather than one option among many, comes to assume 'an ontological priority' (Du Gay, 1996: 181):

> Employers and interested agencies promote a neo-liberal organizational form of competitive self-evaluation that refracts enterprise as a project of personal fulfilment: so that people freely configure and market themselves "as enterprising subjects" through an interpretation of the values associated with enterprise as those embodying social values per se. (Cremin, 2005: 318)

It extends to a more general and embracing 'fiction of autonomous selfhood' (Rose, 1996) or 'compulsory individualism' (Skeggs, 2005b); government through the exercise of personal capacities, whereby 'the language of autonomy, identity, self-realization and the search for fulfilment forms a grid of regulatory ideals' (Rose, 1996a: 145), supposedly a contingent production of contemporary societies.

Foucault's work is ambivalent at best if one is concerned with an ethics of selfhood. In the post-Foucault landscape however, there is clearly thought to be a price to pay for all this compulsion towards 'enterprise' and 'autonomy', hence the inverted commas.[7] Cremin and others assert a common implication of Foucaultian analyses – that the discursive formation of enterprise, self-reflexivity and autonomy serves the interest of a particular group – 'they are simulacra of universal truths inscribed with the interests of, say, a certain class' (Cremin, 2005: 318; Skeggs, 2003; Sabel, 1991; Du Gay, 1996: 145). In his study on work identity Du Gay regularly asserts that 'the price of being "offered" autonomy is accepting responsibility for exercising it in particular ways and for the outcomes its exercise produces' (Du Gay, 1996: 183). That price might include the individualization of risk, resourcefulness and failure (Du Gay, 1996: 182–183; Blackman and Walkerdine, 2001: 104); the pathologization and individualization of dissent and resistance (Flemming and Sewell, 2002: 861); competitiveness rather than cooperation and collectivism (Cremin, 2005: 324); the marginalization of some experiences and individuals (Adams, 2003); and 'the thousand petty humiliations, self-denigrations, deceptions, lies, seductions, cynicisms, bribes, hopes and disappointments' which is the cost, as Rose grandiloquently puts it following Nietzsche, 'of breeding an animal that could feel guilty and bear responsibility for itself and its conduct, against which it must pledge itself as guarantor' (Rose, 1996c: 322).

Enterprise, reflexivity and technologies of self

Unsurprisingly then, for some critical commentators the striving for increased levels of self-reflexivity detailed in the previous chapter tends to be located in this broader normative discourse of 'enterprise' (Miller and Rose, 1990; Cremin, 2003, 2005; Du Gay, 1996). Thus Adkins asserts that 'the self-reflexive subject is closely aligned to neo-liberal modes of governance, indeed is the ideal and privileged subject of neo-liberalism' (Adkins, 2002: 123). The reflexive self becomes recast as 'an entrepreneur of the self' (Gordon, 1987: 300; Du Gay, 1997) or an 'enterprising self' which 'will make an enterprise of its life, seek to maximise its own human capital, project itself a future, and seek to shape itself in order to become that which it wishes to be' (Rose, 1996: 154). Bartky makes the connection between the inhabitant of the panopticon and the contemporary self-reflexive subject explicit: 'in the perpetual self-surveillance of the inmate lies the genesis of the celebrated "individualism" and heightened self-consciousness which are hallmarks of modern times' (Bartky, 1990: 65).

The pervasiveness of reflexivity asserted in the previous chapter is not doubted in these accounts, but it is reconceptualized as the unbalanced co-construction of the power-based interactions played out in the various social fields individuals inhabit. More simply, the reflexive process can all too easily be *appropriated* in the network of power relations we get caught up in, particularly at work: 'The corporate identity becomes individualised through a reflective process in which the needs of the company are emphasised within individual thought as a means for achieving career success' (Cremin, 2003: 118). Furthermore, it can be suggested that reflexivity may regulate those habituated to self-reflexivity, *as well as* those who find themselves adversely and powerlessly positioned in relation to the self-reflexivity of others, a point of differentiation which is taken up in chapter six.

The problem with the 'reflexive project of the self', in sum, is not simply that it is being benignly misunderstood at an analytical level, but that regulatory normative expectations in the guise of individualized empowerment via self-transparency, self-scrutiny and personal responsibility systematically obfuscate processes of government which are fundamentally social and relational. A defining feature of Furedi's 'therapy culture', for example, is 'not an openness towards emotions, but the unusual interest it takes in managing people's internal life' (Furedi, 2004: 197). Captured here is a vital aspect of the regulatory power of 'being reflexive' in post-industrial societies – that at work, school and university, in therapy, on welfare, or at leisure the space of selfhood is colonized by expert systems promoting normative consensus whilst paradoxically signifying self-discovery, self-expression and empowerment (Furedi, 2004; Rose, 1989). Thus the practice of self-reflexivity *cannot* unequivocally be thought of as indicating the privileged equation of perspicuity-knowledge-power; it can alternatively be conceptualized as a contemporary form of government via self-regulation.

It is in this context that arguments which decry Giddens's analysis and those like it as symptomatic of a hegemonic individualism, which takes for granted the premises of that individualism rather than questioning them, can be best understood (Adams, 2003). Giddens's theorization of the self and its relation to the social is capable of being read, even if not intentional, as an assertion of 'individualistic neo-liberalism' (Hay *et al.*, 1997: 93); an unwitting assertion of neo-liberal forms of government and discipline, a contribution to that particular discursive formation. Authors such as Mestrovic (1998), Alexander (1996) and Hay *et al.* (1997) accuse Giddens of offering up a 'lite' or 'hollowed out' social theory which engenders feelings of optimism and completeness, but is in fact more of a distraction from persistent and problematic issues of self-identity than an inclusive account. All these critiques offer-up something of a caricature of the extended reflexivity thesis at its least subtle. In fact there are some parallels between Foucault's recognition of the disciplining dimensions of individualization, Beck's more critical moments and Giddens's earlier work (e.g. Foucault, 1998: 161–162; Beck and Willms, 2004; Giddens, 1979, 1984). However, situated in a Foucaultian framework of governmentality, conceptualized in terms of a contemporary discursive formation and technology of self, the reflexive project of the self lends itself to a more politically and personally problematic reading, reiterating and extending the critical points raised in the previous chapter.

Criticism of Foucault: visibility and agency

If in acting the subject retains the conditions of its emergence, this does not imply that all of its agency remains tethered to those conditions and that those conditions remain the same in every operation of agency.

(Butler, 1997: 13)

There is not the space here to give Foucault's critical reception and legacy the attention it warrants.[8] There are many routes into a critical discussion of Foucault and Foucault-inspired study; here we will focus on one specific problem that has been raised in regards to Foucault's work and Foucaultian analyses – their perceived overdeterminism and subsequent undervaluing of human agency – which impacts upon numerous other critical points. The accusation of excessive social determinism is now a well-worn critical path. Rather than treading it again in general terms here, it will first be approached through a discussion of a specific Foucaultian assertion already discussed: 'visibility is a trap' (Foucault, 1977: 200). Key to this claim is the assumed relationship between visibility and vulnerability. Even critical developments which have attempted to deny, revise or qualify the social reach of panopticism (e.g. Hannah, 1997; Norris, 2002; Norris and Armstrong, 1999; Whitaker, 1999) have tended to accept the logic of 'visibility-vulnerability-subjectification' (Yar, 2003). But does this logic capture the nature of visibility as constituted via governmental discipline and the technologies of self, or is it, as Yar suggests, of a more 'polyvalent and complex nature' (Yar, 2003: 258)?

For Foucault, permanent visibility becomes an internalized, ever-present, self-monitoring gaze. Visibility equals self-subordination. Yar rehearses Martin Jay's assertion that Foucault's under-valuing ('subjected to relentless suspicion and denigration') and over-valuing (at the expense of other dimensions of subject-formation) of vision reflects a French intellectual tradition (2003: 253). For Yar, 'it excludes all other possibilities afforded to visuality in human experience' (2003: 260). The look of others is caught up in an exchange of innumerable possibilities involving approval, dissent, affirmation, and therefore a much more active reception of, and co-construction of 'norms' in some contexts, as well as coercive disciplining (2003: 261). The possibility of a more complex agency in relation to the gaze of authority is indicated here.

Yar goes on to assert how Foucault's claim that it is the *interiorization* of visibility which renders it so powerful, is at odds with his broader understanding of consciousness as a product of discursive positioning. Thus:

> If the subject is not conscious of (does not attend to) his [sic] visibility, [then] the relationship between visibility and discipline collapses. In Foucault's terms, the trap isn't sprung. The introduction of subjective consciousness into the equation effectively surrenders the Panopticon as a generic technology of power to the sense-making activity of situated individuals, upon which it stands or falls. (2003: 261–262)

To put it bluntly, 'people who are blind, ignorant or irrational would be immune to the effects of panoptic power' (Simon, 2005: 7). If consciousness is necessary to mediate disciplinary forms, to transform them into the minutiae of self-governance, then the possibility of disavowal, resistance and partial compliance becomes inevitable too. Consciousness is reinstated as a central battleground in the machinations of social and self-regulating power, and thus all sorts of questions about intentionality and motivation resurface in the cracks of a contradictory account of psychic overdetermination.

Yar claims, for example, that although surrounded by many forms of surveillance in contemporary settings, individuals rarely take conscious notice of these forms and regulate their behaviour accordingly:

> If the logic of panoptic power is conditional upon the subjective awareness and sense-making activity of the individuals 'subjected' to it, then it is by and large liable to have only limited impact in terms of the 'normalisation' of their actions. (Yar, 2003: 264)

An emphasis upon subjective awareness as a mediating dynamic means that it can no longer be understood as something that exists only as an internal signification of a disciplinary economy; by extension panopticism can no longer be uncritically accepted as wholly underwriting situated subjectivities. Its refraction through already-existing psychic space creates the inevitability of differentiation – of forms of visibility, comprehensions of, and responses to them (Koscela, 2003: 300–302; Norris and Armstrong, 1999). Any simplistic causal link between visibility and self-surveillance is thus broken (Yar, 2003: 262–263). The subject becomes 'creative and active...in the management of his [sic] own visibility' (2003: 264). According to this logic, any account of governmentality as a technology of self, panoptical or otherwise, thus needs to take account of the transformative potential of the meeting between self and a normative social order (Elliott, 2001: 96). This does not mean it is necessary to succumb to a 'pristine notion of the subject...whose agency is always and only opposed to power' (Butler, 1997: 17). Instead it is necessary to acknowledge the contradictory tensions of an ambivalent subjectivity, '*neither* fully determined by power *nor* fully determining of power'; to accept the reality of the subject's potential for agency as an 'excrescence of logic' (1997: 17).

It follows that visibility and surveillance can also be resisted and appropriated into subjectivities rather than enacted by docile bodies within the productive exchange of a discursive position (Skeggs, 2005b: 976). Yar provides the example of the 'Surveillance Camera Players', a group of loosely affiliated international performance groups who stage 'shows' for state and corporate CCTV which mock, question and invert their visibility – 'to point out to the guardians of the spectacle that they are being studied...if the enemy is going to clutter our landscape with watchful eyes, we should look into those eyes and let them know how silly we think they are' (New York Surveillance Camera Players, cited in Yar, 2003: 266). A growth in surveillance, in potential visibility, is not what is in question here; rather, it is its integration into a system of total control which incorporates self-awareness. Unless supported by clearly enforceable interventions and punishments, those more familiar governmental mechanisms, panopticism is argued to be more fragile, 'the increasing intensity of visual scrutiny does not necessarily yield a corresponding amplification in subjective self-discipline' (2003: 266).

Yar's argument goes some way towards achieving this balance, but I am not convinced that it offers much of an advance on a more sympathetic reading of Foucault. To be 'creative and active...in the management of [one's] own visibility' places the knower on the *inside* of a disciplinary economy of visibility, not outside of it. Yar is perhaps referring to the contemporary formation of what Foucault calls body-power; the social moulding of the body through a facilitation of individual 'empowerment' and reflexivity which can potentially make unpredictable resistances (Foucault, 1980: 56). So no external point is reached from where a 'pure' agency can be wielded; Foucault, in this instance, seems right to be wary of basing criticism on a point external to discourse. That said, assuming the quote from Butler which opened this section captures the Foucaultian sense in which even a 'radically conditioned form of agency' may take on unforeseeable dimensions (Butler, 1997: 15), it is still unclear to what extent this agency is authored, or why it takes one direction rather than another, and thus questions the appropriateness of the term 'agency' in any meaningful sense; it is merely randomized activity. The issue of agency in relation to Foucault's work thus needs pursuing a little further.

Agency and resistance

Assertions of agency against Foucault's determinism are heard beyond discussion of the connotations of visibility, of course. In the sociology of work, for example, numerous studies have illustrated the ways in which strict demands for emotional labour, and even 'enterprising conduct', are resisted and appropriated through practices such as feigning conformity, jokes, emotional expression and exaggerated deference (Bain and Taylor, 2000; Barton, 2005: 7–8; Bolton and Boyd, 2003; Bryman, 2004: 149–154; Fleming and Sewell, 2002; Hughes, 2005; Knights and McCabe, 2000; McKinlay and Taylor, 1996; Taylor and Bain, 2003). The fit between management norms, however sophisticated in their construction and application, on the one hand, and processes of self-construction on the other, is not so readily assumed. A disjuncture is more likely to be revealed in qualitative accounts which can reveal the subtlety of worker's interpretations rather than the coherence of discourses, and reveal a more rounded conception of subjectivity more generally. For example, an employee might 'seemingly embrace organization initiatives aimed at enhancing quality and service with such ostensible zeal, for example cramming the suggestion box full of not completely useless offerings, that management may be forced to question the wisdom of such measures themselves' (Hughes, 2005: 614; Fleming and Sewell, 2002: 868). Whether explicitly utilized as such or not, examples of dissent and resistance question more broadly a Foucaultian emphasis on total systems of government and the production of subjectivity, and returns the discussion to the more general critique of overdeterminism cited earlier (McNay, 1994: 102; Ransom, 1993: 114; De Certeau, 1984).

Apparent instances of resistance in relation to regulatory norms could, like responses to visibility, be seen as the internal products of a particular discursive formation rather than indicating reflexive and autonomous transgressions of them. It is worth reiterating Foucault's emphasis upon the productivity of government and disciplinary techniques:

if certain activities are enjoined by the policing process…others are engendered by it, so that the elaboration of rules *and the rebellion against them* are bound together dialectically in spiralling definitions of their relationship to one another'. (Hutton, 1988: 127, emphasis added)

As discussed earlier in this chapter it is possible to reinstate some of Foucault's explanatory power by locating the exercise of agency and autonomy *partially* within a broader regulatory discourse of personal enterprise, autonomy and individualization. Simon here reiterates the self-regulating, discursively-bounded understanding of agency reached if the logic of a Foucaultian critique of entrepreneurialism is pursued:

while late modern populations are more mobile and exercise more agency than Foucault seems to account for it also seems that the mobility and agency of populations is still produced by cultural perceptions of when and where it is permissible or even desirable to move and act. This late modern condition of high mobility is arguably one of relative enclosure not the absence of enclosure…Once enclosed not just by walls, but also by the cultural perception of limits, isolation and differentiation are possible; in front of the television or computer, at one's desk, in one's seat or in one's car. At these moments our gaze may be turned inward, to reflect on, to police or even to calculate one's behaviour. (Simon, 2005: 10)

If we add 'for whom' it is 'permissible or even desirable to move and act', as well as when and where, we have a model of regulation which acknowledges differentiation in the ability to exercise agency and self-reflexivity, and inherent, perhaps unavoidable, contradictions in its connection to governmentality and its articulation as a technology of self.

The possibility of agency

This is at best a partial resolution of the myriad of issues thrown up by a Foucaultian analysis of the relationship between self and social change; not least there are questions of intention, desire and motivation which remain; they be will be discussed further in the remaining chapters. It also leads to an evasive feeling of circularity stemming from his account of agency more generally. The circularity seems to emerge from the options for individuals to mould their own subjective space. Although Foucault is at pains to accentuate the productive dimensions of power, there is a 'slippage from a positive to an essentially dominatory model of power' (McNay, 1994: 100) in his work, which is none too easily remedied.

On the one hand, what makes Foucault's position so radical is his contention that there is no space outside of discourse from which we can cast a neutral analytical eye upon it. As Rose has put it: 'the gaze of our inner eye is configured by words, phrases, explanations and valuations: we can experience ourselves as certain types of creatures only because we do so under a certain description' (Rose, 1996b: 234). As discussed above, this allows for a Foucaultian defence against simplistic proclamations of the power of choice, autonomy and personal responsibility to construct an authentic self. Discourses create subject-positions, so our gaze is always outwards from a position held in place by discursive formations; to repeat an earlier quote, we are always 'already in [ourselves] the effect of a subjection much more profound than [ourselves]' (Foucault, 1977: 30). The notion of 'pure' or progressive agency and freedom is thus a myth, as once we approach reality as interlocking discourses, 'the transfigured face of their author is never discernable' (Foucault, 1991: 71). This leaves us with a sense of social reality and its normative moulding of subjectivity as hermetically sealed. If rebellion, denial and disavowal confirms the disciplinary process, what options are left open to the individual? Or as Butler asks 'if subordination is the condition of possibility for agency, how might agency be thought in opposition to the forces of subordination' (Butler, 1997: 19)? There appears to be no viable space for a genuine expression of critique, autonomy, dissent.

On the other hand, an optimistic reading of Foucault suggests that he is providing the individual who comes across his work with the tools of liberation. By bringing him or her up against the historically contingent nature of 'truth' s/he is showing him or her that what s/he accepts as steadfast 'facts' about who or what s/he can be are actually revisable, plastic; he is making a 'finally utopian gesture' (Butler, 1997: 59). In other words, Foucault's analysis creates a space for hope: 'ideas which go without saying, which make possible existing practices and our existing conceptions of ourselves, may be more contingent, recent and modifiable than we think' (Gordon, 1991: 48). Or in Foucault's own words:

> My role…is to show people that they are much freer than they feel, that people accept as truth, as evidence, some themes which have been built up at a certain moment during history, and that this so-called evidence can be criticized and destroyed. (Foucault and Martin, 1988: 10)

An entreaty to 'experiment with the possibility of going beyond' the 'limits that are imposed on us' (Foucault, 1984: 49) is a comforting resolution to the problem of agency and change in Foucault's analysis, and the sense of total enclosure his understanding of the mechanisms of power can suggest. However, I think it is problematic in the context of his broader project. If, as suggested by Foucault and Gordon, we *can* be 'freer' what exactly can we free ourselves from and into? Or, as Walzer frames the problem:

> But what will be left? Foucault does not believe, as earlier anarchists did, that the free human subject is a subject of a certain sort, naturally good, warmly sociable, kind and loving. Rather, there is for him no such thing as a free human subject, no natural man or woman. Men and women are always social creations, the products of codes and disciplines. And so Foucault's radical abolitionism, if it is serious, is not anarchist so much as nihilistic. For on his own arguments, either there will be nothing left at all, nothing visibly human;

or new codes and disciplines will be produced, and Foucault gives us no reason to expect that these will be any better than the ones we now live with. Nor, for that matter does he give us any way of knowing what 'better' might mean. (Walzer, 1986: 61)

So we are 'free' simply to choose one discourse rather than another? What discursive formation is Foucault's work itself a part of? Is it one we should embrace or submit ourselves too? Do we have a choice? If so, then is there a subject that *can* stand outside of discourses and reflect upon them? Is there a brief realm of freedom, a momentary suspension of discourse, a pregnant readiness or anticipation from where we engage all over again with a discourse and enmesh ourselves in a particular regime of truth? I am not sure a Foucaltian approach can satisfactorily answers any of these questions.

Foucault and feminism

Feminism in particular has a tenuous relationship with Foucault's work on this matter. Although his deconstructivism usefully contributes to a laying-bare of patriarchal traditions and the enmeshment of subjects within them whilst revealing their historical contingency (Bordo, 1993), his proscribed notion of agency fits uneasily with the explicitly 'emancipatory project' (Alcoff, 1999: 75) of the more radical applications of feminism:

> On the one hand, Foucault's argument that power inscribes, saturates and even constitutes every human relation ties closely to feminist critiques of language and culture. On the other hand, that argument specifically challenges the very idea of emancipatory politics and individual or collective agency. (Rhodes, 2005: 7)

In the failure to resolve the problem of agency, what haunts Foucault's work, despite his attempts to exorcize it, is the ghost of a universal subject. The qualities of this subject can be inferred from Foucault's occasional freedom-calls, amounting to what McNay refers to as a 'covert appeal to the ideals of autonomy, dignity and recipricocity' (1994: 158). A discussion of agency and determinism is here necessarily broadened out to other points of critique: particularly Foucault's supposed implicit support for the Enlightenment values of masculinist rationality and individualism which feminist work has sought to elucidate.

In terms of individualism, for example, Foucault and Foucaultian analyses have been criticized for failing to acknowledge the importance of interpersonal relationships in self-construction (Burkitt, 1999; Gardiner, 1996), privileging 'the individual's relations with the self over relations with others' (McNay, 1994: 152). Foucault's selves appear as isolated monads, reduced to their capacities to cognize the realities espoused by interlocking discourses. Inner-experience and inter-experience is lost, a mere epiphenomenon to the dynamism of discourse, and 'we assume that cognition dominates people's lives, that we only have ideas and those ideas come to us from the outside, from the social world; we take them in and act on them' (Craib, 1998: 2–3). In Butler's words, Foucault assumes a 'vacated interiority'; 'a malleable surface for the unilateral effects of disciplinary power' (1997: 88). We all seem to respond to discourses as individuals cut-off from each other, when in fact we are in constant negotiation with others about how to understand and express ourselves – 'self-realization is itself embedded within realms of mutuality, trust, intimacy and affection' (Elliott, 2001: 108).

To briefly return to the specific issues of surveillance in contemporary society, Koscela claims that 'urban space is far more complex than the concept of space in Foucault's interpretations of the prison' (Koscela, 2003: 297). An issue of transposability is also one of excessive saliency granted to the *individualization* of contemporary forms of control and surveillance. For though Bentham's form of imprisonment may be a suitable metaphor for some aspects of the urban experience, individuals 'are not under isolation but quite the opposite: a city is a space of endless encounters' (2003: 297).

An aesthetics of care

Although Foucault's work on governmentality and its subsequent application allows for a more complex understanding of the relationship between self and regulative/productive social discourses, concerns about the possibility of autonomous agency persist, as we have seen. However his later work, which is in part an attempt to elucidate the agential possibilities for subjectivity more comprehensively, actually slides into more philosophically and politically problematic positions (e.g. Foucault, 1986).[9] Foucault returns to the Enlightenment in the search for a genuinely reflexive ontology, and retains its critical attitude, though ambivalently, whilst turning his back upon the essentialist and humanist fallacies of Enlightenment thinking in a move reminiscent of Adorno and Horkheimer (Adorno and Horkheimer, 1979; Foucault, 1984). He finds in Greek culture an ideal of self-mastery which allows more space for autonomy in relation to social rules and morality, an ethics of self which allows for the authored stylisation of self (Foucault, 1986).

Foucault's argument is complex, but it is primarily an assertion of the principle of self-determination which is capable of sustained critical ontology, of standing apart from the normative demands of discursive formations and potentially transgressing them in 'ethical moments' of self-reflexivity. In terms of the problem of agency then, Foucault again retains 'some notion of the transcendence in the sense of being able to go beyond the limits that historically have been imposed upon us' (McNay, 1994: 144). McNay and others suggest Foucault's assertion of autonomy in the aestheticization of the self – the self as a work of art – can provide a dialectical counterpoint to the essentialization and naturalization of processes of selfhood which occurs in normative discourses (1994: 145).

However, running parallel to the aforementioned tendency towards individualism, Foucault's aspirations in this later work for a new aesthetics, stylistics or care of self similarly draw uncritically on notions of self-mastery which are at once individualist and masculinist – 'an unexamined and nostalgic fantasy of masculine agency' (McNay, 1994: 153; McNay, 2002). For Foucault, a genuinely radical self-self relation is transported unchallenged form his interpretation of Greek culture, elaborated via notions of 'heroization' and 'virile self-mastery' (McNay, 1994: 149). Brown's defence of Foucault's treatment of the non-discursive, for example, perpetuates an aesthetics of self described in terms of individual self-mastery, 'ordering', 'formulating' and 'stylizing' environmental components in the art of living (Brown, 2001: 188). The Foucaultian ideal fails to extricate the conceptualization of autonomy from problematic normative underpinnings, indicating a lack of critical reflection when it comes to the possibility of critical reflection itself! Foucault's notion of the self in fact 'covertly represents aspects of a specific male experience' (McNay, 1994: 153), unreflexively reproducing some of the traditions of philosophical thinking, rather than transgressing them. As well as accusations of individualism and the universalization of historically gendered self-practices, Foucault's assumption that an 'art of self' inherently opposes essentialism is argued to be misplaced. There is no reason why 'aesthetizations of self' should not draw on essentializing constructions of gender, for example, in highly contestable areas such as gender identity and women's reproductive rights.

Christopher Bollas's outline of an 'aesthetics of care', steeped in the object-relations school of psychoanalytic thought, offers a counterpoint to Foucault's approach which reveals some of its individualist preoccupations (Bollas, 1997). Bollas understands individual development in profoundly intersubjective terms. As discussed in chapter three, the child experiences its first 'object' (usually the care of the parent/s) as a transformative part of its own self-structure. The very building blocks of the self are constituted in and through the dynamics of this relationship with the other: 'the baby and then the child internalizes as structure a process that is a dialectically negotiated composition of his [sic] own instincts and ego interests and the mother's handling of them' (Bollas, 1987: 50). Care and management of the self in adult life depends upon the partial transfer of the parental care system over to self-structure. It also relies, in part, on the search for substitute objects in the mutual management of selves. Put simply, how we are handled by others is the basis for how we handle our self. The implication of Bollas's analysis is that an aesthetics or 'care of the self' is intimately wrought with the process of relationship, a 'grammar of being' learnt prior to the rules of language (1987: 36). Even as it is briefly stated here, the Foucaultian ideal of 'techniques of self' is conditioned and contextualized in the formative concrete relationships of past and present.

Reinforcing this deficiency is a lack of awareness of the gendered nature of subjecthood, perhaps reflecting Foucault's 'blind spot' towards women's experiences more generally (McCallum, 1996: 90; Morris, 1988; Bartky, 1988). His notion of the subject is impersonal, presenting a 'chimera of neutrality' (MCallum, 1996: 90) or discursive abstraction which makes no attempt to deal with subjective experiences of difference, and so is 'unable to distinguish between the different kinds of power relations that cut across women's lives' (Ramazanoglu, 1993: 15). Thus, despite Foucault's emphasis upon the intersection of power, knowledge and embodiment, he fails to pay sufficient attention to the fact that historically, subjective experiences of embodiment differ along gendered (as well as other) lines: 'female embodiment is different from male embodiment' (Ramazanoglu and Holland, 1993: 251).

The substantial range of feminist critique which has engaged with Foucault is discussed in detail elsewhere (e.g. McNay, 2002; Hekman, 1996; Ramazanoglu, 1993; Diamond and Quinby, 1988), though we will return to a concern with the socially differentiated and particularized nature of self-identity in the final chapter. Before concluding this chapter however, it is worth noting an unexpected point of *convergence* between Foucaultian versions of self-identity and those discussed in terms of the extended reflexivity thesis, which come into view more clearly in the light of critique. Though Foucault might be talking more about an ideal, his hopes for an aesthetization of experience actually mirror key tenets of the reflexive project of selfhood conceptualized by Giddens *et al*. In the previous chapter the notion of the self as a reflexive project was accused of the valorization of rationaility, excessive voluntarism and individualism and an at best partial recognition of the relation between reflexive capabilities and a differentiating social structure. Whilst a Foucaultian analysis goes some way to deconstructing the privileging of a rationalized and atomized self-self relationship, in Foucault's later work it ends up in danger of reproducing it, being equally 'disembedded and disembodied' (McNay, 1994: 155). The final chapter will consider the analytical possibility of self-reflexivity in connection to a contemporary society understood as regulated by complex social discourses but not reducible to them whilst avoiding the slippages of both Foucaultian analyses and the extended reflexivity thesis.

Conclusion

It is essential to remain wary of the possible valorization of an authentic 'self' when critiquing contemporary discursive formations of the enterprising/reflexive self for fear of reverting to an essentialist error. However, dismissals of any account of ontological primacy find it difficult to avoid reinstating it somewhere in their schemes, just as the discussion of Foucault's logic has suggested in this chapter (Fraser, 1996: 24). The development of Foucaultian analyses may not require a return to the psychological so much as an acknowledgment and extension of the subject that is already there. To pose this problem another way, asking what the basis is for criticizing the discourse of, say, enterprise and defending another seems to a reasonable question. A common answer appears to be that it serves the interests of established powers by producing a certain kind of self. Does that matter to any of us, as selves? If not, the discussion ends there. If so, who and why? One can only assume it is because they cannot be produced as an enterprising self so easily and end up excluded, marginalized, or can and feel uneasy or that there are better ways of being than an 'entrepreneur of the self'. Even this would not matter unless it matters to those excluded, marginalized or distortedly realized; it must be part of their felt experience. If so some kind of interiority, an affective, embodied awareness which comes to discourse becomes important. Object-relations approaches are perhaps an interesting counterpoint here, as discussed in chapters three and five, for whilst the self they posit is a product of social and discursive formations, it holds onto a notion of a 'core subject' which is nonetheless constituted in relational forces (Hekman, 2000: 301). Indeed, if the limitations of both Foucaultian and neo-modern analyses necessitate a 're-turn to the psychological' (Blackman, 2005: 202), as has been numerously suggested in one form or another (e.g. Bendle, 2002; Burr and Butt, 2000; Elliott, 2004; Frosh, Pheonix and Patman, 2003; Hekman, 2000), then a reconsideration of the object-relational and interactionist approaches discussed in chapter three may be productive. We must be able to say, I think, that the attempt to govern selves through the exercise of autonomy is problematic, and this is because it serves the interest of a pervasively unequal society; and because there are alternative conceptions of self, of social relations, and of experience, that we wish to value.

Rose makes this problem for discursive approaches explicit when he says the following about the relationships between selves and their government: 'Analysis of these novel relations is not critique – no past or future moment is posited when a self, freed from the weight of political expectations and ethical obligations, could relate to itself in some unmediated manner' (Rose, 1996c: 322). But he goes on to say that nonetheless contemporary forms of neo-liberal, enterprising government do exact a cost; those same costs mentioned earlier. Forms of government may always exact costs as Rose suggests. But to me, highlighting the costs of this form of government in particular *does* inevitably amount to critique, and consequently *does* at least imply the possibility of alternative forms of government, alternate selves, which may be more acceptable, less violent and coercive. Moreover it implies a pre-formed ontology, a subject who cares, desires, feels the humiliations to which it refers and is potentially consciously aware of them as such.

Foucault has provided a language with which we can more readily understand the processes of subjection, particularly his conceptualization of governmentality as both social and subjective; the point of 'contact between the technologies of domination of others and those of the self'

(Foucault, 1988b: 19). Panopticism is just one example of a technology of government, which has been fruitfully worked into an understanding of the relationship between contemporary discursive formations, for example 'enterprise', and the technologies of self-construction. As the discussion of enterprise has suggested, a Foucaultian analysis can incorporate more simplistic critiques of overdeterminism, for the dynamics of reflexive agency are themselves argued to be particular embodied subject-positionings, constituted by historically contingent discursive formations. Clearly though, relating individuals ridicule, appropriate, invert, defend, resist, enjoy and ignore whatever normative disciplining technologies attempt to govern them, as well as accepting and being interpellated by them. Some have more to gain or lose in any one of these endeavours depending on other elements of their situated existence (such as employment, age, gender, ethnicity, nationality, education and sexuality). A Foucaultian response may be that selves still come to be constituted *within* a particular discursive economy, not apart from it; or at the other pole of Foucault's concept of power, he might emphasize the possibility of self-mastery; but both reduce the complexity and heterogeneity of psychic life, intersubjectivity and social structure to too simple an equation.

Notes to the text

1 This is not to suggest that Foucault 'reduced everything to discourse', an often-voiced criticism. His definition of discourse itself is productively broad, but he also attended to the 'non-discursive' dimensions of human activity. He perceived them to be both equally subject to the dynamics of social construction and equally important in the production of reality (Foucault, 1972; Deleuze, 1988). See Brown (2001) for a detailed discussion of Foucault's account of the non-discursive.

2 A more recent phenomenon in global employment trends is the well documented migration of call centres from 'developed' to 'developing' countries, in an attempt to reduce labour and other costs. The call centre operations of larger corporations in the United Kingdom, for example, already strategically located in geographical clusters to reduce costs, are increasingly being transferred to India. It is interesting to note the findings of initial research into this new generation of call centres (Taylor and Bain, 2004) which argue that the control and regulation of the conduct of Indian agents is further extended as it takes on a more explicit 'culturalization' role, often with the aim of concealing the call centre location from 'developed' country customers: 'The widespread adoption of anglicized pseudonyms, of having to conceal their Indian locations, and the obligation to speak in "neutral" accents, or even emulate their customers' dialects contribute greatly to a pressurized working experience…These neo-imperialist – and indeed racist – practices add significant, culturally-specific dimensions of psychological strain to pressures associated with the emotional labour that call centres engender' (Taylor and Bain, 2004: 274–8). We might add that they are a further dimension of panopticism in the workplace; an attempt to reach into and modify the processes by which agents come to understand themselves via neo-colonial discourses.

3 Although on a smaller scale here, the relationship between corporate culture programmes and work identity seems reminiscent of the 'depersonalization'

process mental hospital 'inmates' endured in Goffman's *Asylums* (1961). In fact if we imagine society as a total institution, and the depersonalization process as the shift from one discursive subject position to another rather than a loss of an 'authentic' self, the metaphor is a crudely illustrative metaphor of the Foucaultian world-view.

4 The television series *The Apprentice*, originally a US show but now a global franchise, and various spin-offs like *Into the Dragon's Den* (BBC) and *Risking it All* (Channel 4) in the United Kingdom, perhaps attest to the cultural valorization of the 'entrepreneur of the self'.

5 'Enterprise' may be on its way out as an explicit organizing principle of management discourses, which are notoriously short-lived. New terms such as 'emotional intelligence' have risen to prominence (Goleman, 1996; 1998). Emotional intelligence refers to being able to recognize one's own and others' emotions, managing them, and channelling them into self-motivation and drive, gratification deferral and an ability to embrace flexibility and adaptability. Sociological work in this area has suggested that emotional intelligence, like enterprise, 'embodies the meritocratic ideal that we are in control of our own destinies at work and beyond' and the normative 'reinvention of character as reflexive, intelligent and as residing within the realm of individual discretion' (Hughes, 2005: 609, 620; Fineman, 2004, 2000). So although ostensibly novel, the organizing principles of emotional intelligence appear very similar to those of the 'enterprising self'.

6 Reay's analysis of children's experiences of assessment draws similar conclusions to Cremin, but is more attuned to the affective dimensions of their impact upon identity, and the ways in which they are differentially experienced depending on class and gender (Reay, 2005; Reay and William, 1999).

7 See Du Gay (2004) for a detailed differentiation of different forms of 'enterprise' and 'autonomy'.

8 For examples of feminism's critical engagement with Foucault see Diamond and Quinby (1988), Hekman (1996) and McNay (1992). More general critical overviews include Dumm (1996), Hoy (1986) and Simons (1995).

9 For an excellent introduction to critical commentary on Foucault's later work, see McNay (1994), to which the following discussion is indebted.

5

The Narcissistic Self

The introduction of the concept of narcissism counts among Freud's most magnificent discoveries, although psychoanalytic theory has still not proved quite equal to it.

(Adorno, 1968 [1955]: 88)

To pursue the psychological and social relations of narcissism is to enter a swamp.

(Kovel, 1980: 88)

Critical theory and psychoanalysis

Critical theory has long sought to forge psychoanalysis and marxism into a productive dialectic to elucidate the forms of subjectivity possible in late-capitalist societies. One of the most important fundamentals to have emerged from the development of psychoanalysis in object-relations approaches and beyond is the one underpinning this book, that changes in social environment and self-identity are interwoven.

Contemporary schools of psychodynamic thought thus provide a 'conceptual framework for appreciating the interpenetration of external experience with internal psychological structure' (Frosh, 1991: 72). A psychoanalytically-informed critical theory shares with Foucaultian analyses the belief that human interactions which make up our social world do not mould the basic material of the self into a certain shape so much as constitute the basic ingredients of that material. For Foucault, this means that the 'self' is always a product of discourse; self is a secondary production of the reality of discourse. For psychoanalysis however, unconscious dynamics are posited as the conduit via which the social environment constructs psychic life. The machinations of repression and sublimation are real, pulsing dynamisms which utilize the libidinal charge of object-relations in one's environment to progress along the slow, tortuous, uneven and uncertain path towards individuation.

A critical social theory which utilizes psychoanalysis asserts that the self is contingent upon the social environment; more specifically on the quality of human relations it allows, encourages and engenders, at an unconscious level. It rests on the conviction that psychoanalysis can be appropriated to trace 'the origins of intrapsychic conflict to the conditions under which social authority recreates itself in the unconscious mind' (Lasch, 1981: 24). Thus the power of the social environment we find our-selves in is found in 'the way it enters unbidden and unnoticed into the foundation stones of our psychic structure' (Frosh, 1991: 2).

A key offspring in the union of critical theory and psychoanalysis is the explanatory power invested in the concept of *narcissism*, one of the 'core dimensions of the Freudian account of selfhood' (Elliott, 2000: 134), later understood as a psychic building block with strong cultural underpin-nings in late-capitalist societies. As a consequence it was appropriated by some as an emblem for modern times and modern selves towards the end of the last century (Lasch, 1979). Since Adorno's assertion of the value of Freud's concept of narcissism, cited at the opening of this chapter, psy-choanalytic theory has undoubtedly taken up his challenge to substan-tially develop it, though often in divergent directions (e.g. Kohut, 1971; Kernberg, 1975). The subsequent difficulties involved in integrating a developed psychoanalytic concept into sociological analyses are pithily illustrated in the second of the opening quotes. Such difficulty has been mirrored to an extent in the relative lack of interest in the concept as a social and cultural phenomenon today (Valadez and Clignet, 1987).

This chapter is an attempt to reconsider the usefulness of the concept of narcissism in the relationship between self and social change. More gen-erally it is an opportunity to explore if and how psychoanalytical asser-tions of psychological interiority, dynamism and affect can combine with social theory to offer any advance on the debates engaged with up to this point. What follows is a brief explanation of the concept of a psychologi-cal disorder as it has been clinically documented before opening out to survey more sociologically-minded analyses and their critical reception.

Narcissism as a psychological disorder

Overviews of the psychoanalytic literature on narcissism agree that it is at the same time both one of the most important and one of the most per-plexing concepts to have emerged from the discipline (Bromberg, 1982: 438; Cooper, 1986: 112; Pulver, 1986: 91). Freud's initial treatment of the term was influential but brief in – 'a seminal but confusing paper' (Lasch, 1979: 24; Freud, 1914) – not least because his early ideas concerning nar-cissism were not fully incorporated into later revised notions of the struc-tural forces of the self (Freud, 1923, 1924; Frosh, 1991). Consequently there is a consensus that his 'theory of narcissism was left in quite a sketchy form' (Whitford, 2003: 28). Contemporary understandings of narcissism in psychoanalytic discourse draw from an abundance of clinical literature, as well as the writing of influential figures of various branches of psycho-analytic thinking such as Chasseguet-Smirgel (1985a, 1985b), Grunberger

(1979, 1989), Kernberg (1975, 1986a, 1986b), Klein (1952, 1957, 1988 [1975]), Kohut (1966, 1971, 1977), Kovel (1980, 1988), Lacan (1975, 1977), Mahler (1979 [1958], Mahler *et al.*, 1975) and Winnicott (1964, 1965, 1974).

Object-relations terminology – which rests on the conviction that 'there is no instinctual urge, no anxiety situation, no mental process which does not involve objects, external or internal; in other words, object-relations are at the *centre* of emotional life' (Klein, 1988 [1975]: 53) – is the most accessible and convincing explanation of narcissism in my mind and is what will be leaned most heavily upon here. Such a brief overview will inevitably mask the controversies and debates which still mark the evolution of the concept of narcissism in the work of such authors as those listed above, but which are not centrally relevant here.[1] Our summary will be geared towards the broader explanatory brushstrokes most likely to find consensus across various schools.

Freud distinguished between primary and secondary narcissism, and that distinction has mostly been maintained and developed in later revisions by others. Primary narcissism is encountered by everyone – it is the experience of the womb-encased prenatal infant and the neonate. At these times, according to psychoanalytical accounts, the child's needs are met instantaneously. Because there is no delay between need and gratification, the fledgling self feels as if it is the sum of the world; need goes hand in hand with its satisfaction, and no distinction is made between 'within' and 'without', between an internal and external world, between self and other. This is the state of primary narcissism. There are no beginnings and ends to the experience of reality, no 'self', for that indicates separation, but an undifferentiated amalgam of experiences which coalesces into an unconscious omnipotence. There are object relations – namely with the breast or teat – however 'the object that is sought…is not distinguished from the subject that seeks it' (Kovel, 1980: 89).

Primary narcissism provides an important defence mechanism against the helplessness and dependency which actually define the infant's early relations. However the 'expulsion from Paradise' is inevitable (Richards, 1989: 39). Soon after birth, the infant is confronted with feelings of hunger and separation, a devastating experience which starkly contrasts with the previous 'oceanic' oneness of the womb. In these feelings, the infant comes face-to-face with 'its helpless, inferior and dependent position in the world' (Lasch, 1979: 241). To cope with this powerlessness initially the infant indulges in unconscious fantasies which attempt to regain the omnipotent equilibrium of the womb. For Mahler this coping attempt amounts to a second stage of primary narcissism, a symbiotic phase (Mahler, 1979 [1958]). During this phase there occurs a psychic fusion of all existing memory and experience of sensation with stimuli from external world (e.g. mother's breast, hands, face) into a symbiotic state of omnipotence (White, 1986: 147). In Kleinian terminology, the infant directs hate and rage towards the 'bad' aspects of the world (incorporating self and others), those objects which have failed to meet their needs (Klein, 1988 [1975]).

Symbiosis is a fantasy which provides a developmental bridge between primary narcissism and a growing awareness of the separateness of need and its gratification, self and other objects; 'the record of transition from the dyadic person to the individual' (Kovel, 1980: 90). The 'bit-by-bit withdrawal' of instantaneous need-gratification creates a state of 'optimal frustration' in the parent-child relationship at this early stage, which generates consistent experiences of satiation combined with modest steps towards a mastery of the environment (White, 1986: 151). The caregiver's total attention is mourned, internalized and incorporated into the child's self-relations, creating the basis for self-soothing capacities (Kohut, 1971: 61–64). Although a narcissistic enterprise, the latter phase of primary narcissism clarifies the infant's separation, initiating a 'dawning awareness of mother's ministrations along with the dawning awareness of the self that is gratified' (White, 1986: 148).

Normal development follows the symbiotic phase with individuation and separation, initially experienced 'not a sense of *who* I am but *that* I am' (Mahler *et al.*, 1975: 4). The individual's increasing awareness of the reality of the tension between their growing independence and continued dependency demands the dissolution of a psychological reality initially set up as a tenuous fortification against an encroaching outer reality. The infant gradually emerges from an environment of close and caring attention to their needs, in which their fantasy of omnipotence is gratified, into one where he or she is:

> increasingly aware of [his or her] need for the mother's care and help...those infants who are able to begin gradually to delegate their own sense of omnipotence to a parent for whom they have loving feelings, and to share that omnipotence while gaining a feeling of greater effectiveness, both individually and through sharing, are likely to develop a sturdy and joyful sense of self. (Cooper, 1986: 133)

Additionally, a less narcissistic reality is allowed into the relational construction of self, because 'as the infant learns to distinguish itself from its surroundings, it begins to understand that its own wishes do not control the world' (Lasch, 1979: 242). This is the basis for emotional maturity, which lies in 'a recognition of others not as projections of our own desires but as independent beings with desires of their own' (1979: 242). This early experience of unwilling relinquishment is vital to most psychoanalytic accounts, which from Freud's pervasive tone of pessimism onwards, are particularly suited to biographical trajectories in which loss and deprivation are central to individuation: 'one can become a distinctive, functioning human subject only through emerging, dispossessed, from the narcissistic matrix of early experience' (Richards, 1989: 39).[2] The zenith of the individuation process is commonly argued to be reached in the playing out of the oedipal drama. In sum, for these approaches passing through primary narcissism is vital for the fledgling sense of self to emerge, and it is fundamentally an intra-psychic process located within the context of object relations.

Secondary narcissism: aetiology

Narcissism is never totally abandoned and the subsequent degree and value of narcissism and/or symbiosis in healthy psychological development has been debated at length, not least in relation to Freud's own understanding of the ego-ideal (Freud, 1914; e.g. Becker, 1973; Barrett and McIntosh, 1982; Bollas, 1987; Engel, 1980; Kristeva, 1984 [1974]; Lash, 1981).[3] Despite important differences however, most approaches would agree with Kovel that whilst the narcissistic investment of libinal energy in one's own self as an object is vital for self-worth, assertion and esteem, there is a delicate balance to be maintained between too little and too much narcissism (Kovel, 1980). As a 'failed power', 'exaggerated narcissism is an aspect of real, if difficult to conceptualize, disorders' (Kovel, 1980: 88), and is often referred to as secondary narcissism or narcissistic personality disorder (Kohut, 1971). Before considering how narcissism might be defined as a disorder in adult psychology, it is necessary to outline its supposed aetiology in the context of the developmental processes so far discussed.

There appears to be general agreement on the triggers for the development of secondary or pathological narcissism: the actual nature of that most primary of object relationships, the mother-child bond. Thus Frosh encapsulates much psychodynamic thinking on the causes of narcissism in asserting that the successful or unsuccessful incorporation of narcissistic object relations into an integrated self depends upon,

> the mother's ability to maintain a state of 'reverie' – an intense empathic connection with the child which nevertheless leaves the mother separate enough for her to retain her own emotional centre and hence to survive what otherwise might feel like murderous attacks. (Frosh, 1991: 71–2)

Generations of feminist engagement with psychoanalysis has questioned the assumption of the primacy of the mother's role in the child's environment, but the basic components remain the same: 'the total environmental provision of reliable, predictable, empathically attuned attention to the physiological and emotional needs of the child's whole self' (Bjorklund, 2000: 93).[4] Thus is takes no great leap of the imagination to predict what can go wrong: 'the development of pathological forms of narcissism is largely dependent upon the actual failures of the environment to provide appropriate empathic responses to the infant's needs' (Cooper, 1986: 135).

The details of an inadequate 'reverie' vary from the remarkably specific, such as a 'mechanical', non-tactile method of breast feeding (Mahler *et al.*, 1975; White, 1986: 151) to the perhaps overly-general: 'massive disapproval, rejection and neglect instead of interest in encouragement' (Kohut, cited in White, 1986: 153). Basically, it is thought that if a child experiences an environment of contradictory, inconsistent and/or detached care then they may find it difficult to progress from the production of fantasy-based parental objects or *imagos* (which may be a more accurate representation of their perception of reality) to the construction of more concrete object relations: 'their interactions reflect very intense, primitive, internalized object relationships of a frightening kind and an incapacity to depend on internalized good objects' (Kernberg, 1975: 84). Others emerge only as ill-defined extensions of an equally ill-defined self, 'she or he can only relate to others as imagos, as split-off, idealised or denigrated, reflections of a depreciated and unintegrated inner world' (Frosh, 1991: 76). The child thus remains possessed of their insecure craving for omnipotence; now split off from the conscious ego in the form of a 'grandiose self' (Kernberg, 1975; Kohut, 1971).

Basically, if a child's initial narcissistic self-expression is adequately held and mirrored by its environment, it will eventually dissolve the powerful desire for omnipotence into significant others and internalize it into an important dimension of self-structure, the ego-ideal; and accept the individuation furthered by the oedipal complex. If it is not, then an over-expanded but needy sense of self is established as a defence mechanism. This 'grandiose self' has a ravenous dependency on others for confirmation of its existence, which looms behind an everyday detached self, built to prevent any recognition of that vulnerability to its fragile sense of omnipotence. The grandiose self thus serves as an 'intermediate between the official persona presented to the world and an innermost state of affairs against which it defends' (Kovel, 1980: 92); hence the pathological narcissist is caught between the 'mirror and the mask' respectively: 'a reflected appraisal of himself [sic], or a disguised search for one, through which the self finds or seeks affirmation of its own significance' (Bromberg, 1982: 439–440). It is destined to be a frustrated and frustrating recourse to the formative myth of omnipotence.

Secondary narcissism: characteristics

In alluding to the 'grandiose self' we begin to describe the structure and symptoms of secondary or pathological narcissism, as it might be experienced. The unceasing self-aggrandizement characteristic of narcissism is associated with a number of qualities but what makes the disorder more than 'mere' vanity is the fact that is it a defence against an otherwise overwhelming fear of engulfment. The main job of the grandiose self is the maintenance of a defensive fantasy: 'to be perfect…that is, to achieve approbation, to never be dependent, and never to feel lacking in any way' (Bromberg, 1982: 440). As early narcissism has not adequately been internalized as a self-sustaining ego-ideal, the pathological narcissist is paradoxically dependent on the attention of others to shore up their sense of omnipotence. Paradoxical because whilst relations with others are vital, acknowledging this fact is constantly held at bay as it is an admission of vulnerability, of incompleteness, which cannot be allowed access to the fragile ego's defensive grandiosity:

> The hell of the narcissist is the tyranny of his [sic] need for the other…For the narcissist in his unmisgiving project of self-sufficiency, there must be no

outside. No others to ruffle his arrangements. He is not an object-relations theorist. (Phillips, 2002: 214–215)

Relations with others thus tend to be marked by oscillations between extreme neediness and cold aloofness and excessive expectations. The narcissistically disturbed person,

> may view the other (person, ideal, or institution) in an unrealistic and fantasy-bound manner, wishing and hoping that the other will magically identify and satisfy his or her needs. When a partner is unable to do so, feelings of rage, rejection, humiliation and helplessness frequently ensue. (Bjorklund, 2000: 87)

Other people are vital as 'need-satisfying objects' but are variously regarded with hostility, contempt or idealization rather than related to as separate human beings with equally important needs and sensitivities of their own (Bromberg, 1982: 440). Relations with others are disturbed further by aspects of the narcissist's attitude towards his or her own self borne of self-aggrandizement: an excessive sense of the uniqueness and extent of one's own talents, importance, worth to others, and problems (American Psychiatric Association, 2000). The threat to self-esteem posed by the plethora of possible challenges to omnipotence generates extreme rage in the narcissist as it is experienced as an overwhelming threat to a brittle, reactionary if routinely hidden, self-image.

Horney summarizes the twin essences of the diagnostic understanding of narcissism concisely, describing it as 'appearing unduly significant to oneself and craving undue admiration from others' (Horney cited in Cooper, 1986: 120). The key to these two 'always present' tendencies is their exaggerated – 'undue' – nature and the impact they have on interpersonal relationships. In the interactions of everyday life it is likely that inflated versions of self end up punctured by humiliation, but due to the nature of narcissistic defence mechanisms, leads to the generation of yet-greater self-distortions, further humiliation and so on in a downward spiral towards 'disorder', faced with a rage fuelled by its impotence (Cooper, 1986: 121; Kernberg, 1986a: 214; Lasch, 1979).

Brief excerpts from case studies of narcissistic disturbance illustrate some of the diagnostic criteria. An over-idealization of others and relating to them only as 'need-satisfying others':

> [pleading] for instructions on how to understand something or how to feel about it. Sometimes Abby's presentation evoked images of her waiting for me to magically solve her dilemmas. (Bjorklund, 2000: 89)

Self-aggrandizement co-existing with sense of self-doubt and inferiority and painfully ambivalent relations to others:

> She thought others saw her as aloof, unapproachable, or uninterested in relationships with them, while Abby saw herself as 'fun, vivacious, interesting, smart' and a very desirable companion for anybody. (2000: 90)

> Abby seemed anxious, insecure about herself and her attractiveness to others, and intensely desirous of an intimate relationship while also very fearful of it. (2000: 89)

Inter-relatedness is treated with contempt in others but also desired:

> [Abby] was deeply envious of other women's ability to engage in meaningful relationships and attempted to hide this envy by expressing scorn for them. (2000: 87)

Another client, James, was depressed at the termination of a three-month relationship by another, 'unable to understand why his girlfriend wanted to end the relationship' (Czuchta Romano, 2004: 24) and his subsequent rage incorporated inflated ideas of his own abilities, claiming that he was integral to the authorship of her doctoral thesis, despite the short time-span of their relationship (2004: 25). Attitudes towards a college tutor who failed James also suggested a grandiose sense of self-worth and entitlement:

> [James had made] verbal threats against a professor who, according to James, 'unjustifiably made him fail a course'. James describes himself as 'academically brilliant' and in fact, 'could have done a much better job in teaching the course' than the professor who failed him. (2004: 25)

Though of course, there's always the possibility that he was right! The clinician was also analyzed in some detail in terms of the extent to which it was perceived she could meet the exaggeratedly unique and important needs of the client:

> James insisted on knowing my academic preparation, the name of the university I attended, and how many years of clinical experience I had...he was not impressed with the amount of junior staff on the unit...he voiced how upset he was for not getting the private room he requested so 'his special issues' could be discussed privately with his assigned staff...he was unsure whether he could share a room with such 'unatttractive individuals'. (2004: 25)

Another clinical vignette illustrates the narcissistic strategy of appropriating other's knowledge as self-generated expertise, thus denying any reliance on others:

> He did not resent interpretations, but on the contrary took them up quickly and talked about them in his own way, feeling very self-satisfied with his knowledge since he did not feel that the analyst had made any contribution. (Rosenfeld, cited in Whitford, 2003: 32–33).

Other traits include overwhelming feelings of vulnerability (Kovel, 1980: 91); sensitivity to criticism (Bjorklund, 2000: 86); envy and a belief that others are envious of self; persistent fantasies of 'success, power, beauty, brilliance or ideal love' (American Psychiatric Association, 2000); fear of old age and death; and pervasive feelings of emptiness or unrelatedness (Lasch, 1979: 33), the latter in terms of the self as much as other objects, amounting to 'a failure in development of a spontaneous, stable, taken-for-granted self experience' (Bromberg, 1982: 439). These and the other characteristics described above are, most simply, misplaced attempts to emulate the illusory equilibrium of primary narcissism.

The culture of narcissism

Christopher Lasch's work in the late 1970s and early 1980s brought the concept of narcissism to a new audience (Lasch, 1974, 1991 [1979], 1984). His accounts are the most celebrated and documented for representing narcissism as a *cultural* trait as much as a psychological one. Lasch's was the most sustained application of the term to social and cultural processes if not the first (e.g. Adorno, 1968 [1955]; Jacoby, 1975; Marcuse, 1955). Despite the flourish of critical dialogue which followed Lasch's seminal publication (Lasch, 1991 [1979]), today the concept of narcissism is utilized little beyond the confines of self-help literature, mainstream psychiatry and personality psychology, and the occasional piece of social commentary (e.g. Hotchkiss, 2002; Brown, 2001; Payson, 2002). At worst it is recycled as a tired conservative heuristic which associates the concept with irresponsible hedonism, libertarianism and vanity to rail simplistically against the erosion of community-spiritedness, authority, and 'traditional' values (e.g. Lipovetsky, 2005: 10; Lerner, 1999; Turner, 2003). As suggested at the outset of this chapter, it is generally absent from recent sociological debates (Valadez and Clignet, 1987), and is no longer thought of as a key concept in critical social theory (e.g. Crossley, 2005).[5] The remainder of this chapter is concerned with a reappraisal of Lasch's and related analyses in terms of the themes of self and social change as they have been developed in this book.

Re-reading Lasch's seminal social critique getting on for 30 years later, two themes dominate which have slipped from the common vocabulary of a great deal of contemporary social theory: capitalism and humanism. Lasch places 'late capitalism' rather than modernism or post-modernism at the heart of his social theory. He understands contemporary society as strongly determined by capitalism, one of his primary concerns being 'the cultural and psychological devastation brought about by industrial capitalism' (Lasch *et al.*, 1991 [1979]: 194). Lasch attempts to describe how the conditions of modern capitalism encourage psychological responses which, to a lesser degree, parallel the characteristics of pathological narcissism. His account is also marked by a pervasive humanism (Frosh, 1991: 63). This is largely because his critique is aimed squarely at the *losses* it imposes upon the psyche and human relationships; consequently Lasch's project consistently implies a better, more authentic self which might be reinstated or rediscovered. This emphasis upon capitalism and authenticity is far from novel, it shares a great deal with the accounts discussed in chapter two, psychoanalytic dimension aside; but it is notable that few are as critically focused or ethically explicit in today's turn to culture, language and representation.

Lasch's starting premise is that clinical psychology has noted a shift in the most common causes of complaint (Lasch, 1991 [1979]: 36–41; 1984: 42–43), which he argues to have significance for a cultural diagnosis: 'In the last twenty-five years, the border-line patient, who confronts the psychiatrist not with well-defined symptoms but with diffuse dissatisfactions, has become increasingly common' (1991 [1979]: 37). The shift is recognized clinically as a growth in narcissistic personality disorders (Kovel, 1980: 91; Cooper, 1986: 126–127; Elliott, 1991: 73), which is important for Lasch, because it is indicative of a general change in the way we experience our individuality. It is a disorder which is claimed by Lasch to: 'in less extreme form appear in such profusion in the everyday life of our age' (Lasch, 1991 [1979]: 33). Or, as Joel Kovel puts it, a Marxist psychoanalyst whose perspective has many affinities with Lasch: 'different historical epochs will select different pathologies wherein their characteristic form of domination may be reproduced on intrapsychic soil. And pathological narcissism is a leading candidate for the archetypal emotional disorder of late capitalism' (Kovel, 1982: 104).

Late capitalism is a culture of narcissism mainly because it disintegrates the primary interpersonal ('object') relations necessary for the development of autonomous selfhood and instates commodified ones in their place. An explanation of how this is accomplished in three of the key areas Lasch discusses – the family, the commodity form and the therapeutic sensibility – now follows.

The family

In previous times, including earlier forms of capitalism, Lasch argues that the boundaries of self-identity were more clearly demarcated by established routines and habits. They were constructed and maintained within family units and at the level of small communities. The others central to the infant's self-development were consistent in their presence, character and beliefs. At the level of the individual psyche, progress from primary narcissism to individuation via the early mother-child bond and the later oedipal complex was supported by the institution of the family and its interconnection with other social institutions. However rigid and authoritative the family was, Lasch argues, at least an individual had a clear sense of who they were, what their role was, and what was expected of them, with a clear sense of the reality of the world and how to act in accordance with it. Lasch refers to these aspects of family life as 'the work of reproduction'; not just the facts of sex and childbirth, but the bringing up of a child and the nature of that child's environment (Lasch, 1991 [1979]: 154). Children may have developed into adults susceptible to whatever ticks and foibles such a family structure may encourage, but they were likely to develop with clear boundaries in terms of their sense of self, and a realistic sense of dependency and balanced affirmation of independence – they were not likely to be narcissistic.

Lasch contrasts this state of affairs with a key element of social change – what he sees as the 'invasion' of family life, by 'agencies of socialized parenthood' (1991 [1979]: 169). Modern bureaucracies, experts and consumer capitalism have, in combination over the last hundred years or so, gradually taken over the authority and resources necessary for the 'work of reproduction':

> the advertising industry, the mass media, the health and welfare services and other agencies of mass tuition took over many of the socialising functions of the home and brought the ones that remained under the direction of modern science and technology (1991 [1979]: 169).

Thus the 'consensus among the "helping professions" ', soon instilled into experiences of parenting, was that 'the family could no longer provide for its own needs'. The result is the 'socialization of reproduction' (1991 [1979]: 154–155). Questions involved in the 'work of reproduction' such as how to have a child, when, how to bring it up, what it should learn and when, where it will be cared for, etc. have all become subject to bureaucratization and the cult of expertise according to Lasch; clearly overlapping with Donzelot's emphasis on the family as a site of government in the previous chapter (Donzelot, 1979) and Reisman's analysis of parenting (Reisman, 2000 [1961]: 46–48). Parents encouraged to be 'afraid of repeating the mistakes of their own parents' are the new consumers of 'professional' advice, and so embrace the 'routinized half-truths of the experts as the laws of living' (Lasch, 1991 [1979]: 164). However, expert opinion is not uniform, and neither is it consistent. It is constantly updated, redefined and contradicted, and here it elides with contemporary capitalist culture. 'Knowledge' is offered up as part of the cycle of mass production and mass consumption and never stands still for long. It is according to this logic that Lasch labels psychiatry 'the handmaiden of advertising':

> It lays the emotional foundation for the insistence of the advertising industry that the health and safety of the young, the satisfaction of their daily nutritional requirements, their emotional and intellectual development, and their ability to compete with their peers for popularity and success all depend on consumption of vitamins, band-aids, cavity-preventing toothpaste, cereals, mouthwashes and laxatives. (Lasch, 1979: 164)

As a result, parental care, besieged by conflicting, chronically revisable advice, and allowed an increasingly marginal role, is nervous and vacillating. Parents are kept 'in a state of chronic anxiety' (Lasch, 1991 [1979]: 164). Parental authority is similarly unstable, emptying the parent-objects of the characteristics needed to guide the infant through the 'symbolic matrix of the Oedipus complex'. The matrix sets limits, creates boundaries, and brings reality to the necessary process of individuation, without which 'the ego is left to be absorbed back into the object; no longer is there a self with an integrity and boundary of its own' (Frosh, 1991: 87). In Lasch's account, the problem is considered in the traditionally gendered terms of psychoanalysis as 'the decline of the father's role in child-rearing and moral instruction' (Lasch, 1981: 32; Barrett and McIntosh, 1982: 37).

The situation is consolidated by the fact that the family no longer enjoys mutual connections with other institutions. As a unit, it has been severed from its social context, 'de-sociated' in Kovel's terminology. As a result the family is excessively focused on the child, exacerbating the 'superheated' nexus of parent-child relations:

> When the particular traumata which lend an individual stamp to each case fade out, we are left with the distinct impression that what crushes the developing person under a weight of sick narcissism is nothing but the family itself...For the scission of the family from organic, productive and reciprocal relations with the community forces the energy of that family in upon the developing individual. In the superheated environment which results the person is moulded in the direction of pathological narcissism. (Kovel, 1980: 94–95)

On the one hand parental roles have been usurped by external authorities, on the other, what remains of their authority is increasingly isolated, pressurized, scrutinized and uncertain. These factors have 'subtly altered the quality of the parent-child connection' (Lasch, 1991 [1979]: 169–170). The increasing socialization of the family conjures up 'an ideal of perfect parenthood while destroying parents' confidence in their ability' (1991 [1979]: 170). Consequently, parents become indistinct forms of authority, who attend to their children with nervous energy and partially-suppressed disdain. The infant is provided with 'an excess of seemingly solicitous care but with little real warmth' (1991 [1979]: 171), and 'suffocating yet emotionally distant attentions' (1991 [1979]: 172).

Aggrandized and unattainable images of parenthood combine with the normative promotion of narcissism to trap parents themselves in an unattainable ideal, which they simply do not have the experience or motivation to fulfil:

> The modern parent's attempt to make children feel loved and wanted does not conceal an underlying coolness – the remoteness of those who have little to pass on to the next generation and who in any case give priority to their own right to self-fulfilment. (1991 [1979]: 50)

The vicarious self-esteem of the parents is thus perpetuated. The infant is encouraged to relate to 'idealistically inflated impressions' of one or more parent, which are nevertheless constantly frustrated. These relationships encourage what Lasch refers to as a 'family tautology'; whereby 'the family members tacitly conspire to indulge' the exaggerated expectations of the infant so as to 'maintain the family's equilibrium' (1991 [1979]: 172). The family can no longer meet the basic requirements of the child for psychological development:

> As people become interchangeable, as their lives become losing battles for a sense of location and roots, they can do less and less for their children, who are asking, more poignantly and desperately and urgently, for exactly the same things. (Frosh, 1991: 100)

It will no doubt be obvious that Lasch makes a firm link between the type of family relations depicted and those which object-relations theory attribute to the formation of narcissistic disturbances, outlined earlier. In late capitalism the 'integrity of the parental object is violated' (Kovel, 1980: 98), laying the ground for the internalization of omnipotent fantasies in the developing psyche, a vicariously-inflated sense of worth and a failure to establish firm boundaries between self and other objects. The child's own grandiose aspirations and feelings of omnipotence are encouraged yet unsuccessfully realized, and so all the more devastating when unfulfilled. Cults of expertise, the therapeutic sensibility, and the commodity form empty out the seemingly essential object relations of the family, and encourage a generational cycle of narcissism:

> the narcissistic parent carries the distress of the culture in which he or she is embedded, then replicates this state of affairs through distorted treatment of the child – through relating to the child as a commodity or as a mirror – producing another narcissistic personality. (Frosh, 1991: 100)

Thus both parents and children are primed for narcissistic manipulation by the structures of late capitalism.

The commodity form

Ideally perhaps the indistinct authority of parenting could be assuaged by links to significant others outside of the family in the developmental process of the individual. However, Lasch's problem with late capitalism besides its hand in the dissolution of the family and parental authority is that it also undermines the object relations necessary for the development of a coherent, meaningful self capable of relating to others empathically and genuinely *beyond* the family nexus. Specifically, he is critical of another perceived social change: the increasing 'propaganda of commodities' or what Kovel refers to as 'the hegemony of the commodity form' (Kovel, 1980: 96), which consolidates narcissism as a requisite and adaptable psychological response.

On the one hand the 'culture of consumption' encourages a view of the 'world of objects' as an 'extension or projection of the self': 'The consumer lives surrounded not so much by things as fantasies. He [sic] lives in a world that has no objective or independent existence and seems to exist only to gratify or thwart his desires' (Lasch, 1984: 31). The world external to the self is presented in terms of how its objects relate back to the self, their exchange-value for the self, not in terms of relating to intrinsic qualities of the objects; a 'social correlate' of the omnipotence described earlier – 'things exist in order to be incorporated, devoured or controlled' (Richards, 1989: 64). Images, representations, abstractions come to be represented back to the self rather than concrete things and people, 'under the sway of the sign and the logic of the commodity form itself' argues Kovel; 'in sum a non-human *other* has emerged as the dominant cultural form in late capitalist culture...now the human representations are themselves palpably stooges for that infinite fluid that is the commodity itself'

(Kovel, 1980: 96). The reification of the other into a commodity form also reifies interpersonal relations: 'consumption no longer symbolises care and affection...it is the whole of love, the way in which intimacy is negotiated' (Frosh, 1991: 100). Thus the narcissistic character is one 'under the spell of the image' (Levin, 1987: 518).

Consequently deep and long-sustained relationships become a rarity in a culture of 'sanitized relating', whereby 'we replace the few depth relationships with a mass of thin and shallow contacts' (Bauman, 2004: 69). Relationships are flitting and fleeting, built as they are on the unstable foundations of a culture of narcissism: 'if you skate on thin ice your salvation is in speed' (Bauman, 2004: 70). The family, emptied of its defences by commodity capitalism and expert systems, cannot help but reflect and maintain this state of relational impoverishment in Lasch's analysis.

Mass consumerism glorifies a concern for self-image, Lasch argues, and encourages the identification of the self with various consumption-oriented 'lifestyle' packages, whilst eliminating or marginalizing any alternative: 'they reduce choice to a matter of style and taste, as their preoccupation with "lifestyle" indicates' (Lasch, 1984: 34). It is a consumption-orientation which encourages an identification with surfaces, appearances, and how exchange-value, in terms of how they reflect back upon the self. Based as they are on mass consumption, they cannot be allowed to become static. They have to keep moving, so that individuals keep consuming. In this sense prescribed object relations make a constant, independent sense of self difficult, and instead encourage a fleeting, ephemeral and uncertain self-identity, symptomatic of the narcissism described earlier. Or perhaps more precisely, 'the world of consumer goods *does* offer some kind of integration to the disoriented, disenchanted modern self', particularly in terms of 'regressive psychic satisfactions in fusion with or possession of needed objects' (Richards, 1989: 126).

However, 'the citizen-turned-consumer is then even further removed, as a result of immersion in the fragmentary imagery of advertising and consumer culture, from any possibility of more authentic integration' (1989: 64). Thus, on the other hand, the modern individual, as a consumer, worker, family member, cannot grasp the complexity of the social world, and can only accept her dependence. 'Reality thus presents itself...as an impenetrable network of social relations' (Lasch, 1991 [1979]: 91). It is 'a world of giant bureaucracies...and complex, interlocking technological systems' (Lasch, 1984: 33). The consumer's dependence on such 'intricate, supremely sophisticated life-support systems...recreates some of the infantile feelings of helplessness' (1984: 33–34). The individual is thus caught between a hazy, distant and impenetrable social world and a promissory, seductive, representational world. Faced with the apparent reality of fantasies and the phantasmagoric nature of reality, representation, and imagery, the individual retreats into an inflated, grandiose self, mirrored by commodities and mediated imagery which masks a pervasive sense of indistinctness and vulnerability.

Narcissism is further encouraged by the *nature* of the fantasies individuals are encouraged to consume, according to Lasch. Specifically, 'images of the good life' envelop the consumer, and are associated with glamour, celebrity and success (1984: 181). Lasch argues that mass culture and advertising thus do not provide realistic, authentic or attainable goals: 'mass culture encourages the ordinary man [sic] to cultivate extraordinary tastes...Yet the propaganda of commodities makes him acutely unhappy with his lot. By fostering grandiose aspirations, it also fosters self-denigration and self-contempt' (1984: 181). Thus the individual is further encouraged to harbour feelings of dependence and worthlessness with fleeting promises of omnipotence. The result contributes to object relations which can undermine both a firm sense of self, and of the reality of external objects, including other people; a key tenet of narcissistic disorders and the defensive creation of a 'grandiose self' from a psychoanalytic viewpoint. Without this distinction in place, the individual is susceptible to the oscillations of omnipotence and fearful dependency.

The therapeutic sensibility

Lasch argues that subjectivity has also been colonized by 'cults of expertise', centred on the notion of 'therapy'. The turn to therapy represents for Lasch another example of the self's dependence on external expert systems. For the modern individual, 'plagued by anxiety, depression, vague discontents, [and] a sense of inner emptiness' he associates with narcissism, therapy offers the promise of an autonomous overcoming of alienation. Therapists 'become his [sic] principal allies in the struggle for composure; he turns to them in the hope of achieving the modern equivalent of salvation, "mental health" ' (Lasch, 1991 [1979]: 13). The problem for Lasch is that the salvation therapy offers is unattainable. The therapeutic climate encourages dependence on external definitions of well-being which discourage autonomy and realistic appraisal of the limits to selfhood. It fosters a psychological state of constant mindfulness – 'the notion that health depends on eternal watchfulness' (1991 [1979]: 48) – encouraging anxiety and self-doubt.

The therapeutic climate is 'another cultural change that elicits a narcissistic response and, in this case, gives it philosophical sanction' (1991 [1979]: 48). These two factors – the encouragement of narcissism and its rationalized endorsement – stem from a therapeutic ideology which attempts to prescribe the definitions of mental and physical well-being. The individual must constantly judge him or herself against these definitions, engendering a climate of relentless self-examination: 'the emergence of a therapeutic ideology upholds a normative schedule of psychosocial development and thus gives further encouragement to anxious self-scrutiny' (1991 [1979]: 48). For Lasch, the therapeutic sensibility encourages new levels of self-awareness, and here he may be in agreement with Giddens.

Lasch may thus be inclined to view Giddens's emphasis of the positive qualities of reflexivity as bringing an air of grandeur and authenticity to what Lasch reads as a narcissistic retreat. Some critics have indeed suggested that Giddens's work obscures the true nature of the opportunities for contemporary identity by transforming negative attributes of modern life into positive ones. Mestrovic argues that 'Giddens is not mindful of the fact that he is really promoting, albeit unwittingly, excessive narcissism' (Mestrovic, 1999: 155). Alexander proposes a similar shortcoming in Giddens's work:

> The pathologies and alienations of modernity are converted into positive reaffirmations about the powers of the modern self and the emancipating contributions that apolitical scientific experts make to the reconstruction of the society. (Alexander, 1996: 135)

It is along these critical lines that reflexivity as perpetual self-scrutiny might be transformed from harbinger of choice to emblem of pathology. For Giddens personal health is increasingly about making reflexively-informed choices. Choosing from a range of expert advice, the individual can make an informed decision if they reflexively involve themselves in those knowledge systems – 'reskilling' – in Giddens's terminology: 'if a person takes the time to reskill appropriately, a reasonably informed choice can in fact be made' (Giddens, 1991: 141). Giddens takes an individual with a bad back as an example. She may be disillusioned with orthodox medicine, and become aware that a range of other therapies are available. She could then learn about the structure of the back, and the basics about a number of therapies. With these resources she could make a reasoned choice from the range of therapies available. This is the act of 'reskilling' or 'reappropriation' (1991: 140).

However, Lasch sees the abundance of 'choice' and self-awareness as a banal and pseudo-liberatory characteristic of the contemporary self. It is an awareness facilitated and shaped by consumer capitalism, lauded and propagated by therapy, against a backdrop of powerlessness and uncertainty, in which authentic expression and autonomous selfhood are marginalized. Modern medical and psychiatric professions, and 'the therapeutic outlook and sensibility' in general, foster narcissistic patterns of anxiety and striving self-doubt:

> in which the individual endlessly examines himself [sic] for signs of ageing and ill health, for tell-tale symptoms of psychic stress, for blemishes and flaws that might diminish his attractiveness, or on the other hand for reassuring indications that his life is proceeding according to schedule. (Lasch, 1991 [1979]: 49)

Furedi makes similar points regarding the 'therapy culture' of the early twenty-first century (2004). It is a culture which 'continually endorses the project of self-realisation and holds out the promise of individual enlightenment through the exercise of autonomous behaviour' (Furedi, 2004: 106); it promotes, in other words, something closely resembling Giddens's 'reflexive project of the self' (Giddens, 1991). On the other hand, in Furedi's estimation, therapy culture also promotes a standardized cultural narrative for the trajectory of the project of selfhood, making a mockery of the valorization of self-chosen individuation. That mockery is extended by the nature of the cultural narrative: one which encourages *dependency* on the very expert systems which promote autonomy. Dependency is configured in terms of the risk of illness, a widening definition of psychological distress, the dangers of coping without support, and the encouragement to seek professional help at every turn via the mechanisms of careful self-scrutiny (Furedi, 2004: 111–112). For Furedi, echoing Lasch, there is 'a growing sense of being ill' in the reflexive construction of self (2004: 108–109); reflecting a 'distinctly feeble version of human subjectivity' (2004: 107).

Thus an obsession with the self is encouraged, a kind of hypochondria of the soul, rather than genuine self-actualization or self-development.[6] In psychoanalytic terms, the individual seeks reassurance in an attempt to overcome his or her gnawing self-doubt, and bolster his or her 'fantasies of omnipotence and eternal youth' (Lasch, 1991 [1979]: 40). The narcissist is thus susceptible to therapeutic and commodified solutions, which in fact perpetuate narcissistic traits.

It follows that the hypochondriacal self indicates another possible inversion of the extended reflexivity thesis, but this time along psychoanalytic lines, in its broadest terms, rather than Foucaultian. The advocacy of the reflexive formation of self-identity mirrors, in some respects, elements of the therapeutic climate which Lasch criticizes, particularly the state of hypochondria. The reflexive project of the self encourages, or at least accepts, 'endless self-scrutiny' as a foundational principle of identity. As Giddens states, 'the reflexivity of the self is continuous, as well as all pervasive', in terms of 'a self-interrogation of what is happening' (Giddens, 1991: 76). Giddens undoubtedly focuses on concepts such as self-development and self-actualization, and sees these as authentic possibilities in the context of a post-traditional world. In the view of Lasch then, Giddens's work might itself be seen as encouraging narcissistic responses, and bestowing a further 'philosophical sanction' upon it (Lasch, 1991 [1979]: 48).

To summarize, for Lasch and others, the power of contemporary culture lies in its ability to destabilize interpersonal relationships, particularly within the family. Once the primary self-defences of firmly established object relations derived from relationships with caregivers are undermined, capitalism is poised to reach in and seduce exposed psychic structures with its narcissistic hall of mirrors and promises of omnipotent self-sufficiency. The rootless self-scrutiny apparently encouraged ironically shares many similarities with the extended processes of reflexivity highlighted by Giddens, but inverts their value by equating them with narcissistic aspects of modern self-identity.

The type of social analysis offered by Lasch is primarily one of psychosocial fragmentation, and it has much in common with the arguments put forward in chapter two. More recent work in this tradition basically supports Lasch's portrayal of culture, perhaps even pointing to an acceleration in the kinds of social change he indicates (Bauman, 2004; Furedi,

2004; Sennett, 1999). Lasch's detailed psychoanalytic reading tends to have disappeared from many of these accounts, though the basic claim that the building blocks of a stable, autonomous self are undermined by the interpenetration of a morally and socially fragmented socio-cultural structure and psychological development remains. However, I think it is Lasch's take up of object-relations theory and his particular 'psychoanalytic gloss' (Frosh, 1991: 64) that has the potential to advance an understanding of the relationship between self and social change, beyond theories of psychosocial fragmentation, and in dialogue with the Foucaultian and neo-modern perspectives discussed in earlier chapters. Before we can consider which, if any, elements of Lasch's approach can be taken forward however, the critical literature his work has generated must first be considered.

Positive narcissism

Lasch has been accused of downgrading the importance of the mother-child bond and 'feelings of attachment, mutuality, identification and relatedness' more generally in his critique of narcissism (Barrett and McIntosh, 1982: 45; Engel, 1980). They are devalued by what is argued to be an exaggerated emphasis upon the oedipal struggle in the formation of self which systematically underplays the power of pre-oedipal relationships, particularly that of child and mother (Benjamin, 1988; Barrett and McIntosh, 1982: 38). We reconnect here with the common assertion that the experience of primary narcissism is in fact a positive formative experience; it stays with us as an important aspect of the 'ego-ideal', here conceived of as an aspect of self-structure distinct from the super-ego. A re-emphasis of pre-oedipal relationships is integral to object-relational feminist critiques, stressing the role of the mother-child bond for psychic development, not just the oedipal shift towards individuation and super-ego formation (1982: 45–46). The denigration of narcissistic desire and the valorization of individuality mirrors normative patriarchal authority and its (narcissistic!) insistence upon independence and separateness (Barrett and McIntosh, 1982).

This claim has been debated in complex but fascinating terms, arguments revolving around the degree to which the narcissistic desire for unity is responsible for positive states such as creativity, empathy, resistance, and coping with mortality, or more problematic ones like the group psychological processes supposedly involved in fascism (Aronowitz, 1980; Becker, 1973; Benjamin, 1980; Chasseguet-Smirgel, 1985a, 1985b; Chodorow and Contratto, 1982; Engel, 1980; Jacoby, 1980; Marcuse, 1955). What can be derived from these arguments for our purposes is that 'primary narcissism is to some extent rehabilitated and given a positive rather than exclusively negative inflection' (Barrett and McIntosh, 1982: 46; Frosh, 1991: 94).[7] Asserting the need for a more balanced 'dual reign' of superego, 'heir to the Oedipus complex', and ego ideal, 'heir to the state of primary narcissism' in psychological development is a claim which

Lasch later conceded to, whilst much of his analysis remains intact as a critique of *excessive* narcissism or perhaps of the 'culture of the uninhibited ego ideal' (Engel, 1980: 101; Lasch, 1981: 33).

Caricatures of past and present

A second commonly-cited criticism of Lasch, and the 'culture of narcissism' critique more generally, is its implicit conservatism: 'It hints of past and better times, when people were less self-obsessed. It...is suspected of secreting a love of authority...an affection for obedience, and families and societies which did not spare the rod or gallows' (Jacoby, 1980: 59). An atmosphere of conservatism penetrates in particular a lament for the apparent disappearance of patriarchal family structures (Aronowitz, 1980; Jacoby, 1980). There is undoubtedly an 'elegiac tone' and 'evident regret' in at least some of his descriptions of the disappearance of the traditional family; and this tone is paralleled by an unreflexive hypostatization of 'the family' of the past (Barrett and McIntosh, 1982: 38–39). His evocation of an idealized 'golden age' of the family glosses over the violence, inequality and socially stratified variations which impacted upon the patriarchal family as well as their contextualization in religious, feudal/industrial structures which makes romantic appraisal an insufficient portrayal.

What seems to be demanded is a move towards a more Foucaultian position. Jacoby poses for Lasch the kind of question a Foucaultian critique would probably ask: 'is there a *decline* of authority per se...or a *deflection* of authority' (Jacoby, 1980: 61; emphasis added)? Foucaultians would surely side with the latter interpretation; as we saw in the previous chapter, forms of authority and regulation are seen to be colonizing or 'governing' many areas of life, including the family in historically novel ways, and in the end, such claims are not that far away from Lasch's (e.g. Donzelot, 1979). Here narcissism can easily be re-imagined as a particular cultural configuration with interlocking discourses (such as Lasch's 1991 [1979] discussion of politics, sport, education, therapy and the medical profession) which incorporate the family and processes of subjectification. In fact Kovel, a contemporary of Lasch's, introduces his critique of narcissism in more Foucault-friendly terms, 'it is useful to see how a historically significant segment of people are led to develop self-experience of a specific kind' (Kovel, 1980: 98). It suggests a historically-contingent constellation gradually built up from countless micro-processes, rather than a *declension* in authority *per se*. This re-imagining can be accommodated by a Laschian analysis. This is not to say there can be an easy union of Foucaultian and psychoanalytic positions however, as later discussion will indicate.

A parallel critical point is that Lasch's view of the present also emerges as something of an over-simplification in terms of the family and social change more generally. On the one hand, Lasch's view of any remnants of paternal authoritarianism as a 'pseudo-problem' and 'secondary formation' deflecting from 'real problems' is far too casual a dismissal for those still 'on the receiving end' of patriarchal forms of power (Lasch, 1981: 28, 33; Barrett and McIntosh, 1982: 44). On the other hand Lasch tends towards a blanket criticism of the contemporary 'family' as it emerges from colonization of state and commerce and the supposed libertarianism of the 1960s (e.g. Lasch, 1991 [1979]: 176–180). This is not to suggest that Lasch's analysis needs to be inverted and families are still universally in the grip of patriarchal authority, or that the present be accepted as the ideal it is presented as in populist politics or its packaging as a commodity. Jacoby pithily states it thus: 'if the banners for a sexual revolution are sagging, the bumper stickers for family revival are worse' (Jacoby, 1980: 60). Instead it indicates that Lasch rests on over-simplified and undifferentiated caricatures in his binary understanding of the archetypal family figures of past and present: 'the old, terrifying father is pitted against the new absent father-pal; the old, highly cathected mother, and the new, narcissistic, distant, self-absorbed mother' (Elshtain, 1980: 109). If Lasch's work does have any lasting value, his cultural and psychological diagnoses must be made more reflexive of the normative constructions of past, present and future they can so easily generate.

A question of agency

A related consequence of Lasch's tendency to play a generalized view of the past off of one of the present is thus its failure to capture the varied and multiple experiences which constitute family and everyday life in contemporary capitalist societies. The image of the family as unwitting conduit for the one-way traffic of the depersonalizing processes of late capitalism has been questioned by those who take a more ambivalent approach to the human impact of recent social changes. Jacoby asked 'is the newer, fragmented family composed of passive and accepting individuals?' (Jacoby, 1980: 61), and Elshtain's comments epitomize the critical response:

> Most of the time families, for better or worse, remain the locus of the most powerful, ambivalent, and meaningful emotional ties. The family may be Lasch's dessicated husk but thus far it has stubbornly refused to blow away, despite the chill winds of apocalyptic social criticism. (Elshtain, 1980: 108)

The most significant aspect of this third critical point, at least in terms of the scope of this book, is that it tackles the *passive* version of human agency Lasch arguably relies upon. Out of his apparent misreading of the nature of the family comes the accusation that Lasch and others mistake the necessary emergence of new forms of identity for social withdrawal and introversion (Aronowitz, 1980; Gendlin, 1987). Although these forms may for some slide into pathological narcissism, they represent a necessary and active engagement with the dissolution of long-established identity positions engendered by social change; they have 'problematised the traditional "self" and encouraged serious experimentation around the historical opportunity to develop, out of need, a genuinely different way of being' (Levin, 1987). This critique dovetails with the more celebratory versions of post-modern theory, wherein fragmentation, difference, uncertainty and ambiguity are to be embraced in a collage-like approach to the make-up of one's own identity, and of course Giddens's conceptualization of agency.

It should come as no surprise that Giddens has offered a particularly trenchant critique of Lasch's perspective on the family (Giddens, 1991). He tackles Lasch's view of the family as a springboard for a broader questioning of his negative depiction of the possibilities for human agency thrown up by the social changes integral to what Giddens prefers to call late modernity or post-traditional society. What Giddens does is attune a history of criticism to his own theory of extended reflexivity and its explicit fore-fronting of human agency. Lasch and similar critics overlook the possibility of a 'positive appropriation of circumstances in which globalised influences impinge upon everyday life' according to Giddens (1991: 124). The problem with Lasch's account, he argues, is its prevailing current of social determinism. In other words, the individual as reflexive agent is under-theorized in Lasch's analysis: 'the individual appears essentially passive in relation to overwhelming social forces' (1991: 175).

In order to produce an accurate account of agency, Giddens argues that social theory must 'accomplish three tasks', tasks which, he claims, Lasch overlooks (1991: 175). Firstly, accounts must recognize that 'human agents never passively accept external conditions of action' (1991: 175). Individuals are always reflecting upon, and contextually reconstituting, those conditions. Secondly, individuals and groups appropriate the conditions of their social life, particularly in modern settings where social life has eschewed traditional authority and opened up areas to reflexivity. Thirdly, it is incorrect to distinguish between malleable 'micro-settings' of action, such as family life and intimate relationships on the one hand, and impenetrable social systems on the other hand, which form 'an uncontrolled background environment' (1991: 175). In avoiding these factors, Lasch's account, as far as Giddens is concerned, fails 'on an empirical level to grasp the nature of human empowerment' (1991: 175). As a result the individual emerges as a powerless, socially-shaped entity; a pinball knocked from side to side, his or her movement dependent on external causes. Narcissism is read off as the psychological consequence of a narcissistic culture, and the effective intervention of agency is thus excluded from Lasch's account.

Consider Giddens's claims in terms of the family. Like Lasch, Giddens argues that we live in a society where traditional family patterns are gradually being unravelled. Once there were clearly defined gender roles, a clearly defined patriarchal authority, submissive childhood and extended family support networks. These have all been eroded. If they have not disappeared, they have certainly been fundamentally challenged as the 'natural' state of affairs. Now we can acknowledge that there are plenty of macro reasons for this happening, such as the decline of religion, and of a morality of chastity and faithfulness, easier divorce, advances in contraception, the impact of the women's movement, urbanism, geographical mobility, the communication revolution, and so on. So, marriage is now a very different institution to what it was even 50 years ago. It depends on little other than what Giddens refers to as 'enduring voluntary commitment'. It is increasingly a relationship for the sake of a relationship – other perks and pitfalls have dissolved. One *possible* response is undoubtedly the one highlighted by Lasch, Giddens argues – narcissistic withdrawal – individuals may indeed feel beleaguered and belittled by such changes (Giddens, 1991).

But, individuals also actively restructure new forms of gender and kinship relations, they do not just withdraw from social engagement and retreat into themselves. Step families, communal living, single parenting, two-family arrangements, non-religious weddings, alternative vows, same-sex marriages, partnerships and child-rearing, new gender roles, demands for paternity leave, and new models of child development all suggest an active reconstruction of the institution of the family. This is not localized, trivial, narcissistic withdrawal: it is a restructuring of what a family is, what family life means. And it is done by example, in practice, in everyday routines, at the same time as coping with the uncertainties of these new forms. Thus, 'individuals appear not as withdrawing from the outer social world, but engaging boldly with it' (Giddens, 1991: 178).

So transformations at the 'micro' level of family life and intimate relationships can also generate 'macro' social changes too like the legalization of same-sex weddings and increases in statutory paternity leave. We can now look back at Giddens's three-point check list for adequate accounts of agency in terms of the family. Firstly, people do not just accept a decline in family life; secondly, they are capable of appropriating the space of family life and to some extent deciding its fate, constructing its parameters; and thirdly changes at the 'micro' level can become broader social changes which then reinforce personal changes – the traffic of transformative power can flow both ways.

Giddens makes similar points in relation to Lasch's more general critique of capitalism and the commodity form. Giddens argues that: 'In assessing the prevalence of narcissism in late modernity, we have to be careful to separate the world of commodified images, to which Lasch frequently refers, from the actual responses of individuals' (1991: 178–179). Giddens, in my mind correctly, criticizes Lasch for conflating the proliferation of commodified images with an assumed narcissistic response. While he acknowledges that commodifying influences are 'powerful', Giddens contends that 'they are scarcely received in an uncritical way by the populations they affect' (1991: 179).

Lasch does not pay much attention to opportunities for individual appropriation, which may indeed be a serious shortcoming. Lasch's critique is problematic, in that he theorizes any kind of *successful* resistance at all out of his account of narcissistic culture. The individual appears to be locked into a culture which offers no option but the perpetuation of that culture and, consequently, increasingly narcissistic leanings. As Tucker states: 'The requirements of consumer capitalism and the personality structure of the narcissist fit into a coherent whole which leaves few possibilities for alternative paths of social change' (Tucker, 1998: 169). While this level of pessimism may not be wholly displaced, it seems to negate the myriad ways in which the social conditions Lasch elaborates upon are, and can be, challenged by individuals and social groups. Lasch admits that 'much could be written about the signs of new life' emerging, and in this admission the shortcomings of Giddens's analysis discussed earlier are replicated in reverse. That said, Lasch serves as a useful reminder of the challenges that the contemporary self faces, and the dangers of associating the rise of a vocabulary for self-development with authentic progress too unequivocally. The concept of narcissism, as utilized by Lasch, suggests a darker side of the reflexive project for the psyche, which must be taken seriously.

The value of a Laschian analysis

What is the value of Lasch's analysis in hoping to understand the relationship between self and social change? Can today's societies be adequately captured as 'cultures of narcissism'? Anecdotal evidence suggests a number of social processes fit broadly into his critique. Growing rates of cosmetic surgery suggests an enduring fascination with surface appearances, a denial of ageing and perhaps an inability to accept perceived flaws, all possible characteristics of narcissism as culture; celebrity lifestyle is both increasingly documented and yet packaged as accessible; 'reality' television immerses viewers and participants in an atmosphere of spectatorship, that the meaningfulness of human activity derives from how it is perceived by an imagined or actual audience; developments in genetic science may soon provide parents with choices over the sex of their child, possibly the first of a number of 'options' encouraging children to be thought of as narcissistic reflections of parental desire. On the other hand social movements such as fair-trade, anti-capitalism, make poverty history, anti-fascist and anti-racist and anti-homophobic suggest an engagement with the outside world, with others, and with a sense of identity that suggests Lasch's analysis is excessively pessimistic. Anecdotal examples can be played off of each other indefinitely. One way to assess the relevance of a Laschian account of self and social change is to compare it with the other dominant perspectives discussed in this book so far.

Lasch himself conceded the first critical point raised here, and although the value of narcissism is still debated, any further discussion on that point is beyond the scope of this book.[8] Criticism of Lasch's conservatism undoubtedly has substance, though perhaps his analysis can be rescued from its conservatism by acknowledging a need to avoid the idealization of the past in a critique of the present. Kovel, for example, although offering a critique very similar to Lasch's, is careful to point out that 'in actual history the isolated, pure family, has been only a phantasm in the minds of people who yearn for consolation against the rigours of society and the indifference of nature' (Kovel, 1980: 96). There is also a need to be unequivocal about the authoritarian and patriarchal aspects of 'traditional' family life and the renunciation of the desirability of any return to such a state of affairs, without necessarily eschewing the requirement of forms of authority, independence and autonomy. It may thus be possible to avoid Lasch's 'unhappy conclusion' that 'the evils of the traditional family form and the good go together' (Elshtain, 1980: 107).

The issue of agency, or lack of it, is perhaps the most penetrative and inescapable criticism directed at Lasch. However, although Giddens is right to be wary of any model of social change which reads off psychological responses automatically (Giddens, 1991), on closer attention it is not always apparent that Lasch *is* making such assumptions. As has been indicated above, Lasch relies on a complex psychoanalytic framework and the domination of commodity capitalism for his concept of narcissism, but this does not necessarily exclude an adequate theory of agency. Just as Giddens connects the extension of reflexive awareness to the individual's 'disembedding' from previous certainties, Lasch describes 'an escalating cycle of self-consciousness' arising from the lost 'immediacy' of external reality (Lasch, 1979).

For Lasch, the consciously constructed self is a severely limited one, but not necessarily because individuals passively accept the narcissistic culture's offerings and then malfunction as a self. It is arguable that the individual in Lasch's account is actively involved in the construction of their sense of self. The problem for Lasch is that commodity capitalism offers such a poverty of options as resources for that construction, whilst making any alternative difficult. Foucaultian analyses might point in the same direction but here there's a more explicit normative/ethical position taken on the destructive nature of the available discourses; problems are also located more firmly in the realm of interpersonal and intra-psychic dynamics.

Whether this is a benefit or a hindrance theoretically depends on one's appreciation of the psychoanalytic perspective, particularly the object-relational approach, to which Lasch's analysis is indebted. Lasch seems in agreement with Giddens in that as the traditional contexts of reality have retreated, contemporary reality has become increasingly mediated. However, for Lasch, the forms of mediation are problematically shaped by capitalism, and other factors, narrowing an individual's options for how they make sense of themselves, others and the external world:

> the only reality is the identity he can construct out of materials furnished by advertising and mass culture, themes of popular film and fiction, and fragments torn from a vast range of cultural traditions, all of them equally contemporaneous to the contemporary mind. (Lasch, 1991 [1979]: 91)

The individual in this quote could quite easily be Giddens's reflexive individual, constantly constructing a narrative in the choices he makes in the 'openness of the world' (Giddens, 1991: 189). Lasch argues that choices are not limitless however; they are shaped by the forces of commodity capitalism, amongst others.[9] In this sense individual agency may be limited, but not because the individual is seen as excessively passive, as Giddens suggests. The problem according to Lasch is that, even as agents, we are all caught up in narcissistic responses; they are reasonable adaptations to a social structure, from the intimacies of the family to the impersonality of the bureaucracy, which rewards and encourages narcissistic responses across the lifespan.

Craib similarly argues that Lasch *does* discuss how individuals engage with the world, but with a detail which more effectively captures the complexity of the individual's association with an external world:

> Lasch's argument…is that what comes from the outside world, *including expert knowledge*, is not being used to change the world, but to protect oneself, unrealistically, from unpleasantness and eventually from death. We're not finding better, wider identities but rather manic false selves. (Craib, 1990: 188; emphasis added)

In a menacing and impenetrable outside world, the search for personal identity is encouraged to attach itself to fantasies of omnipotence and obliteration. Mass consumerism and expert systems encourage these fantasies, suggesting individuals can make choices which add up to an unblemished selfhood: 'expert knowledge itself conspires in this, appearing to offer an insurance against growing old, growing ill, growing to a socially disapproved size' (1990: 189). In this context, the quest for a meaningful self-identity is seen in a different light. 'It becomes a search which destroys both the fabric of our interdependence, as relationships cannot be sustained, and which leaves the outside world moving along whatever course it is following' (1990: 189). Giddens's reflexive project is here disputed, with Lasch's analysis confounding Giddens's belief in an increasing and beneficial interdependence, a transformation of intimacy and a dialectical relationship with the social world.

In the light of his psychoanalytic foundations, Lasch asserts that narcissism is a co-construction of culture and self, each mutually constituted in the other. Narcissism is thus a perfectly understandable way of making sense of one's self in contemporary social contexts: 'Narcissism appears realistically to represent the best way of coping with the tensions and anxieties of modern life, and the prevailing social conditions therefore tend to bring out narcissistic traits that are present in everyone' (Lasch, 1991 [1979]: 50).

It could be argued that Lasch, in this instance at least, is not conceiving of individuals as passively accepting the world. Relying on a psychoanalytic model, they are actively involved in it and appropriating their environment as best as they can. The problem for Lasch is that, in doing so, individuals, unwittingly or not, become involved in a downward spiral of narcissistic, psychological activity. The opportunities and choices opened up by post-traditional society are in a sense inverted by Lasch, and regarded as pseudo-opportunities which in fact further ensnare the individual in a narcissistic culture. The purpose of his analysis is to bring a sense of shared meaning to hitherto personalized difficulties in the 'struggle to become a self'; understanding it as such is a more realistic base for change (Frosh, 1991: 67–8).

Revisiting surveillance

Lasch and Giddens have been tentatively compared, but how does a Laschian analysis stand up to the introduction of a Foucaultian one? The difficulty in comparing these three positions resides in the extent of their differences and it is not always easy to find specific points of comparison. The roots of their difference lie in their different models of self more than their accounts of social change. Giddens's model of self relies on a 'tidy' unconscious in thrall of a rational ego; Lasch's, on the psychoanalytic assumption of hidden dynamics, partial penetration of psychological states and intra-psychic constitution, cannot be allowed into either Giddens's model of a 'tidy' unconscious in thrall to a reflexive ego or Foucault's discursively inscribed subject, for which stories of internal dynamism are merely another inscription.

One theme which unites these perspectives, disparate though they are, is *self-surveillance*. It is, of course, variously interpreted and we began with the extended reflexivity thesis which takes self-surveillance as an aspect of self-reflexivity. The reflexive project of selfhood was theorized with some ambivalence in terms of uncertainties, anxieties and loss but these were relatively minor satellites revolving around the central concept of choice in the constitution of a self increasingly aware of itself, and its free-dom to make choices in making up itself. There is a noted tendency to marginalize the ways in which reflexive processes involved in identity construction can be appropriated by regulative and normative demands and expectations, and compromised by embodied, partially or non-reflexive processes of subjectivity.

In some sense Lasch's is the less sophisticated analysis, for the detail of the ways in which individuals are unavoidably bound-up in processes of subjectification are more fully realized in Foucault's account of discursive formations, technologies of self and subjectivization. And yet the individ-ualized constitution of subjectivity in the intersections of historically con-tingent discourses leaves a hollowed out, atomized self, primed at the heart of a Foucaultian analysis. Rather than the removal of a psychic entity all together, the image of an amorphous, perspicuous self, ripe for construction, remains. A Laschian analysis is far from complete, and its psychoanalytical borrowings can no doubt be contested, but they do at least attempt to provide a dynamic account of the human struggles, plea-sures, anxieties and relationships which invest the mutual constitution of self and cultural configurations with meaning and power.

We saw in the previous chapter how a Foucaultian position poses different questions about self-scrutiny. Conceptualizations of 'govern-mentality' and 'enterprise' have built upon Foucault's assertion that 'visibility is a trap'. The 'opening' up of the self to reflexive scrutiny is utilized to interpret it as a vehicle for psychological subjection. However, despite usefully inverting Giddens's analysis, limits to the explanatory power of self-scrutiny as a technique for inscribing normative discourses upon the self were discussed. Basically, despite Foucaultian arguments to the contrary, their accounts inevitably imply a pre-existing subject. Attempts to theorize it out of the society-subject equation means it is under-theorized as a consequence, rather than successfully avoided. As with Lasch an emphasis upon the determinism of discourse leads to an accusation of an implied lack of human agency; but a Foucaultian analysis struggles to theorize the psychic basis for self-investment in discourses, to govern oneself in particular ways, other than an ambiguous will to power.

Is it possible that a psychoanalytic perspective developed out of a Laschian analysis can lead to a more meaningful explanation of the intimate process of subjection-through-surveillance/reflexivity? It potentially allows theorization from the subject-up as well as from culture- down more fluently. In terms of the relationship between visibility, culture and selfhood, an emotional, possibly unconscious, investment in or disavowal of, processes of self-surveillance is acknowledged as foundational in a socially-oriented object-relational approach. A space is reopened for an embodied, dynamic, emotional, partially reflexive, object-oriented being, shot through with the promises and problems of a psychodynamic perspective. More specifically, Lasch argues that a *desire* to be seen makes sense in a culture of narcissism, as a simple question such as 'what does it feel like to be seen?' surely indicates. Other work has similarly acknowledged an emotional dimension to processes of surveillance in contemporary cultural and self-understandings.

Koskela has argued that our engagement with surveillance, our being rendered visible is an ambivalent or mutable experience, an 'unstable, nebulous and unpredictable engagement' which 'evokes a variety of feelings: the objects watched can feel guilty without a reason, embarrassed or uneasy, shameful, irritated, fearful; also secured and safe' (Koskela, 2002, 2003: 300). It is not simply that those involved in criminal or subversive activity feel uneasy, law-abiding citizens feel safe and secure, exhibition-ists pleasurably exposed. The main character of Hari Kunzru's recent novel *Transmission*, for example, is Guy, a wealthy company director who lives in a state-of-the-art high-rise development. The building is equipped with 'blanket electronic surveillance' which is supposed to reassure its corporate clients. However, for Guy, it begins to have the 'opposite effect. He tended to walk a little faster as he passed beneath the smoked-glass camera domes in the car park. Fitting his key into his front door he felt furtive. Closing it behind him was a guilty relief' (Kunzru, 2004: 118).

There is also a potential 'fascination' in being seen, sometimes sexual; 'the algebra of surveillance structures the reveries of voyeurism, exhibitionism and narcissism' (Tabor, cited in Koskela, 2003: 302). The pleasures derived from being visible are perhaps an element of healthy narcissism; in Lasch's analysis it becomes a pervasive, self-validating 'pleasure' beset with contradictions stemming from a complex development of object-relations and observable in countless aspects of late-capitalism's particular cultural configuration. Such a formulation requires a complex account of the relationship between desire, visibility and its psychic manifestations beyond that offered in the discussion of Lasch here, but it is uncertain that Foucault could ever take us there with his emphasis upon subjectivity as a discursive positioning from start to finish.

In a Foucaultian sense the fears and pleasures involved in visibility may be an element of the productive economy of disciplinary mechanisms. Almost all human action and expression, for Foucault, is generated by the rules and regulations of a particular discursive formation or regime of truth of an episteme more generally. All forms of self expression are an aggregate of what is sayable and doable within socially inscribed parameters; they do not transcend, or penetrate from outside, those parameters (Foucault, 1980a). Consequently, pleasure in one's sense of visibility is viewed as an inherent aspect of the productivity of the policing process of visibility contained within it. So, rather than inverting the disciplinary mechanism Foucault might view pleasure, fantasy, etc. as a productive consequence of panopticism. In other words, maybe the apparent phenomenon of an increased desire for visibility in some contemporary cultures (*Big Brother*, television confessionals, docu-dramas, etc.) confirms its disciplinary function. Discipline works through rewards as well as punishments, resistance as well as compliance.

Foucault may thus be better equipped than Lasch to incorporate questions of agency which signify resistance and appropriation into his overdetermined portrayal of subjectivity. But if we *are* to claim that the experience of pleasure is purely a consequence of the internal dynamics of a discursive formation, we perpetuate a peculiar circularity. It allows nothing to be said of a *priori* or intersubjective psychic structures which in turn engender and constitute forms of social control, discursive formations and disciplinary techniques in such different and complex ways. The association of visibility with pleasure, amongst other emotions, raises interesting questions about object relations, narcissism and desire which take us deep into the realm of psychodynamic theory.

To reiterate Lasch's analysis, an individual judged on the presentation of themselves as a surface, a collection of images decoded in the self-aggrandizing vocabulary of mediation shared by real or imagined audience, comes to rely on that image of themselves, one of as-seen-by-others, for its verification. In terms of surveillance in its broadest sense, an individual is increasingly likely to see themselves in terms of 'a theatrical view of [their] own "performance" ' (Lasch, 1984: 30; 1991 [1979]: 32), noticeable perhaps, in the growth of reality-television, following the day-to-day dramas as they unfold in hospitals, airports, armies, etc. and competitions which expose individuals to new levels of scrutiny – *Pop Idol, X-Factor*, etc. – and demands for confession-type levels of reflexivity by 'performers', including 'celebrities'. Lasch argues that there consequently emerges a 'new kind of self-consciousness' in the way the subject takes itself as an object (Lasch, 1984: 29). It is marked by a vacillating, uneasy self-scrutiny, encouraging the narcissistic blurring of boundaries between self and outside world.

Lasch illustrates this state of affairs further: 'we cannot help responding to others as if their actions – and our own – were being recorded and simultaneously transmitted to an unseen audience or stored up for closer scrutiny at some later time' (Lasch, 1991 [1979]: 47). Personal recording devices extend a sense of self-as-performance, others-as-audience for Lasch, and accentuate process of self-surveillance. Not only because they provide 'the technical means of ceaseless self-scrutiny' but because they render 'the sense of selfhood dependent on the consumption of images of the self, at the same time calling into the question the reality of the external world' (1991 [1979]: 48). We have become unable to separate the self as a public performance or marketing exercise from any firm or consistent 'inner' senses of self. We live in 'a world of mirrors' where the boundaries between the self and the social world in which it operates become blurred (Lasch, 1984: 30). 'In a mirror-fixated world', argues Frosh, 'the centring of the object's self in something deep and stable becomes impossible' (Frosh, 1991: 73).

Reinstating a subject?

As with Foucault the subject is rendered as an object on its own horizon by the discursive practices of contemporary societies. As with Foucault, Lasch offers a very different analysis of some of the processes which are elsewhere interpreted as a much less problematic extension of self-reflexivity. Unlike Foucault, processes of surveillance and self-scrutiny can be more fully worked out in terms of the tenuous pleasures they provide to an *already existing* embodied subject by developing Lasch's analysis. This pre-discursive entity is not the bounded bag of traits and drives which is the caricatured target of Foucaultian criticism of psychoanalysis, however; it is the always porous, 'never completed' psychically charged and ambivalent interplay between the boundaries of 'self' and 'object', be the latter parents, significant others, mediated others, literally objects or cultural configurations (or 'disciplinary economies') more generally (Winnicot, 1974: 13).

Social structure and self structure are thought to be mutually intertwined but based upon an acknowledgement of essential characteristics nonetheless – a libidinal drive towards other objects in which the self is constituted: 'it is through a creative involvement with others that and the object-world that the self becomes enmeshed within socio-symbolic forms' (Elliott, 1999: 143). With an analysis of what is, comes an assertion of what ought to be. More generally, a psychoanalytically-informed critical theory cannot help but express an ethical commitment to the integrity of the self, to what *is* and to what is *lost* in the denigrations of a culture of narcissism or similar. Thus Kovel's more explicit attempt to acknowledge the historical contingency of all constructions of self-experience is followed by the assertion that contemporary constructions are of 'a kind, moreover, that reproduces on subjective terrain the sense of alienation and estrangement which we recognise as the signature of capitalist relations' (Kovel, 1980: 98). To be 'alienated' and 'estranged' there must be something one can be alienated or estranged *from*. In that simple assertion we move into the complex debates over essentialism, constructionism and the foundations (or lack) of selfhood discussed in the previous chapter and returned to in the next, but a few words are justified here.

Lasch's account, shorn of some its more problematic assumptions and implications, rests on the analytical and normative assertion of object relations as foundational in the co-construction of self and culture. What is being *valued* here then, asserted as a normative requirement, is a particular configuration of object relations, not just within the family but in terms of human relations more generally. These relations mediate, in turn, partially unconsciously, something which must be thought of as the essential needs of the libidinal drives. The specifics of this configuration are often implied in critique rather than spelt out but they are akin to the expression and fulfilment of 'transhistorical human needs – such as infantile helplessness, the need for warmth and nourishment, separation and individuation, attachment and so on' expressed in an environment of collective, relational autonomy (Elliott, 1999: 247).

Needs only become constituted in the constellation of relations which make up a particular cultural configuration of course. Even with this qualification, the assertion of 'better' interpersonal relationships to meet 'needs' is an anathema to a Foucaultian approach. Foucault cannot take us towards the relational basis of subjection because the power of interpersonal relationships is oddly lacking in his accounts, and because for him there is nothing to be alienated from, nothing to *lose*. But perhaps an account of needs necessarily 'provides something of a baseline for social critique and political judgement' (Elliott, 1999: 247).

On the basis of those aspects of a culture of narcissism discussed here, pleasures and anxieties derived from a phenomenon such as surveillance potentially make more sense. Laschian analysis incorporates a theory of interpersonal psychic structures and individuals with needs and motives to invest in the discourses and technologies of self-scrutiny and surveillance rather than being inscribed by them in an individualist fashion. Whether narcissistic struggles with the porousness of self-other boundaries are a consequence of a culture of narcissism in particular, or as Lacan would have it, the developmental process universally, is a point for further discussion. While Foucault describes some of the processes of self-scrutiny so convincingly, a Laschian analysis again brings a sense of the psychodynamic travails involved. The emotional power of self-surveillance – the anxieties and pleasures which both propel and can be evoked by it, both regulative and productive – is brought to life rather than being a shadowy, at times disavowed implication of an abstract historical development impinging on neutral subjects.

Conclusion

In summary, if anything of a Laschian analysis is to be held on to it first of all has to be balanced with an understanding of the positive valuing of narcissism in self-structures established by feminist and object-relations theory; it also has to accommodate the possibility of agency in terms of resisting, appropriating, disavowing and subverting the discourses of a culture where the commodity form dominates and colonizes spheres of human activity and self-identity; and it needs to be capable of differentiation of subjective experience in relation to social structure. Where does that leave his arguments today, and in light of the perspectives previously discussed? Lasch was actually saying something similar to Foucault and the theorists of governmentality: basically, the process of subjectification is usurped (though it always is for Foucault) by dominant social forces. Lasch gives the dynamics of subjectivization more of a psychic charge which brings it further resonance and gravity whilst at the same time opening it up to familiar philosophical and political problematizations from a post-structuralist perspective.

What Lasch does offer is an important counterbalance to the banal optimism of some contemporary approaches to identity. Giddens's dialectical approach allows him to incorporate many of the ideas Lasch develops, but that dialectic stops short in much of Giddens's social theory, leading to an imbalance which seems to stress the optimistic portents for self-identity over and above the kind of critical analysis which Lasch details so convincingly. This can suggest an over-simplifying tendency in neo-liberal accounts which effectually reduces the importance of problematic issues that do not quite fit into the sunny individualist disposition of this tendency. Reflexivity and choice were located in discursive formations of 'governmentality'; active techniques taken up by individuals to constitute themselves in particular ways. Here similar processes are portrayed as severely conditioned and defined, but by the *specific* conditions of modern corporate-capitalist relations with the added consequence of a *distortion* of ontological and interpersonal processes. Foucaultian analysis has captured some of the machinations of cultural processes of regulation with remarkable sophistication but its refrain from essentializing equates to a refrain from any sense of why we might care what changes occur in cultural configurations, psychological subjection, or opportunities for self-identity, beyond the advocacy of a banal pluralism.

A Laschian analysis, though flawed and partial, pessimistic and normative, is a picture of a self-identity which seems to capture an important dimension of contemporary existence which is lacking in much recent theorizing. However, Lasch makes little attempt to consider the diverse ways in which the dynamics of modernity impact upon different individuals and social groups, and as a result, the differentiated opportunities for the construction of self-identity. Similarly, Lasch sees narcissistic culture as a blanket term, affecting all individuals in roughly the same fashion.

Neither reflexivity, nor its critical nemesis, narcissism, can be adequately understood as homogeneously experienced phenomena. In the concluding chapter the discussion will return to focus on issues around the distribution of the psychological impact of social change, confronting the 'problem of ascertaining the extent to which the effects of social change are ubiquitous, uncontrolled and invariant' (Valadez and Clignet, 1987: 457).

Notes to the text

1 For a detailed account of the differing perspectives on the definition, aetiology and treatment of narcissism see the papers collected in Morrison (1986); for an overview see Frosh (1991).

2 Gloomy accounts of individuation as frustration are tempered by Mahler and colleagues' observations of the joy and excitement a child can derive from its nascent assertions of independence in the lifelong quest for a balance between symbiosis and separation (Mahler et al., 1975).

3 Feminist critics have argued that the emphasis upon both the oedipal conflict and individuation as the vital processes or end-states is a normative reflection of the cultural superiority of patriarchal 'masculine' processes, which also include detachment, independence assertion and rationality. Along with object relations theory, such criticism has led to an emphasis upon pre-oedipal development, the continuing importance of mother-child relationships, and relations deriving from experiences of primary narcissism, for psychological development in the work cited here. The latter point will be discussed further later in this chapter.

4 The normative role of psychoanalysis in inducing guilt in women and naturalizing their cultural-historical care-giving role has been the main focus of feminist critique. Whether descriptive or prescriptive, the primacy and corporeality of pregnancy, childbirth and breastfeeding can be acknowledged (though all of these are becoming obsolete as vital to the process of reproduction), but it is no longer acceptable to elide primary responsibility for care with the mother. Similarly, the actual and possible role of fathers and other primary caregivers in the infant's early development seem glaringly absent from many psychoanalytic accounts. These are now familiar criticisms, though worth reiterating, whilst conceding that the primary care role does still tend to be carried out by mothers in many contemporary societies.

5 Stephen Frosh's Identity Crisis (1991) is a notable, though now dated exception. Discussions do appear (e.g. Whitford, 2003) but hardly amount to a systematic reappraisal of the concept.

6 There are numerous examples which suggest the cultural prevalence of hypochondriacal tendencies. Screening and self-checking to aid the early prevention of many diseases has become widespread to the point where the anxiety the screening process induces compared to the likelihood of it preventing the onset of the disease has raised concerns (Burne, 2003). If all the public health leaflets recommending self-checks were combined, the procedure for daily or weekly self-examination would be an arduous task. The availability of knowledge about illnesses and treatment choices via the internet can also generate speculation, fear, and disease as much as it can personal empowerment. National newspaper articles

have also suggested that following a survey of GPs, a 'modern epidemic' of 'worried well' – 'people who think they are sick but are, in fact, perfectly healthy' – was increasingly visible, with doctors quoting figures of between 10 and 20% of their patients fitting into the category of 'worried well'. The 'worried well' or 'health anxious' are informed, often after consulting internet sites, or as a result of the increasing number of 'health scares', but nonetheless have no great health problems (Wilson, 1999). Advertising encourages men and women to look carefully at themselves for unwanted signs of ageing as well as providing the appropriate cosmetic or surgical fixes.

7 There is a danger here in reifying 'fathering' and 'mothering' roles in binaries as simplistic as Lasch's, naturalizing the association of women with nurturing and attachment and men with competition and authority. This may be a cultural configuration of lasting power, rather than simply a caricature, but it ought to be stated that neither pre-oedipal nurturing nor oedipal separation are necessarily gendered.

8 The assertion that a balance between ego-ideal and super-ego is vital for the development of a healthily individuated but interdependent self is far from accepted as gospel truth however. Lacanian psychoanalysis throws such assumptions into disarray by arguing that all attempts at individuation are in fact narcissistic denials of the reality of fragmentary and unstable reality of self-experience (Lacan, 1975).

9 In fact, the promise of unfettered self-development and ungoverned choice Lasch sees as one element of contemporary narcissistic culture, which relates to a banal, 'pseudo-self-awareness' characteristic of narcissism rather than any authentic self-liberation. In this context, Giddens's work could be seen as a contributory element to a narcissistic culture, an idea which will be taken up later in this chapter. It is an issue which also connects with the particular ideological reading of Giddens's work discussed in the previous chapter.

6

Repositioning Reflexivity

> Only an ethics or a social science which witnesses suffering is worthy of our
> energies or our attention.
>
> (Frank, 1991: 64 in Charlesworth, 2000: 11)

Although very different, what the perspectives drawn upon in the preceding chapters share is an account of the processes of self-reflexivity in relation to key social changes. A journey through various imaginings of reflexivity has brought us face-to-face with many of the difficulties and limits involved in theorizing the relationship between self-identity and social change, which can now be summarized.

A common failing in most of the perspectives discussed in previous chapters, with the possible exception of Foucault and some Foucaultian analyses, is their tendency to universalize the self-constituting responses to socio-structural changes; in other words little account is made of the *differential* impact of social changes upon social groups and individuals depending on their positioning relative to social structure. Sometimes this absence is obscured by the conceptualization of *in*determinate structures, as in the extended reflexivity thesis, sometimes homogenously *over* determined structures are implied, as in accounts of psychosocial fragmentation and cultural pathology. The challenge is to account for the inter-relationship of self-identity and social structure which somehow manages to capture the differential impact of those structures and the consequently differentiated impact upon self-identities without completely losing sight of a general model. We need a phenomenological approach which can adequately convey the 'corporealized subjectivity' as a site of social differentiation (Charlesworth, 2000: 17), but does not reduce it simply to the deterministic connotation of being 'a site' but acknowledges the subtlety and complexity of being-in-the-world; 'a sufficiently pliable form of theorizing that casts a more critical light on the martial (free) subject that haunts the "subject" of reflexive modernization' (Hey, 2005: 858). An exploration of the possible analytical tools for conceptualizing differentiated self-identity more accurately will close this chapter. The overall aim, in sum, is to produce an account of self-identity in relation to social change which is more firmly *embedded* in complex, differentiating social structures. This aim runs parallel to the requirement for a model of self more adequately *embodied* in a corporal, dynamic and relational model discussed in chapter three.

Access denied

The various new theories of the aesthetic, prosthetic, reflexive, rational, enterprising, omnivorousness and mobile self all describe different relationships to culture (usually as accumulation or experimentation), but what they all have in common is a presumption of *access* and *entitlement* to a range of cultures that can resource their self-making.

(Skeggs, 2005b: 973)

Bauman argues that sociology has over-reacted to the economic reductionism of its past to the point where in terms of 'the economic aspects and roots of human misery…most new visions kept petulantly silent' (Bauman, 2004: 36). Or, as Lawler states the problem, an excessive attachment to the 'cultural turn' in social theory can mean that 'the social-structural dimensions of class inequality are now understood as being embedded *only* in the subjectivities of social actors' (Lawler, 2005: 798; emphasis added). Crompton and Scott, in a discussion of the 'cultural turn' in class analysis, argue that 'a renewed emphasis on identity and difference should not be allowed to obscure or to downgrade one of the major preoccupations of class analysis, which is the study of structured inequality' (Crompton and Scott, 2005: 191).

Bauman claims that social theory has shifted to a concern with issues of representation and recognition, but this is a distant and nebulous idea for much of humankind and remains so if economic aspects are ignored (Bauman, 2004: 37). I disagree; issues of poverty and economic inequality are intimately bound up with issues of recognition and processes of identification. In fact Bauman appears to contradict this last point when he goes on to assert that 'identification' is vital to stratification and that the latter can perhaps be imagined as *limiting* meaningful identities. In fact there is evidence that the 'cultural turn' has been succeeded to some extent, with a substantial amount of recent work, some of which is discussed below, attempting to re-emphasize the 'realities' of social stratification alongside issues of identity and social recognition and some of the broader insights of post-structuralist theory.[1] What must be examined is the relationship between stratification, identity and life chances without reverting to the reductive and largely discredited sociologies of stratification which narrowly emphasized employment, relied on an over-simplified causal model of structure-consciousness-action and unreflexively reproduced its own 'Enlightenment' assumptions, amongst other criticisms (Devine and Savage, 2005: 1–2).

Jenkins argues that it is the 'definitive embodiment' of dimensions of social identity – 'gender/sex, ethnicity/"race", or disability/impairment' – which allows or restricts an individual's access to the resources necessary to play the bigger 'game' of developing and maintaining a meaningful sense of self (Jenkins, 1996: 51):

> The world is not really *everyone*'s oyster: a range of factors systematically influences access to the resources that are required to play this game. In any given context, some social identities systematically influence an individual's opportunities in this respect. The materiality of identity, and its stratification with respect to deprivation and affluence, cannot be underestimated. (1996: 51)

I think Jenkins is correct, though a definition of what is 'definitively embodied' needs to perhaps be more fluid than Jenkins' description: age, sexuality, nationality, locality, housing, medical status and biography, for example, are all 'definitively embodied' if they are interpolated into the nexus of power relationships and stratification; there are extra-individual limits to when these can be effectively 'hidden' or produced as required. Few would disagree with the assertions of Jenkins and Bauman, summarized clearly in the opening quote of this section, but many of the dominant theorists of our era have underestimated these factors by failing to integrate them more fully into a *differentiated* account of the impact of social change (Phillips and Western, 2005).

Polarizing access and entitlement

Bauman argues that at one pole is a global 'underclass' (at the bottom of which is the refugee), who have no access to choice. For Bauman, as for Jenkins, this polarity is as much an issue of recognition and identity as it is resource availability: 'identification and allocation are mutually and reciprocally entailed in each other' (Jenkins, 1996: 169). A lack of recognition equates to a lack of choice which is marked, says Bauman, by the *absence* of identity. Most individuals are located somewhere between these poles. A simplistic polarity of 'poverty equals an absence' and 'wealth equals the presence of identity' must be avoided however, for it has patronizing undertones besides its over-simplification.

Jenkins, in discussing the nature of organizations, usefully extends a Foucaultian analysis to explain how allocation and identification interact (see also Fraser, 2001). He argues that late modernity is defined in part by the existence of large and complex organizations which govern our lives, a point made in chapter one. How they govern is by the detailed *categorization* of individuals and groups. As Foucault has stressed, this is achieved through the minutiae of organizational procedure, 'a cumulative and consistent classificatory process which is anything but trivial' (Jenkins, 1996: 163): the interviews, tests, observations, checks, monitoring, recording and rationalizations which produce categorizations and which legitimate them; whether directed at the worker, pupil, welfare recipient, psychiatric patient, parent or consumer. What may or may not be apparent in Foucaultian analyses is what Jenkins makes explicit – that categorizing judgements are intimately bound to the allocation of resources and/or penalties (1996: 157–158).

Organizations, in connection with the allocatory processes in the broader social environment, have the ability to forcefully reify categories of identity via the selective allocation of resources and penalties to members and non-members alike: 'however achieved, the capacity of organizations to identify people as individuals or collectively – and to make those identifications "stick" through the allocation of resources and penalties, should not be underestimated' (1996: 168). In their most comprehensive form, they combine across social locations to construct a powerful 'regime of truth', an interlocking self-fulfilling prophecy in motion; 'undesirable' identifications such as an address on a 'problem' estate, possibly combined with problematic nationality, name, ethnicity, educational background, and so on, leads to a failure in job applications other than menial service work. This work is often in metropolitan centres at some distance from home, relying on public transport, leaving little time, money or energy to reflexively 'choose' from any of the 'opportunities' which might engender upward mobility and allow other identifications which initiate a cycle of increased resource allocation.

Winners and losers

Our critique can be substantiated by considering how recent social changes stratify opportunities for an effective 'reflexive project of selfhood'. A number of accounts have attempted to do just that, Scott Lash's conceptualization of reflexivity 'winners' and 'losers' being a particularly salient example (Hey, 2005; Lash, 1994; Lash and Urry, 1994; Lasch, 1995; May and Cooper, 1995; Sennett, 1999; Skeggs, 2004; Wacqant, 1999). Lash understands gain and loss in terms of an individual's positioning in relation to burgeoning information and communication structures which are replacing traditional social divisions. Lash and Urry concur with and contribute to the extended reflexivity thesis on some points, particularly Giddens's dialectical reading of agency. Modern forms of capitalism 'do not just lead to increasing meaninglessness, homogenization, abstraction, anomie and the destruction of the subject' (Lash and Urry, 1994: 3). Some of the processes of modern society 'may open up possibilities for the recasting of meaning in work and in leisure, for the reconstitution of community and the particular, for the reconstruction of a transmogrified subjectivity' (1994: 3). Lash and Urry also think through the transformations impacting upon subjectivity in terms of an 'increasingly significant reflexivity' (1994: 3). The authors are also careful, however, to qualify what a 'sociology of reflexivity' means for them: 'we do not argue that this entails some sort of end to the value of structural explanation *tout court*... we propose to the contrary that there is indeed a structural basis for today's reflexive individuals' (Lash and Urry, 1994: 6).

The commonly cited structural bases for the differentiation of reflexivity emerge out of the social changes discussed in chapter one and subsequent discussion: a decline in manufacturing and unionization, the geographical redistribution of jobs, an international division of, and competition for, labour; the salience of unprotected, temporary contracts; technological advancement, the retreat of the welfare state, growth in surveillance, and the various forms of spatial proximity and concentration of various groups hastened by global flows of people, products, ideas and cultures and the dominance of neo-liberal ideology (Wacquant, 1999; Lash and Urry, 1994). Such changes are crystallized as 'information and communication structures' according to Lash and Urry, though many other commentators use similar terms. Via these structures beneficially situated groups and individuals utilize modern technologies to consolidate and create new forms of knowledge and power.

Those at the helm or close to the heart of these structures – such as those creatively involved in the design, finance, publishing and advertising industries, the 'digerati' as they sometimes referred to (Hey, 2005) – are the 'winners' of reflexive modernity. Lash and Urry refer to these as the professional-managerial classes and the skilled working class (1994). But there are also many losers, evident when Lash and Urry ask: 'What sort of reflexivity for those effectively excluded from access to the globalized, yet spatially concentrated information and communication structures?' (Lash and Urry, 1994: 143). In the sweatshops of clothing manufacturers, the assembly lines of electronics firms, the development of crack economies, the rising homelessness numbers, swelling minority ghettos, Lash and Urry see a growing battalion of reflexivity 'losers'. Some have directly benefited from the increased reflexivity of society while some service it from the increasingly wilder margins. The latter have little choice but to occupy these positions as traditional forms of working-and lower-working-class work and leisure have been eroded by these new structures: 'the new lower class represents a sort of structural *downward mobility* for substantial sections of the [previously] organised-capitalist working class' (1994: 145).

As a result, Lash and Urry contribute to a powerful argument, broached in chapter one, that the social world is subject to a heightening polarity, or a 'bimodal pattern', of reflexively organized opportunity (Lasy and Urry, 1994: 148–150, 160–163; Bradley, 1996). On the one hand, new forms of employment for the middle classes depend on new rules of engagement with information and communication structures. Reflecting Jenkins's argument, it is argued that the specialized knowledge, training, and location required to play by these rules operates as a selection process which systematically excludes many via a broader structural coalescence of various forms of capital and their discursive imposition and inscription (Skeggs, 2005: 969).

The new middle classes occupy the management and design end of 'advanced services' which include 'software, personal finance, education and health, business services, the culture industries and parts of hotel, catering and retail services' (Lash, 1994: 163), who are more likely to process, and consume, highly valued 'symbols' rather than material goods (Lash, 1994: 64; see also Lasch, 1995; Sennett, 1999). 'Networking' is key to 'winning'; a process which utilizes characteristics of the reflexive self as capital, accompanied by its own procedures and protocols (Wittel, 2001; Hey, 2005). Reflexivity winners have extensive access to numerous cultural activities and repertoires, as well as consumer goods, services, and travel which might make possible something akin to a 'reflexive project of selfhood'.

On the other hand these reflexivity 'winners' rely on an increasingly service-intensive lifestyle which, as well as providing a market for each other, provides a market for 'the casualised labour of the new lower class' (Lash, 1994: 165; Lawler, 2005b: 442–443); 'urban domestics', to use Wacquant's term, who cater to 'the full gamut of household needs of the new corporate nobility: driving children to and from school, walking the dog, cooking, cleaning as well as provisioning the home and providing personal security' (Wacquant, 1999: 110–111).

Sennett's study of the 'personal consequences of work in the new capitalism', discussed in chapter one, is one of a number which highlight the concrete experiences of a global lower class, similarly arguing that the benefits of modern working practices are reserved for an elite few (Bales, 2004; Bauman, 2004; Ehrenreich, 2001; Ehrenreich and Hochschild, 2003; Klein, 2000). Sennett argues that the 'flexibility' of modern capitalism *seems* to offer new opportunities to the individual: 'flexibility is used today as another way of lifting the curse of oppression from capitalism. In attacking rigid bureaucracy and emphasizing risk, it is claimed, flexibility gives people more freedom to shape their lives' (Sennett, 1999: 9–10).

There are some similarities between Sennett's definition of flexibility and Giddens's concept of reflexivity, and Sennett does go on to discuss themes which partially parallel Giddens's work, such as the dissolution of traditional routines, the re-articulation of time, increasing interdependence, and questions of identity in the context of these changes, but there is a much more explicit attempt to account for divergent experiences. He argues that when transposed to the world of work, the uncertainty, diffusion of responsibility, short-term-ism and mobility associated with the project of reflexivity obscures already complicated systems of control and fragments temporal narratives. The consequences parallel those highlighted by accounts of psychosocial fragmentation and to some extent the culture of narcissism. Put simply, a coherent, consistent and meaningful identity is difficult to maintain, and is consolidated rather than alleviated by the contemporary structuring of work. In the words of Lois Wacquant:

> Employment no longer supplies a common temporal and social framework because the terms of the labour contract are increasingly diverse and

personalised, job tenures are short and unstable, and a growing number of positions do not carry with them protection from material deprivation, illness, joblessness, not to mention adequate retirement. (Wacquant, 1999: 112)

Sennett considers the process of de-skilling, as does Giddens, but his analysis illustrates his understanding of work and identity as polarized experiential worlds rather than uniformly and neutrally constituted spaces waiting to be re-skilled.

Sennett's work in particular is useful because it roughly maps on to the stratification of experience which make up the winners and losers of Lash and Urry's information and communication structures, whilst portraying those experiences in some concrete detail. Ehrenreich's first-hand account of surviving on a subsistence wage in America, and similar British efforts, also powerfully convey the sense of entrapment contemporary options for employment impose upon the 'working poor' (Abrams, 2002; Ehrenreich, 2001; Toynbee, 2003). Combine the effect of de-skilling with lower wages in real terms, increased competition, the spatial ghettoization of the poor, their intersection with other social signifiers of 'lack' (e.g. gender, race), state withdrawal from social support and assistance, and normative discourses of cultural inferiority and personal responsibility, and a clearer picture of the distinction between Lash and Urry's reflexivity 'winners' and 'losers' comes into view as well as the polarization of life-chances in general. A stratified map of opportunity emerges, where individuals and social groups are differentiated in terms of their ability to be reflexive, the context in which reflexivity is required and defined, and the ability to utilize that reflexivity effectively by converting it into life-chances. The detail of these processes can still appear uncertain however, particularly the extent to which the reflexivity of winners and losers differs, if differences ought to be seen as constitutive or merely symptomatic of the structuring of inequality, and how 'winning' relates to 'staking a claim' amidst changing social structures (Hey, 2005: 858).

Bourdieu and reflexivity

Reflexivity 'winners' and 'losers' have also been conceived in terms of gender (Adkins, 2003; Ehrenreich and Hochschild, 2003; Jamieson, 1999; McNay, 1999). McNay argues that gender identity is 'less amenable to emancipatory processes of refashioning' than the extended reflexivity thesis suggests. She particularlizes the experience of reflexivity in contemporary stratification, beyond that indexed by Lash and Urry in their account of information and communication structures. McNay combines a critical interpretation of Bourdieu's work, particularly his concept of *habitus* and *field* with a reconsideration of the possibilities for self-reflexivity (Bourdieu, 1976). In fact, for many contemporary theorists and researchers of social stratification research 'Bourdieuvian perspectives now command the stage' (Devine *et al.*, 2005: 13); thus it is worth summarizing his use of these terms briefly.[2]

The *field* refers to the always-existing boundaries of our experiential context; 'a relational configuration endowed with a specific gravity which it imposes on all the objects and agents which enter it' (Bourdieu, cited in Widick, 2003: 684). We move through different fields but the collection of fields we confront tends to be common for different class groupings. Habitus, basically understood, is the way individuals act within and towards those fields. The habitus is not constituted by freely-chosen dispositions however. The field itself engenders and requires certain responses, 'hailing' the individual to respond to themselves and their surroundings in certain ways. In this sense the field instantiates us as subjects and reproduces social distinctions via the enactment of habitus.

For Bourdieu the habitus is fundamentally an *embodied* phenomenon. It signifies not just how we think about the world but the bodily 'system of dispositions' we bring to a field: 'a way of walking, a tilt of the head, facial expressions, ways of sitting and using implements, always associated with a tone of voice, a style of speech and…a certain subjective experience' (Bourdieu, 1977: 85–87). Though thoroughly individualized, the habitus in fact reflects a shared cultural context. The cultural commonalities of a class become inscribed upon the body and are reproduced in personal deportment in the field, which is forever a constitutive response to already-existing social conditions. Thus, for Bourdieu: 'the body is a mnemonic device upon and in which the very basics of culture, the practical taximonies of the habitus, are imprinted and encoded in a socialising or learning process which commences during early childhood' (Jenkins, 1992: 75–76). Habitus is also an unconscious formation. The various characteristics of the habitus are enacted *unthinkingly*; that is partly what defines them as habitual.

Reflexive awareness of this production would rupture the fit between habitus and field, and is rare: 'principles em-bodied in this way are placed beyond the grasp of consciousness, and hence *cannot* be touched by voluntary, deliberate transformation' (Bourdieu, 1977: 94; emphasis added). Consequently, the reproduction of class identities happens via unwitting determinancy: 'what they do has more meaning than they know' (1977: 35). Thus Latour describes how Bourdieu 'subjugates the multiplicity of expressions and situations to a small number of obsessively repeated notions which describe the invisible forces which manipulate the actors behind their backs' (Latour, cited in Boyne, 2002: 119).

Bourdieu's concept of habitus/field, and their subsequent development in a wealth of research, asserts the persistence of socially stratified identity positions and the pre-reflexive enactment of an embodied class typology in areas as diverse as the experiences of students and pupils (Bufton, 2003; Willis, 1976); working-class women (Skeggs, 1997); parental choice of schools (Ball *et al.*, 1995); the agency of visually-impaired children (Allen, 2004); and social work practice (Houston, 2002). Such a conceptualization appears to be at odds with the extended reflexivity thesis, which sweeps away class as an important social structure and identity peg, replacing it with the ascendancy of individualization and reflexive awareness. In fact the two could hardly be more different, one stressing the unconscious, social determinism and embeddedness, the other pervasive self-awareness, voluntarism and a process of social and cultural disembedding.

Drawing critically on Bourdieu's work, McNay argues that there *may* increasingly be 'ambiguities and dissonances that exist in the way that men and women occupy masculine and feminine positions'. An increased exposure to other 'fields' of normalized activity (e.g. women entering the workforce) potentially creates the necessary dissonance which allows reflexivity 'in'; individuals potentially become aware of previously taken-for-granted belief structures, habits, ways of being and doing, initiating a cycle of reflexive awareness-dissonance-more reflexive awareness, etc. Rather than embracing reflexivity as a universally extended capacity in a dialectic with indeterminate social structure however, McNay imagines reflexivity as a much more 'irregular manifestation', that is 'unevenly realised' (McNay, 1999: 109, 111). In terms of gender, no plateau has been reached where the power imbalance of gender relations has finally been excavated and undone, or where the allocation of resources has been equalized. Power is still articulated, imposed and challenged and incorporates various degrees of reflexivity in the minutiae of relationships. It arises in the concrete, specific negotiation of specific fields, not in a conclusive and comprehensive prize won via abstract exposure to a pliable social backdrop of multiple choice.

More generally resource allocation operates according to carefully policed definitions of 'normality', to which allocation is directed, and against which all possible deviations are measured, punished and/or denied resources (Jenkins, 1996: 166–167). The symbolic, the imagined and the material are forged together in the stratification of identity. Of particular relevance for our discussion is that contemporary aspects of 'normality' might include the expectation of self-reflexivity. Recent work by Skeggs and Adkins amongst others tackles exactly this normative element of reflexivity and how it inter-relates with social categorization and the implications for resource allocation follow closely (Adkins, 2002; 2003).

In terms of gender and sexuality Adkins argues that 'theories of reflexive modernity propose not a reconfiguration of gender and sexuality in the context of increasing reflexivity but their dissolution' (2002: 4). By contrast, reflexivity is argued to be a socially ascribed characteristic, unequally inscribed in social relationships, appropriating for some, but denying for others. Thus reflexivity is not a prism through which social differences are dispersed, but rather one 'through which classification itself may take place' (Adkins, 2002: 8; Skeggs, 2002). In its broadest terms, the mobility necessary for 'exposure' to other fields, and thus transformative self-reflexivity, may be conditioned by already-existing delineations of field, capital and habitus: 'it is those with stakes in many fields, namely male members of dominant social classes, who thereby find it easier to develop various kinds of reflexivity' (Devine and Savage, 2005: 15). In this context, reflexivity is itself a resource, allowing further mobility and thus 'privileged positions' in late modernity which qualify certain groups and individuals for the allocation of further resources (Adkins, 2002: 130); it is a 'cultural logic' in relation to which 'subjects are positioned in contradictory ways' (Blackman, 2005: 199). It is not, therefore, a simple outcome of social change but a vehicle for the re-edification of social differences and divisions and the entrenchment and polarized redistribution of resources. Thus: 'techniques such as experimentation are not understood as unproblematically involving free play and free will and hence as "liberatory" or detraditionalizing, but rather are understood as techniques which rework and are constitutive of differences' (Adkins, 2002: 131).

Adkins draws on Skeggs's recent work to argue that self-reflexivity relies on 'specific techniques for knowing and telling the self' (Adkins, 2002: 8) which imbues the speaker with a naturalized epistemological authority (Skeggs, 2002). These characteristics are 'more available to some than to others' and 'rely on forms of appropriation, which dispossess certain "selves" of such properties' (Adkins, 2002: 8). Reflexivity and associated demands upon the subject for autonomy, flexibility, choice and self-regulation are thus implicated in power relationships and the maintenance of privileged positions, often tied to masculinity (Skeggs, 2002: 130; Walkerdine, Lucey and Melody, 2001) and/or 'less privileged' groups more generally (Nilan and Threadgold, 2005). Adkins offers a thorough and detailed analysis in arguing that women often end up as 'reflexivity losers', being denied the positions of reflexive authority and mobility. In terms of gender and class at least, the fault lines of an effective reflexivity seem to run a similar course to long existing social structures, rather than transcending them once and for all.

Apportioning reflexive capabilities

These arguments substantially contribute to a more situated, socially differentiated understanding of processes of self-reflexivity, attuned to its political and ideological nuances. However there is a problem in perceiving a valorized reflexivity as solely a highly-classed and gendered luxury securing resources and beneficial identifications. Despite the complexities of these nuanced critiques of extended reflexivity, there is a danger here of reinstating the patronizing overtones of a 'false class consciousness' interpretation. To say that poorer and/or culturally and socially marginalized groups might be 'less' reflexive, even if this is a regrettable product of a particular social positioning, could be interpreted as saying that such individuals are not as capable as those further up the hierarchy of making sense of their lives as it 'really is'. Indeed Charlesworth claims that the experiential field of the working classes is 'encountered as an unquestioned universe' (Charlesworth, 2000: 12), a world of 'realized automacy that leaves individuals less affected by consciousness' (2000: 6).

As has been argued throughout this book, in as much as it is possible to conceive of reflexivity in general terms, it is almost always structured by, and embedded in already-existing cultural discourses, wherever they are socially positioned. People are capable of a partial reflexivity towards their circumstances in ways which those same circumstances have, to a greater extent, prescribed. If a 'genuine' reflexivity is at all possible, then there are no convincing arguments which suggest that such a capability would be more available to socially dominant groups, that they can somehow make themselves more transparent to themselves. As I will argue below, they key issue is reflexivity's relation to, or refraction through, other dimensions of social existence. The hierarchization of self-reflexivity as an unproblematic resource unwittingly reproduces some of the dividing lines it seeks to explain. As Hey warns, 'there is always a danger in engaging in the debates about material inequality that one disappears into the "lack" discourse one is critiquing' (Hey, 2005: 868). What Charlesworth and others may be indicating then is not a lack of reflexivity *per se* but a number of ways of being reflexive, which are performed in relation to, confined and engendered by, the particulars of differentiated social locations.

It is also worth reiterating at this point that reflexivity has not been conceived of as an unequivocal 'good' in the preceding chapters of this book. To do so is to apportion too much faith to the promises of choice, actualization and agency made with the hegemonic framework of commodity capitalism. Even for those for whom it is said to represent cultural capital and personal advancement, the normally white and male middle- and upper-class 'winners' at the helm of networking human relations and the cutting edge of symbolic production, reflexivity can also equate to levels of anxiety and pervasive self-scrutiny. An ironic but gnawing sense of detachment, personal meaninglessness and disassociation, leisure time commodified by consumerism and time-poverty are all correlational diagnoses. In the previous chapter such processes were interpreted as narcissism, undermining meaningful human relationships and identities as much as it can resource them.

If explicit psychoanalytic readings of pathology do not convince, the stresses and strains of the 'reflexive project' or the instrumentalism with which it is necessarily adopted by all classes may more readily be accepted (Wittel, 2001; Skeggs, 2005: 971). An analysis of the 'effortfulness' involved in 'working up the resources of a highly serviceable reflexivity' may point to the social and psychological ambivalences involved in demands for reflexivity, deepening 'an appreciation of the "losses" such winning entails' (Hey, 2005: 863–864). May and Cooper's disjunction of visibility and availability (cited in Frost, 2005: 70) – 'this multiplicity of images and possibilities is increasingly visible. But this need not mean that it is increasingly available' – here takes on a double meaning. Not only are many excluded from the choices made visible by technologically advanced mediation, those choices themselves are presented as exaggerations and distortions of what they really offer, a point made repeatedly by a Laschian analysis in chapter four and here by Frost in relation to young women:

> Even leaving the question of resources aside for a moment, is it possible to have a 'good' relationship, a fulfilled mind, a great job, 'well-adjusted' children, and a worked, lean and fit body? People may identify with illusions, against which any achievement induces a sense of disappointment. (2005: 70)

There are more dimensions to reflexivity, more poles between which it can be conceptualized than reflexivity-extended-equals resources/ social advantage, reflexivity-diminished-equals some form of impoverishment. The practice of self-reflexivity may be a 'badge' of identity which qualifies one to be categorized in a particular way. But it does not stand alone or apart from other forms of identification. Reflexivity can be utilized as a badge of shame or a badge of pride, of failure or of success, perceived as a right or a compulsion, depending on how it combines with other aspects of a 'definitively embodied' identity. Between alternatively conceptualized poles, for example, reflexivity can be thought of as a regulatory process appropriated in the power imbalances of employer-employee relationships and all manner of areas of experience such as parenting, criminality, welfare-to-work programmes and mental health, as discussed in chapter four, as well as an accessory of the identity projects of the elite. Thought of in this way, reflexivity is not simply a scarce resource of the wealthy and/or cultural elite, or another form of capital from which a poor majority are routinely and systematically excluded, much less a 'disembedding mechanism'.

Instead it is, as Adkins argues, a process firmly embedded in the social structuring of inequality, but not only in terms of its distribution. As an imposed 'technique of self' it can work as tool of self-regulation upon/for those individuals who we might think of as excluded from the 'benefits' of self-reflexivity. A key consideration is the specific discourses which generate and police reflexivity, as we saw in chapter four, *and its connection with genuine choices* and socio-cultural resources, a point discussed later in this chapter. 'Reflexivity' means different things and has different outcomes for individuals and groups depending on social positioning. Social stratification may work through the forms of reflexivity made available, or be consolidated despite them. The relationship between reflexivity and differentiated social positions will now be considered further.

Polarization and post-reflexive choice

A notion of habitus/field tempered by an ambiguous, complex, contradictory reflexivity suggests how social categorizations can be reproduced but also challenged and overturned if in more situated, uneven and 'piecemeal' ways than the extended reflexivity thesis suggests.[3] It is *not* clear however that changes afoot in gender relations, however patchy, are also happening in terms of other areas of social stratification such as class, which always intersect with and thus problematize accounts of 'advancement' in other areas of stratification. In fact it could be argued that in terms of the lived experiences of the globe's poorest and wealthiest, the distinction between fields has *increased* whilst transposability is decreasingly viable for the overwhelming majority of the poor, leaving them adrift and bereft in their 'fields'.

Numerous accounts have detailed the lifestyles of the underprivileged: the 'wasted lives' of refugees and impoverished migrants (Bauman, 2004); the urban slums, 'warehousing the twenty-first century's surplus humanity' (Davis, 2004: 28), the total population of which was recently estimated at 921 million, or a third of the global urban population (2004: 13); or the working poor, who's working lives only serve to perpetuate their continual state of impoverishment (Ehrenreich, 2001; Wacquant, 1999). There are accounts too of an equally bounded and separate existence at the other end: the rich and powerful, increasingly hidden behind gated communities and moving through secure, defended spaces (Blakely and Snyder, 1997; Caldeira, 1996), to the point where 'some odd optical property of our highly polarized society makes the poor almost *invisible* to their economic superiors' (Ehrenreich, 2001: 216; emphasis added). The increasing invisibility and silence of the poorest groups is commonly recognized in empirical and theoretical analyses (Charlesworth, 2000; Skeggs, 2004).

Many studies point to a growing polarity in the distribution of wealth and associated life chances (see chapter one; also Bradley, 1996; Joseph Rowntree Foundation, 1995), particularly between skilled and unskilled workers across the globe (Feliciano, 1993; Lawrence, 1994; Wes, 1996). Poor health, bad housing, limited employment, fewer rights of movement, even toxic waste 'will always run downhill on an economic path of least resistance' (Bauman, 2004: 59) and mark out the field of a growing number, as will the minutiae of surveillance and regulative techniques discussed in chapter four – they have a socially differentiated purpose and impact. The in/ability to escape from that field may be the most accurate definition of class, or of stratification more generally (Bottero, 2004: 987), if for the poor, 'the reality is that mobility is closing down across post-industrial societies' (Byrne, 2005: 812). Wacquant similarly argues that the consequence of new forms of marginality and inequality are increasingly polarizing, '*entrapping* populations situated at an increasing remove from the middle and upper tiers of the class structure' (Wacquant, 1999: 107; emphasis added).

But these increasingly exclusive, inescapable fields of resource inequality, experienced as obdurate realities, are *not* maintained primarily by the 'behind-the back' workings of the habitus, *nor* are they dissolved by concentrated reflexivity. An acknowledgement of the complex co-existence of reflexive awareness and habitual dispositions can only take us so far in coming to terms with the generation of contemporary identities and their relation to an increasingly differentiated social structure. One's habitus may restrict and condition a proportion of 'choices'; social change may be facilitating a reflexivity which penetrates the fog of structured dispositions; but identities are formed in the ability to translate the choices which emerge from this complex interplay into meaningful realities. Even a heavily qualified reflexivity can only tell a partial story of contemporary identity. The key focus in understandings of contemporary identity and the social basis for their distinction thus becomes what will be tentatively referred to as *post-reflexive choice*.

The point can be reiterated by some recent research in Britain, Wendy Mitchell and Eileen Green's study of working class mothers' support networks (Mitchell and Green, 2002). It offers illustrative support for a more complex portrayal of the co-existence of reflexivity, habitus and post-reflexive choice. The authors interviewed a number of young mothers in 'Townsville', who were defined as working-class and predominantly white. They found women whose reflexive and creative capabilities were tightly bound-up with broader inequalities:

> Townsville's young mothers may be increasingly individualised self-reflexive actors but one cannot and should not ignore, the continuing importance of their 'habitus'...Here, their everyday experiences and discourses of motherhood, kinship and their own self-identity as a mother still remain closely interwoven with the wider socio-economic inequalities which permeate their lives. (Mitchell and Green, 2002: 2)

In other words, reflexive actors are still grounded in the 'externalities' of class, locality and kinship (Savage *et al.*, 2005). In the lives of those participating in Mitchell and Green's study at least, the prevalence of reflexivity did not equate with the choice to move beyond the parameters set by these externalities.

Situating reflexivity

More specifically, the young mothers did reveal the characteristics of reflexivity highlighted by Giddens and others such as attitude flexibility, the centrality of the individual and relationship plasticity (Mitchell and Green, 2002: 9). However, this does not lead inevitably to a freedom to construct individualized biographies. In fact, 'making life-style choices' in the context of a reflexive project of selfhood would 'frequently require practicalities such as socio-economic resources and opportunities, which many of Townville's young mothers do *not* have access to' (2002: 10; emphasis added). Despite the Townville women stating an awareness of, and desire for, more varied activities in their free time, 'their leisure was usually home based, such as watching television/reading due to child-care issues and financial considerations' (2002: 16).

In a study of life in the urban ghettos in America, it was found that maternity was often sought by young women as one of very few identity 'choices' on offer (Fernandez Kelly, 1994). To opt for mothering was not, as it may appear from the 'outside', a decision lacking in an appropriately reflexive consideration of life chances and choices: 'This mothering identity allows girls to signal their version of autonomy, that it might also foreclose other "opportunities" is completely beside the point, since these are deemed non-realizable' (Hey, 2005: 866).

One aspect of Savage *et al.*'s account of life in Cheadle, an 'unfashionable' Manchester suburb, relates similar findings (Savage *et al.*, 2005). Residents' intention to stay in the area were rarely couched in terms of unreflexive acceptance of 'their lot' but rather a resigned acceptance that their options were severely limited (Savage *et al.*, 2005: 118). Common escape routes were nostalgic narratives – 'the retrospective projection of hope into a lost world' – or a half-hearted investment in the vagaries of chance. Apparently a third of all the Cheadle respondents said that they would be staying in the area 'unless they won the lottery': 'in a fantastic world they would live somewhere else, but in their day-to-day life they had little choice'; or that without the lottery or a similar windfall, their own plans and goals – one is tempted to say their reflexive project of selfhood – could not practically be realized (2005: 118).

A fascinating study of the perceptions of the 'good life' in indigenous Fijian youth, amongst other groups, reached similar conclusions (Nilan and Threadgold, 2005). For these respondents, a reflexive ordering of identity was present, but the *language* of aspirational, actualizing self-reflexivity takes much more of a back-seat in the reporting of what a good life is and what the obstacles are to getting there. Their analysis of some of the comments of the indigenous Fijians respondents is worth quoting at length:

> The stark reality of their impoverished material circumstances is reflected in the simplicity of some future visions – *employment, good house, a job*. We see some evidence of the construction of individual life courses…but the sense of actual *choice* was singularly absent…Any reflexive emphasis was on *self-discipline*, which may connote the making of a self-trajectory…but it seems 'internally referential' (Giddens, 1991: 244) to perceptions of extreme material risk. (Nilan and Threadgold, 2005: 21; emphasis in the original).

Thus the authors indicate the importance of variations in the *forms* self-reflexivity takes in the habitus of distinct social groups, particularly as it relates to choice, but not necessarily the *extent* of reflexivity. Reay similarly found that whilst middle-class children drew on discourses of entitlement, ordered choice and self-realization more readily in the confident presentation of themselves and their futures, poorer children, like the young girls in Walkerdine *et al.*'s study, framed their identities with hesitancy, ambivalent defensiveness, shame and the fear of shame as well as pride and hopefulness (Reay, 2005).[4] These feelings co-exist with, and are often confirmed by, a perceptive awareness about their own treatment by teachers, family history, social expectations, but this is a very different reflexivity from the one of middle-class children. Charlesworth found a pervasive form of reflexivity based not so much around 'how should I live' as a kind of Foucaultian ideal of self-care, but rather an incessant dread of 'what if', in terms of losing one or more interlocking and fragilely-held stakes in employment, financial, housing and childcare (Charlesworth, 2000: 77). Structures and discourses of class thus operate differentially on the emotions and the psyche, but do not systematically circumscribe 'genuine' self-reflexivity wherever we are positioned.

Interestingly, but perhaps unsurprisingly, recent empirical research suggests that discourses of reflexivity are refracted through gendered locations as well as class (Gill *et al.*, 2005; Walkerdine, Lucey and Melody, 2001). In her later theoretical developments of a study of young women's identity and appearance issues (Frost, 2001, 2003, 2004, 2005), Frost argues that:

> Within [the] self-reflexive project, people remake themselves in relation to 'available' versions: perfection, or the 'best version' is pursued. So, having a 'better' relationship, a 'better' family life, new career possibilities and a healthy, fit and physically attractive body are all consciously 'worked at'.
> (Frost, 2005: 68)

However, reflexive self-construction is beset with problems of dissatisfaction and disassociation as many women are unable to incorporate available versions 'comfortably or successfully into their sense of self' (2005: 69). Thus Blackman argues that one's positioning in relation to the logic of reflexivity and flexibility can be highly injurious (Blackman, 2005: 199), expressed by the young girls participating in Walkerdine *et al.*'s study as feelings of 'humiliation, hatred of self, anxiety, paranoia, depression and anger...through gaps, silences and contradictions between their self-presentation and their bodily leakage' (Blackman, 2005: 1999; Walkerdine, Lucey and Melody, 2001). Clearly, there are personal and emotional consequences in not being able to follow the injunction to self-reflexivity in particular ways (Hey, 2005; Reay, 2005).

The examples drawn upon briefly here suggest that reflexivity *is* an expressive and affective capability of the respondents in these studies. It is not reducible to a capability of the fortunate (or the sociologically inclined), a regulatory form of self-presentation or a transformative process of identification. Considering degrees of reflexivity in the context of persisting socially structured and structuring habitus may in fact be misplaced if what matters for individual experience and opportunity is the capacity to convert 'reflexions' into meaningful realities which requires material resources that some individuals simply do not have access to. A complexly imagined extension of reflexivity amounts to very little if it is detached from its immediate embeddedness in a differentiated resource context. Thus the specifics of *post-reflexive choice* were vital for the life-chances and subsequent identities of the individuals interviewed by Mitchell and Green.

Clearly, the point being made here is not that reflexivity is necessarily attenuated by habitus, nor that reflexivity should be interpreted as a form of regulation. Whilst acknowledging degrees of independence and reflexivity, 'underlying structures and inequalities' are still vital for making sense of identity, but not just behind the backs of subjects via the enactment of a Bourdieuvian 'habitus'. The respondents in most of the studies mentioned here may be somewhere near the bottom of Lash's pile of 'reflexivity losers' but the term is something of a misnomer. For a lack of reflexivity neither underpins nor is a significant outcome of 'losing' necessarily, anymore than it is a surfeit of unconsciousness. It is not a lack of reflexivity which underpins this loss, nor deprivation created by the reflexivity of others. As I understand it Lash does not actually envisage a lack of reflexivity *per se* as marking out those at the bottom; rather they 'lose' in relation to reflexivity because they are marginalized by a social structure which empowers reflexivity in others, as Adkins and Skeggs have argued. But reflexivity may also be utilized as a form of regulation for structural 'losers' (or be viewed as an aspect of a cultural pathology) as the discussion here and in previous chapters has indicated. In this light reflexivity is far from an unequivocally positive 'resource'.

But a further point is that the lack of ability to shift fields can persist *whatever* the reflexive awareness of individual subjects, and is of course vital in resulting identifications. To repeat Lash and Urry's question – 'What sort of reflexivity for those effectively excluded from access to the globalized, yet spacially concentrated information and communication structures?' (Lash and Urry, 1994: 143) – a suitable answer would be that it is a reflexivity separated from meaningful choices, potentially avoiding two problematic claims: that a lack of or pseudo-reflexivity somehow marks out the most marginalized; or that reflexivity is necessarily socially or personally transformative. Thus the specifics of *post-reflexive choice* are vital for the life-chances and subsequent identities of the individuals studied.

Being as nothingness

Diane Reay argues that there is a 'new sociology of class' that 'has begun to carve out a space for affective dimensions in analyses of class' (Reay, 2005: 913), some of which is being drawn upon here. Although the empirical studies of this 'new sociology' may focus on particular geographical areas, the arguments made about the polarization of inequality are more general: 'it is a global phenomenon leaving disempowered, dispossessed people the world over invisible within their own national cultures' (Charlesworth, 2000: 9). The value of this work, at least for our purposes, lies in the extent to which it can 'explore the embodiment' of the neo-liberal cultural logic of self-reflexivity and choice 'in the lives of people struggling to cope and survive' (Blackman, 2005: 199). A painful sense of invisibility and nothingness is a recurring emotional expression of those lives in a number of recent accounts which might broadly fit into Reay's categorization of a 'new sociology'.

Global flows of people in all directions, incorporating 'downward' as much as 'upward' mobility mean that extreme polarities, interdependent but mutually exclusive, can exist not only between rich and poor nations but within, spatially located side by side, and across the globe. The existence of Cancun, Mexico, is an illustrative example of polarization, made vivid by the close geographical proximity of both poles. One of the first purpose-built luxury resorts, Cancun's development destroyed reef and wetlands to build two hundred hotels and associated luxury trappings. Less than 10 miles away, previously empty land has ballooned into a slum of around 30,000 people to service the tourists. One British newspaper reported that as many as 40% 'live without sewerage or piped water' and earn less than $10 a day (Vidal, 2003). Cancun's slums exist alongside their mutually dependent pockets of extreme wealth, but globalization reinforces polarities at, appropriately, a more global level of interconnectedness.

Such spatial proximity, accompanied by the virtual propinquities afforded by the growing technologies of mediation, further exacerbates a reflexive awareness of the polarity of resource allocation, categorization and identity and paradoxically, considering that proximity, a sense of invisibility and voicelessness amongst those 'excluded'. In the globalization of human traffic, more comfortable and self-regarding European nations are not exempt from the messy social and personal consequences of extreme polarization. Young residents of estates in the French suburbs on the edges of metropolitan enclaves of Paris, many of whom were second or third generation north or west African immigrants, rioted for a number of consecutive nights in November 2005, burning cars and property. As in Cancun, the poor live on the doorsteps of the rich but are 'invisible' to them, perceived as 'horrifically near and intriguingly distant' (Lawler, 2005: 442). Proximate but socially positioned as poles apart, the rhetoric of upward mobility, where it persists, rings particularly hollow. They exemplify the increasing polarization of life-chances and the interpenetration of resource allocation, location, social categorization, reflexivity and identity within as well as between nation states.[5]

A former inhabitant of one of these 'difficult' estates says: 'the people who live there live next door to France...we're not citizens. *We don't know what we are.* Not Arab or west African, but not French either. We're *unrecognised* and unremembered. No wonder people rebel' (cited in Henley, 2005: 19; emphasis added).[6] Downward mobility as a polarized response to repositionings of social change again equates with isolation, invisibility and 'non-identity', not as an abstract vehicle of recognition for those with little else to worry about, but as a primary experiential context, closely allied with social categorization and resource allocation. The actions of the French youth, desperate as they were, may reflect a distorted and attenuated realization of the reflexive project of selfhood. Like the actions of residents in urban ghettoes elsewhere, 'it is about making the resources at hand work to deal with the immiseration and exclusion of the locale' (Hey, 2005: 867). Whereas for the affluent choosing 'risky' practices may be a positive (even normative) dimension of the reflexive project of selfhood, signifying adventurousness and promising emotional highs, for the impoverished 'it is likely to result in imprisonment' (Skeggs, 2005b: 971), or perhaps deportation.

Consequently, reflexivity in dismembered fields may actually accentuate and consolidate a sense of muteness and powerlessness rather than alleviate it. For example, it is *via* reflexive capabilities that the Townville women 'perceived a dearth of socio-economic opportunities and life-chances for themselves, which in turn had important ramifications upon levels of self-esteem and future aspirations' (Mitchell and Green, 2002: 14). Others similarly argue that whilst reflexivity is increasingly prevalent, the consequences are far from celebratory for many. Where class once provided a meaningful context for the experience of poverty, the reflexivity of the underclass reveals 'a picture of unadorned exclusion' (Boyne, 2002: 121). Boyne echoes Charlesworth's claims that Camus' depiction of 'the absurd' as a universal existential angst applies more specifically to the field of working-class experience:

> A world that can be explained even with bad reasons is a familiar world. But on the other hand, in a universe suddenly divested of illusions and light, man [sic] feels an alien, a stranger. His exile is without remedy since he is deprived of the memory of a lost home or the hope of a promised land. This divorce between man and his life, the actor and his setting, is properly the feeling of absurdity. (Camus, cited in Charlesworth, 2000: 5)

If 'the connection between class location and cultural identity appears to have unravelled' (Bottero, 2004: 987), Giddens may be correct to associate the contemporary age with broadly felt processes of 'disembedding'. However, the common companion assertion that extended self-reflexivity is *universally* the basis for individualized, reflexively-constituted re-embedding is less apparent. To frame it slightly differently, it may be that the established habitus of working-class practices has been opened up to reflexivity in post-traditional times, but this does not equate to a provision of the necessary material and symbolic resource to exit an impoverished field and enter a more favourable one. Clearly this is a far cry from the vision of reflexivity at the heart of the extended reflexivity thesis. As Hey puts it, it is not the same as 'the "crafted autobiography" of the neo-liberal subject...but a much more equivocal one, subject to a (partial) recognition that the circumstances for choice and agency, much less autonomy, are not evenly distributed' (Hey, 2005: 867). For the poorest, 'it is as if the world now stands out for them as a series of practices they are exempted from' (Charlesworth, 2000: 79).

Non-involvement, non-recognition, invisibility: these are all heavily-charged affective states of being, not simply analytical categories; ways in which class is powerfully inscribed, partially through reflexive processes. The devastating reality of this experience is captured by one of Charlesworth's unemployed respondents' comments on the minutiae of their daily lives (2000: 79), worth reproducing here at length:

X: A've bin rait depressed miseln this week. An' fuckin' boored aht'a mi mind. Ah just an't got a fuckin' thing to du. It is strange, it just meks mi s'upset. Its like beein' fuckin' ill, I feel sick an' I an't bin rait fo' weeks. A'm just wastin' all mi life an' the'r in't a fucking' thing Ah' can du. That's why Ah stay in bed su late. Ah dun't wanna get up to feel su fed-up. [*Pause*] It meks mi feel strange inside... [*Pause*]

S: What du yer mean?

X: Ah feel different, especially when Ah g' aht. Like Ah'll gu' fo' a video or sumaht an' when Ah'm the'er Ah feel worried an' threatened a bit, like, an' Ah sort'a can't decide which t'ave, then Ah'll get 'ome an' Ah dun't wanna watch it but Ah'm boored an' Ah need summaht t'du. So Ah watch it! But Ah don't enjoy stuff at moment.

S: Du things not seem t'matter to yer?

X: No. Nowt seems rait t'mi, not like it wo. It's awful in it, getting' older, fo this! That this is it. Signin' on', crap jobs... [*Pause*]... n'money... this place! [*Laughs*]

In a sense reflexive capabilities may be the beneficiaries of 'disembedding mechanisms' of social change; they enter the fissures which have broken into the habitus of disrupted everyday practices. But considered from a phenomenological view point their impact is socially differentiated in enormously meaningful ways; the reflexivity they bring is a knowingness shorn of the material-symbolic resources of autonomy or empowerment.

In a context of increasing polarization then, for the poorest, self-reflexivity may reflect back 'the bleak darkness of the invisibility of these people's lives to themselves' (2000: 4). This is not to relinquish the heavily-qualified conceptualization of reflexivity which has been established throughout this book; wherever we find it, reflexivity is almost always a partial, ambiguous and embedded phenomenon. But as a culturally-saturated process of individualization and self-referentiality, closely allied to processes of commoditization and surveillance it brings into focus a distinct lack of agency, as individuals are cut adrift from any meaningful social order, 'located within unformed or fractured or multiply chaotic fields' (Boyne, 2002: 124), which nonetheless offer no escape routes. Reflexivity, from this standpoint, does not bring choice, just a painful awareness of the lack of it. The fields Boyne describes separate off the individuals contained within from more 'mobile' others in myriad material, cultural, social and symbolic interpenetrations. They are more like 'permanent enclosures' (Fernandez Kelly, 2004) than the open-ended and abstract systems which the reflexive individual supposedly faces in their post-traditional realities.

Skeggs develops a similar argument in a discussion of 'poor whites' in Britain and the rhetoric of social 'inclusion', still favoured by government ministers, journalists and commentators in discussions of inequality and related matters at the time of writing (Skeggs, 2005, 2004). Skeggs emphasizes the complex interweaving of cultural dimensions and distinctions of class to argue that membership of the 'included' has become heavily culturalized. To be included is to share (middle-class) 'cultural values, aspirations and ways of living' which, she argues, poor whites are automatically excluded from because they have the 'wrong sort' of culture (Skeggs, 2005: 58). Thus 'the problem of class is a problem of getting working-class people to be more like their middle-class counterparts' (Lawler, 2005: 799). Not only do they inhabit and represent an excluded culture, there are no criteria for mobility, no basis for escape:

> They do not have the cultural capital that could enable them to belong…There are no narratives of escape offered here, only pathology and atavism. This is not a matter of taste but being the wrong people in the wrong place at the wrong time. *This is race and class with no value whatsoever.* (Skeggs, 2005: 58; emphasis added)

Social recognition demands a 'refusal' of the labels fixed upon class and race whilst consolidating conditions which makes it difficult to negate them (Savage *et al.*, 2005: 98). In terms of a multi-polar conceptualization of reflexivity, we may find social changes engender at one end a capacity to reflexively construct an identity in the 'project' like terms of choices and realizable goals, and at the other, a kind of reflexivity-of-nothing. 'Nothing' or 'no value' refers to the emptiness and futility generated by a polarized field of existence excluded from either the power to make meaningful decisions or the networks of mutuality, meaning and relative mobility which might perhaps shield individuals from the corporal-psychic extremes of inequality and exclusion. In Charlesworth's phenomenological account of working-class experience in Rotherham, South Yorkshire, 'it is the paucity of the working people to *render the world* that leaves many feeling there is something missing in their lives' (Charlesworth, cited in Savage *et al.*, 2005: 98; emphasis added). Poverty is recast in cultural and individualized terms, represented as a deficiency of culture, 'a problem of dispositions, of not being able to become the right person', which inevitably works through subjectivities (Skeggs, 2005: 64).

Consequently, there is of course an undoubtedly important affective, psychological dimension to this recasting. As Reay asserts (Reay, 2005: 917) in relation to schooling, for example, class and gender intersect and working-class girls commonly (though not always) internalize 'an understanding of their low achievement as pathological'. The effect of these discourses points to the interpenetration of issues of recognition and redistribution: 'These girls, in the context of schooling, inhabit a psychic economy of class defined by fear, anxiety and unease where failure looms large and success is elusive; a place where they are seen and see themselves as literally "nothing" ' (2005: 917). For not having the necessary characteristics necessary to be recognized as a valid and valuable identity – being 'nothing' – equals a failure to qualify for those important material, cultural and social resources which allow for the choice and 'mobility' necessary for a 'reflexive project of selfhood'. The fear of being 'nothing' reflects the spectre of invisibility and non-recognition which is a recurring theme of accounts of the poor and poorest. Hence Charlesworth's 'central issue' is the 'muteness, silence, inarticulacy and the problem of accounting for the available sense that grounds these lives and which the silence rises amidst' (Charlesworth, 2000: 2).

More generally the social valorization of reflexivity as a universal and individualized resource for self-betterment sets up a pervasive discourse which further fixes some individuals in social positions while legitimizing the mobility of others: 'when people do not surmount class barriers, they can be positioned as lacking in some way', even 'blamed for their own domination' (Lawler, 2005: 798–800). In a social and political system which has abandoned broader plans or promises of distribution, the only option for improving one's quality of life is individualized movement up the social hierarchy. Social mobility is thus presented in political discourse as the effective and only legitimate means of betterment for poorer and/or 'excluded' members of society. As Skeggs, argues, mobility makes sense only in relation to something fixed, in this case the 'point zero' of working-class culture which all mobility is projected away from (Skeggs, 2004); 'discourses of mobility encode working classness as something that has to be left behind' (Reay, 2005: 921). Parallel is its signification through 'massification', consolidating working classness as 'both other and unknowable' (Lawler, 2005b: 443). The 'fixing' of the poorest sections of society into closed-off and homogenized fields of existence is further exacerbated, or rather is mutually constitutive of, the rhetoric of mobility and individualization infused in (middle- and upper-class) 'inclusion'. As a productive binary it perpetuates the immobility of the former by denying its social structural foundations as well as blocking access to the amassment of qualifying forms of capital.

The reflexivity of such groups and individuals is distilled into a muted voice, which does not have the power to be heard, to be translated into a language that can qualify it for 'inclusion', or more precisely, the recognition and/or resource allocation which are arguably the foundations of quality of life and a meaningful self-identity. Again Charlesworth's eloquence captures this silence as felt-experience better than my paraphrasing could:

> For how does one sign silence? How can one render a socially acquired condition of something akin to muteness? How does one communicate the intimate process of loss involved in sensing conditions discovered in solicitude, of a being one is connected to in care, having been denied the resources to communicate gesturally, posturally and linguistically with those who share their position? (Charlesworth, 2000: 135)

This is an argument not just about the continuation of inequality, but social change as the polarization and cultural consolidation of inequality; the qualitative *worsening* of the fields of experiences of the poorest and most subordinated (Wacqant, 1999); a downward mobility which generates a pervasive sense of fixity, isolation and invisibility: 'Downwardly mobile populations remain silent, not only because they are busy surviving, but also because their failure prevents them from being listened to' (Valadez and Clignet, 1987: 464); they are on 'the outside of the arena of the public sphere' as McCarthy puts it (McCarthy, 2000: 285). Charlesworth takes this to signify a 'foreclosing of the contemplative condition'. In a sense this may be true, but it is possible that symbolic as well as material deprivation does not prevent self-reflexivity; it is rather that it is not a reflexivity which can translate into the social, material and cultural capital necessary for social recognitions.

It is an unresourced self-relationship so it ends up as an absurdity, a reflexivity-of-nothing:

> this is an absurdity that cannot know itself because it cannot experience the ontological security and social grounds upon which self-justification might be realized. There is only ambiguity and confusion...emanating from a realm that is fractured, perceptually aggressing and negating. (Charlesworth, 2000: 6)

There may be, in sum, a stratification of one's positioning in relation to the transformative logic of reflexivity, one which can have deleterious impact on the losers; thus Hey suggests that the

> coordination of the life projects of the new digerati is professionalized – while the coordinates and coordination for those outside this new sociality takes a fundamentally different form; one that at times translates into a defensive radical pessimism – a fundamental turning in on the enclosed within the enclosure. (Hey, 2005: 869)

Being on the losing end of polarization does not preclude high levels of self-reflexivity; it may in fact pointedly encourage a subject turning-in upon itself, coming face-to-face with its immobility, stigmatization and intransigence in a world where the opposite pole, exposed and visible, is apparently predicated on protean movement and mobility.

Conceptualizing reflexivity across polarities

We have established a number of possible poles in an attempt to make sense of the multiple ways that reflexivity can intermesh with, configure and be configured by other important social phenomenon discussed in previous chapters, some of which have been expanded upon in this concluding chapter. The table below is an attempt to summarize these poles, but a number of qualifications need to be set out first. A first point of caution is that reflexivity can rarely, if ever, exist in a 'pure' state at one end of this pole, nor is it being valorized here as an unequivocally desirable state. It is the 'space' between the poles which is intended to imply the possibilities for the lived reality of self-reflexivity; the poles themselves are only markers of that space. To reiterate, the concept of poles is not an attempt to suggest that reflexivity be thought of as *either* one extreme *or* another. The experiential reality of reflexivity for most people is captured, if it is captured at all, somewhere in between these poles.

A second qualification is that, despite the concept of polarities, some of the more ambivalent dimensions of the phenomena under discussion must be maintained. Although positioned at the negative pole, for example, some degree of narcissism is commonly thought to be healthy, and feminist critics

Table 6.1   The experiential poles of a qualified concept of reflexivity

Positive pole	Negative pole
Reflexivity as driving force behind increasing self mastery.	Reflexivity restrained by reality of embodiment, relational, unconscious and emotional processes, and experiential ambiguity; and socio-cultural narratives which partially disavow reflexive capabilities
Reflexivity further disembeds individuals from cultural/social narratives and processes of stratification accepted as 'given' in the past.	Reflexivity always operates in relation to socially differentiated habitus; more generally it is culturally contingent and contextualized, rather than transcending cultural discourses.
Pervasive self-scrutiny and self-awareness generates programme of self-mastery and 'democratization' of relationships with others.	Narcissism, anxious self-scrutiny, inner-emptiness, instrumentalism, effortfulness and related pathologies pervade weak self-identity.
Contact with more choices, others, ideas, time, services and finance etc. equates to a resource from which a meaningful identity 'project' can be reflexively constructed.	Uncoupled from meaningful choices equals painful awareness of lack; possible disavowal of reflexivity and search for certainty.
Extended reflexivity heralds the retreat of external government of self by prescriptive social and cultural expectations and traditions, and ascendancy of choice, transparency and autonomy.	Surveillance and self-surveillance as related elements of 'trap'. Reflexivity re-imagined as closely governed imposition which regulates and constructs selves; a technique of self inculcated via discourses of self-mastery and self-actualization.

have argued that the search for symbiosis at the heart of narcissism is a potentially positive characteristic overlooked by the masculinist valorization of individuation. Neither are certain groups or individuals intended to be represented at each pole, say men or westerners or rich people on the left and their binary opposites on the right, even though that may at first appear to be a plausible shorthand interpretation. Reflexivity is a phenomenon which intersects with other psychosocial processes in complex and sometimes contradictory ways. To complicate things further, aspects of any one of the positive poles on the left readily criss-cross with any of the negative poles on the right; they are interchangeable. There are also many points of overlap between the different definitions within the 'positive' and 'negative' columns.

Conclusion

In sum, this chapter has considered whether it is possible to particularize the experience of self-reflexivity in relation to processes of social stratification and psychological affect. It has been argued that a psychosocial understanding of stratification does indicate the existence of contemporary forms of self-reflexivity. What we take reflexivity to mean in relation to self-identity has already been heavily qualified in earlier chapters however. Self-reflexive acts have been reconceptualized as partial and *embodied* processes, beset by the ambiguities, contradictions and disavowals argued to be inherent dynamics of a self theorized beyond the priorities and assumptions of the extended reflexivity thesis. The patterns for one's self-development and self-awareness have thus not in any final sense become transparent, that is, open to 'pure' reflexive ordering.

The imagined qualities of perspicuity and self-mastery attributed to reflexivity have been further problematized by accounts which more prominently theorize the relational and social aspects of existence. Meadian and Kleinian analyses, for example, all draw our attention to the interpersonal fundamentals of even the most primary and intimate dimensions of self-knowledge. If what we are and how we comprehend what we are is so infiltrated with the messages and meanings derived from relationships with others, then self-reflexivity has to be understood as something much more embedded in those relations, and more broadly, it is something which is always encultured and socialized in particular ways.

The self is still constructed according to established patterns, set by the cultural norms, traditions and sanctions in which one's self-development takes place. The extended reflexivity thesis may be correct in asserting that as a result of numerous social changes, reflexive awareness has allowed for the relativization of a whole body of cultural patterns which may have once been experienced as taken-for-granted stocks of knowledge. Consequently identity may indeed be a more chronically-reflexive process. Nonetheless cultural understandings of gender, sexuality, relationships, work, leisure, consumption, communication and so on are still loaded with assumptions and practices that persist, are difficult to change and even distinguish in everyday experience, and undoubtedly impact upon self-identity. The valorization of an individualized self-reflexivity, emphasizing ratiocination, rationality and self-mastery is itself argued to be a culturally contingent understanding, normative as much as analytical.

This final chapter has developed a critical acknowledgement of the socially and culturally embedded nature of reflexivity to further complicate its relationship to self-identity. Claims that self-reflexivity is basically a socially distributed resource, a form of capital which both reflects and reinforces an increasing polarization of inequality, were considered. The role of reflexivity was thought to be partially undermined by the continuity of habitual forms of activity within socially-structured fields of action which either reflexivity does not necessarily penetrate or which encourage or discourage the development of reflexivity. Such accounts have developed a more critical and partial understanding of self-reflexivity, and contribute to the theorization of contemporary identity formation. However it was claimed that the attribution of more or less reflexivity to certain groups ran the risk of raising the ghost of 'false consciousness'. A variation on established criticism which avoids this pitfall is firstly to acknowledge that reflexivity is always a partial process, wherever one is socially positioned; the critical claim established in previous chapters.

The work discussed in this chapter lends itself to the suggestion that social changes evident in modern structures of employment, education, housing and health provide reflexive opportunities for some social groups while denying them to others. Even *if* it can be agreed that reflexivity is an increasingly predominant aspect of self-identity, it has been argued that analyses of this growth need to be understood further by examining the distribution of reflexivity. This has to be done by considering the patterns of, for example, work and leisure generated by new information and communication structures, and the gradients and polarities that exist within these structures in terms of opportunities for resourcing a meaningful and reflexive self-identity. The issue here is not simply one of whether or not there is an increased reflexive relationship to one's self-identity detectable in only certain groups within a global society. It is equally important to examine the opportunities individuals have to transform reflexive awareness into an opening out of choices for an effective and autonomous self-identity, focusing on the ways in which opportunity, or the lack of opportunity, gravitates towards particular social groups.

It has also been argued here that self-reflexivity has different manifestations and produces different outcomes depending on one's already existing social positioning. Self-reflexivity is not irrelevant to the life-chances, social and self-recognition of the poor, nor is it absent. The particular configuration of cultural and material stratification denies those already marginalized access to the capital which activates that self-reflexivity as a basis for further recognition and entitlement. For some, reflexivity is refracted through choice, be it in terms of cultural, social, economic resources, for others it is refracted through a lack of choice. For as Bauman argues (Bauman, 1998: 86): 'All of us are doomed to the life of choices, but not all of us have the means to be choosers'.

Notes to the text

1 See, for example, Devine *et al.* (2005), Brannen and Nilsen (2005), Bottero (2004), Crompton *et al.* (2000) and the special edition of *Sociology* dedicated to 'Class, Culture and Identity', Vol.39 (5), December 2005.

2 For a more detailed discussion of the relationship between habitus, field, reflexivity and contemporary self-identity, see Adams (2006). The work collected in Devine *et al.*'s book (2005) is a sustained application of Bourdieuvian perspectives to contemporary issues in stratification theory and empirical research. Not everyone agrees that Bourdieu's work has significantly reinvigorated approaches to stratification; see, for example, Crompton and Scott (2005) in Devine *et al.*'s collection.

3 Interestingly, a conceptualization of 'the unacknowledged conditions and unintended consequences' of action in Giddens's earlier work held out the potential for a more grounded, socially-stratified and embedded version of the reflexive project (Giddens, 1976, 1984). However, the ascendancy of reflexivity as a central process in self-identity in Giddens's later work is paralleled by a rapid decline in the importance allotted to these processes. There is no reference to either factors in *The Consequences of Modernity* (1990), *Modernity and Self-Identity* (1991), *The Transformation of Intimacy* (1992), or *Living in a Post-Traditional Society* (1996). In each of these texts there are, however, lengthy discussions of agency, making the absence all the more conspicuous.

4 Accounts of contemporary forms of middle-class habitus are less common, though see Lawler (2005).

5 An emphasis upon 'place and space' rather than employment has to some extent re-energized localized ethnographic studies of stratification, partially due to the appliance of Bourdieu's concepts of habitus, field and capital (Savage *et al.*, 2005: 100–102). Spatial dimensions of inequality have also gained credence in broader discourses, such as the supposed 'postcode lottery' which relates location to various indices of quality of life such as access to healthcare, employment opportunities and death rates. At the time of writing there is also debate over the extent to which Britain is developing spatial enclaves based on race and class.

6 The actions of these French youth are perhaps unsurprising after reading Bourdieu *et al.*'s *The Weight of the World* (1999). The study flags up a sense of miserable isolation and non-recognition amongst the French working classes again and again. Such concerns are paralleled ambivalently in many aspects of contemporary French culture, such as the novels of Michel Houllebecq and the films of Michael Haneke.

Bibliography

Abrams, F. (2002) *Below the Breadline: Living on the Minimum Wage*. London: Profile Books

Adams, M. (2006) 'Hybridising habitus and reflexivity: Towards an understanding of contemporary identity', *Sociology*, Vol.40(3): 511–528

Adams, M. (2003) 'The reflexive self and culture: A critique', *British Journal of Sociology*, Vol.54(2): 221–238

Adkins, L. (2003) 'Reflexivity: Freedom or Habit of Gender?', *Theory, Culture & Society*, 20(6): 21–42

Adkins, L. (2002) *Revisions: Gender and Sexuality in Late Modernity*. Buckingham: Open University Press

Adorno, T. (1955) 'Sociology and Psychology', *New Left Review* (trans. Irving N. Wohlfarth), two parts: 46 (Nov.–Dec. 1967): 67–80; and 47 (Jan.–Feb. 1968): 79–97

Adorno, T. and Horkheimer, M. (1979 [1947]) *Dialectic of Enlightenment*, London: Verso

Albrow, M. (1996) *The Global Age: State and society beyond modernity*. Cambridge: Polity Press

Alcoff, L. (1999) 'Feminist Politics and Foucault: The Limits to a Collaboration' in A. Dallery and C. Scott (eds) *Crises in Continental Philosophy*. Albany: SUNY Press

Alexander, J. (1996) 'Critical Reflections on "Reflexive Modernization"', *Theory, Culture and Society*, Vol.13(4): 133–138

Alexander, J.C. (1995) *Fin de Siècle Social Theory: Relativism, Reduction, and the Problem of Reason*. London: Verso

Allen, C., Milner, J., Price, D. (2002) *Home is Where the Start is: The Housing and Urban Experiences of Visually Impaired Children*. Bristol: The Policy Press

American Psychiatric Association (2000) *Diagnostic and Statistical Manual of Mental Disorders*, 4th edition text revision (DSM IV-TR), Washington, DC.

Ang, I. (1985) *Watching Dallas: Soap Opera and the Melodramatic Imagination*. London: Methuen

Argyrou, V. (2003) '"Reflexive modernization" and other mythical realities', *Anthropological Theory*, Vol.3(1): 27–41

Arkin, A. (1997) 'Hold the production line', *People Management* (February 6, 1997): 22

Armstrong, D. (2004) *A New History of Identity: A Sociology of Medical Knowledge*. Basingstoke: Palgrave

Aronowitz, S. (1980) 'On Narcissism', *Telos*, No.44 (Summer 1980): 65–73

Atkinson, P. and Housley, W. (2003) *Interactionism*. London: Sage

Bain, P. and Taylor, P. (2000) 'Entrapped by the "electronic panopticon"? Worker resistance in the call centre', *New Technology, Work & Employment*, Vol.15:1: 2–18

Bain, P., Watson, A., Mulvey, G. and Gall, G. (2002) 'Taylorism, Targets and the Pursuit of Quantity and Quality by Call Centre Management', *New Technology, Work and Employment*, 17(3): 154–69

Bales, K. (2004) *Disposable People: New Slavery in the Global Economy*. California: University of California

Ball, S., Bowe, R. and Gewirtz, S. (1995) 'Circuits of Schooling: A sociological exploration of parental choice of school in social-class contexts', *The Sociological Review*, 43: 52–78.

Baron, S., Field, J., Schuller, T., (eds) (2000) *Social Capital: Critical Perspectives*. Oxford: Oxford University Press

Barrett, M. and McIntosh, M. (1982) 'Narcissism and the Family: A Critique of Lasch', *New Left Review*, I/135 (Sept.–Oct.): 35–48

Barrett, M. and McIntosh, M. (1982) *The Anti-Social Family*. London: Verso

Bartky, S.L. (1990) *Femininity and Domination: Studies in the Phenomenology of Oppression*. London: Routledge

Bartky, S.L. (1988) 'Foucault, femininity and the modernization of patriarchal power' in I. Diamond and L. Quinby (eds), *Feminism and Foucault: Reflections on Resistance*. Boston: Northeastern University Press: 61–86

Batt, R. and Moynihan, L. (2002) 'The Viability of Alternative Call Centre Production Models', *Human Resource Management Journal*, 12(4): 14–34

Bauman, Z. (2004) *Identity*. Cambridge: Polity Press

Bauman, Z. (2001) *The Individualized Society*. Cambridge: Polity Press

Bauman, Z. (2000) *Liquid Modernity*. Cambridge: Polity Press

Bauman, Z. (1998) *Globalization: The Human Consequences*. Cambridge: Polity Press

Beck, U. (1992) *Risk Society: Towards a New Modernity*. London: Sage

Beck, U. and Beck-Gernsheim, E. (2002) *Individualization: Institutionalized Individualism and its Social and Political Consequences*. London: Sage

Beck, U. and Beck-Gernsheim, E. (1995) *The Normal Chaos of Love*. London: Polity Press

Beck, U. and Willms, J. (2003) *Conversations with Ulrich Beck*. Cambridge: Polity Press

Beck, U., Giddens, A. and Lash, S. (1994) *Reflexive Modernization*. Cambridge: Polity Press

Becker, E. (1973) *The Denial of Death*. New York: Free Press

Bell, D. (1973) *The Coming of Post-Industrial Society*. New York: Basic Books

Bellah, R., Madsen, R., Sullivan, W. *et al.* (1996) *Habits of the Heart: Individualism and Commitment in American Life*. Berkeley: University of California Press

Bendle, M. F. (2002) 'The crisis of "identity" in high modernity', *British Journal of Sociology*, Vol.53(1): 1–18

Benjamin, J. (1988) *The Bonds of Love: Psychoanalysis, Feminism and the Problem of Domination*. London: Virago

Benjamin, J. (1978) 'Authority and the Family Revisited: Or, a World Without Fathers', *New German Critique*, No.13: 35–57

Bjerrum Nielsen, H. (1993) '"Black Holes" as Sites for Self-Constructions' in R. Josselson and A. Lieblich (eds) *Making Meaning of Narratives in the Narrative Study of Lives*, Vol.6. London: Sage

Bjorklund, P. (2000) 'Medusa Appears: A Case Study of a Narcissistic Disturbance', *Perspectives in Psychiatric Care*, Vol.36(3), 86–94

Blackman, L. (2005) 'The Dialogical Self, Flexibility and the Cultural Production of Psychopathology', *Theory and Psychology*, 15 (Apr. 2005): 183–206

Blackman, L. and Walkerdine, V. (2001) *Mass Hysteria: Critical Psychology & the Media*. Basingstoke: Palgrave

Blakely, E. J. and Snyder, M. (1997) *Fortress America*. Washington, DC: The Brookings Institute

Boggs, C. (2001) 'Social capital and political fantasy: Robert Putnam's *Bowling Alone*', *Theory and Society*, 30: 281–297

Bollas, C. (1987) *The Shadow of the Object: Psychoanalysis of the Unthought Known*. London: Free Association Books

Bolton, C. and Boyd, C. (2003) 'Trolley dolly or skilled emotion manager? Moving on from Hochschild's Managed Heart', *Work, Employment & Society*, Vol.17(2): 289–308.

Bordo, S. (1993) *Unbearable Weight: Feminism, Western culture, and the Body*. Berkeley: University of California Press

Bourdieu, P. (1998) *Practical Reason: on the Theory of Action*. Cambridge: Polity Press

Bourdieu, P. (1990b) *The logic of practice* (trans. R. Nice). Cambridge: Polity Press

Bourdieu, P. (1990a) *In Other Words: Essays Towards a Reflexive Sociology* (trans. M. Adamson). Cambridge: Polity Press

Bourdieu, P. (1977) *Outline of a Theory of Practice*. Cambridge: Cambridge University Press

Bourdieu, P., Accardo, A. *et al.* (1999) *The Weight of the World: Social Suffering in Contemporary Society* (trans. Priscilla Pankhurst Ferguson). Cambridge: Polity Press

Bourdeiu, P. and Wacquant, L. (1992) *An Invitation to Reflexive Sociology*. Cambridge: Polity Press

Boyne, R. (2002) 'Bourdieu: From Class to Culture', *Theory, Culture and Society*, Vol.19(3): 117–128

Boyne, R. (2000) 'Post-panopticism', *Economy & Society*, 29(2): 285–307

Bradley, H. (1996) *Fractured Identities: Changing Patterns of Inequality*. Cambridge: Polity Press

Bradley, H., Erickson, M., Stephenson, C. and Williams, S. (2000) *Myths at Work*. Cambridge: Polity Press

Brah, A. (1996) *Cartographies of Diaspora: Contesting Identities*. London: Routledge

Brannen, J. and Nilsen, A. (2005) 'Individualisation, choice and structure: a discussion of current trends in sociological analysis', *The Sociological Review*, Vol.53(3): 412–428

Breen, R. and Goldthorpe, J.H. (1997) 'Explaining Educational Differentials: Towards a Formal Rational Act Theory', *Rationality and Society*, 9(3): 275–305

Bromberg, P. (1986) '"The Mirror and the Mask": On Narcissism and Psychoanalytic Growth' in Morrison, A.P. (ed.) *Essential Papers on Narcissism*. New York: New York University Press: 438–466

Brown, N. W. (2001) *Children of the Self-Absorbed: A Grown-Up's Guide to Getting over Narcissistic Parents*. Oakland, CA: New Harbinger Publications

Brown, S. D. (2001) 'Psychology and the Art of Living', *Theory and Psychology*, Vol.11(2): 171–192

Brubaker, R. and Cooper, F. (2000) 'Beyond "identity"', *Theory and Society*, 29(1): 1–47

Bryman, A. (2004) *The Disneyization of Society*. London: Sage

Bufton, S. (2003) 'The Lifeworld of the University Student: Habitus and Social Class', *Journal of Phenomenological Psychology*, Vol.34(2): 207–234

Burchell, G. (1993) 'Liberal government and the techniques of self', *Economy and Society*, 22(3): 266–282

Burchell, G., Gordon C. and Miller P. (eds) (1991) *The Foucault Effect*. Hemel Hempstead: Harvester

Burkitt, I. (1999) *Bodies of Thought: Embodiment, Identity and Modernity*. London: Sage

Burkitt, I. (1991) *Social Selves: Theories of the Social Formation of Personality*. London: Sage

Burman, E. (1994) *Deconstructing Developmental Psychology*. London: Routledge

Burne, J. (2003) 'More Than You Need to Know?', *Guardian*, Weekend Magazine (November 15, 2003)

Burr, V. and Butt, T. W. (2000) 'Psychological distress and post-modern thought' in D. Fee (ed.) *Pathology and the Post-modern: Mental Illness, Discourse, and Experience*. London: Sage

Butler, J. (1997) *The Psychic Life of Power: Theories in Subjection*. Stanford: Stanford University Press

Butler, J. (1990) *Gender Trouble*. London: Routledge

Butt, T. and Langdridge, D. (2003) 'The Construction of Self: The Public Reach into the Private Sphere', *Sociology*, Vol.37(3): 477–493

Button, G., Coates, S., Cook, P., Lankshear, G. and Mason, D. (2001) 'Call centre employees responses to electronic monitoring: some research findings', *Work Employment and Society*, 15:3: 595–605.

Caldeira, T. (1996) 'Fortified enclaves: the new urban segregation', *Public Culture*, Vol.8(2): 329–354.

Callaghan, G. and Thompson, P. (2002) ' "We Recruit Attitude": the Selection and Shaping of Routine Call Centre Labour', *Journal of Management Studies*, 39(2): 233–254

Callaghan, G. and Thompson, P. (2001) 'Edwards Revisited: Technical Control and Call Centres', *Economic and Industrial Democracy*, 22(1): 13–37

Cameron, D. (2000) *Good To Talk?* London: Sage

Castells, M. (1997) *The Information Age: Economy, Society and Culture, Vol.II: The Power of Identity*. Oxford: Blackwell (2nd edition, 2004)

Castoriadis, C. (1987) *The Imaginary Institution of Society* (trans. Kathleen Blamey), Cambridge: Polity Press

De Certeau, M. (1984) *The Practice of Everyday Life* (trans. S.F. Rendall), Berkeley, CA: University of California Press

Chandler, M. J., Lalonde, C. E., Sokol, B. W. and Hallett, D. (2003) 'Personal persistence, identity development and suicide', *Monographs for the Society for Research in Child Development*, 68(2).

Charlesworth, S. J. (2000) *A Phenomenology of Working Class Experience*. Cambridge: Cambridge University Press

Chasseguet-Smirgel, J. (1985b [1984]) *Creativity and Perversion*. London: Free Association

Chasseguet-Smirgel, J. (1985a [1975]) *The Ego Ideal*. London: Free Association

Chodorow, N. (1978) *The Reproduction of Mothering*. Berkeley: University of California Press

Chodorow, N. and Contratto, S. (1982) 'The fantasy of the perfect mother' in *Feminism and Psychoanalytic Theory*. New Haven, CT: Yale University Press: 79–96

Claxton, G. (ed.) (1984) *Beyond Therapy: The Impact of Eastern Religions on Psychological Theory and Practice*. London: Wisdom Publications

Cohen, I. J. (1989) *Structuration Theory: Anthony Giddens and the Constitution of Social Life*. London: Macmillan

Coleman, J. S. (1990) *Foundations of Social Theory*. Cambridge: Belknap

Coleman, J. S. (1973) *The Mathematics of Collective Action*. London: Heinemann

Cooper, A. M. (1986) 'Narcissism' in A. P. Morrison (ed.) *Essential Papers on Narcissism*. New York: New York University Press: 112–143

Craib, I. (1998) *Experiencing Identity*. London: Sage

Craib, I. (1992) *Anthony Giddens*. London: Routledge

Cremin, C.S. (2005) 'Profiling the Personal: Configuration of Teenage Biographies to Employment Norms', *Sociology*, Vol.39(2): 315–332

Cremin, C. S. (2003) 'Self-Starters, Can-doers and Mobile Phoneys: Situations Vacant Columns and the Personality Culture in Employment', *The Sociological Review*, 51(1): 109–128

Crompton, R. and Scott, J. (2005) 'Class Analysis: Beyond the Cultural Turn' in F. Devine, M. Savage, J. Scott and R. Crompton (eds) *Rethinking Class: Culture, Identities and Lifestyle*. Basingstoke: Palgrave Macmillan: 186–203

Crompton, R., Devine, F., Savage, M. and Scott, J. (eds) (1999) *Renewing Class Analysis*. Oxford: Blackwell

Cushman, P. (1995) *Constructing the Self, Constructing America: A Cultural History of Psychotherapy*. Cambridge, MA: Perseus

Czuchta Romano, D. M. (2004) 'A self-psychology approach to narcissistic personality disorder: a nursing reflection', *Perspectives in Psychiatric Care*, Vol.40(1): 20–28

Davies, M. (2004) 'Planet of Slums: Urban Involution and the Informal Proletariat', *New Left Review* (March 26/April 2004): 5–34

Dean, M. (2002) 'The regulation of the self' in T. Jordan and S. Pile (eds) *Social Change*. Oxford: Blackwell: 229–272

Dean, M. (1999) *Governmentality: Power and Rule in Modern Society*. London: Sage

Deleuze, G. (1988) *Foucault*. London: Athlone

Dennis, A. and Martin, P. J. (2005) 'Symbolic interactionism and the concept of power', *The British Journal of Sociology*, Vol.56(2): 191–213

Devine, F. and Savage, M. (2005) 'The Cultural Turn, Sociology and Class Analysis' in F. Devine, M. Savage, J. Scott and R. Crompton (eds) *Rethinking Class: Culture, Identities and Lifestyle*. Basingstoke: Palgrave Macmillan: 1–23

Devine, F., Savage, M., Scott, J. and Crompton, R. (2005) (eds) *Rethinking Class: Culture, Identities and Lifestyle*. Basingstoke: Palgrave Macmillan

Diamond, I. and Quinby, L. (eds) (1988) *Feminism and Foucault: Reflections on Resistance*. Boston: Northeastern University Press

Donzelot, J. (1991 [1980]) 'The Mobilization of Society' in G. Burchell, C. Gordon and P. Miller (eds) *The Foucault Effect: studies in governmentality*. Brighton: Harvester Wheatsheaf: 169–180

Donzelot, J. (1979) *The Policing of Families* (trans. R. Hurley). New York: Pantheon

Du Gay, P. (2004) 'Against "Enterprise" (but not against enterprise, for that would make no sense)' *Organization*, Vol.11(1): 37–57

Du Gay, P. (1997) 'Organizing Identity: Making Up People at Work' in P. Du Gay (ed.) *Production of Culture/Cultures of Production*. London: Sage: 285–344

Du Gay, P. (1996) *Consumption and Identity at Work*. London: Sage

Dumm, T. L. (1996) *Michel Foucault and the Politics of Freedom*. London: Sage

Durkheim, E. (1951 [1897]) *Suicide: A Study in Sociology*. Glencoe: Free Press

Dutton, K. R. (1995) *The Perfectible Body: the western idea of physical development*. London: Cassell

Ehrenreich, B. (2002) *Nickel and Dimed: Undercover in Low-wage America*. London: Granta

Ehrenreich, B. and Hochschild, A. (eds) (2003) *Global Woman: Nannies, Maids and Sex Workers in the New Economy*. Basingstoke: Palgrave

Elias, N. (1978/1939) *The Civilizing Process, Vol.1: The History of Manners*. New York: Pantheon Books

Elliott, A. (2004) 'Psychoanalysis, Modernity, Postmodernism: Theorizing for a New Era', *Psychoanalysis, Culture and Society*, 9: 63–73

Elliott, A. (2001) *Concepts of the Self*. Cambridge: Polity Press

Elliott, A. (2000) 'Psychoanalysis and Social Theory' in B. S. Turner (ed.) *The Blackwell Companion to Social Theory*. Oxford: Blackwell: 133–159

Elliott, A. (1999, 2nd edition) *Social Theory and Psychoanalysis in Transition*. London: Free Association Books

Elshtain, J. B. (1980) 'The Self: Reborn, Undone, Transformed', *Telos*, No.44 (Summer, 1980): 101–11

Elster, J. (ed.) (1986) *Rational Choice*, Oxford: Basil Blackwell

Emerson, R. M. (1972) 'Exchange Theory, Part I: A Psychological Basis For Social Exchange' in J. Berger, M. Zelditch and B. Anderson (eds) *Sociological Theories in Progress, Volume Two*. Boston: Houghton Mifflin Company

Engel, S. (1980) 'Femininity as Tragedy: Re-examining the "New Narcissism"', *Socialist Review*, 53: 77–104

Erikson, E. (1950) *Childhood and Society*. New York: Norton

Fernandez-Kelly, M. P. (1994) 'Towanda's Triumph: Social and Cultural Capital in the Transition to Adulthood in the Urban Ghetto', *International Journal of Urban and Regional Research*, 18: 88–111

Fernie, S. and Metcalf, D. (1998) *(Not) Hanging on the Telephone: Payment Systems in the New Sweatshops*, Discussion Paper 390. Centre for Economic Performance, London School of Economics

Fineman, S. (2004) 'Getting the Measure of Emotion – and the Cautionary Tale of Emotional Intelligence', *Human Relations*, 57(6): 719–740

Fineman, S. (2000) 'Commodifying the Emotionally Intelligent', in S. Fineman (ed.) *Emotion in Organizations*. London: Sage: 101–114

Flax, J. (1990) *Thinking Fragments: Psychoanalysis, Feminism and Postmodernism in the Contemporary West*. Berkeley: University of California Press

Fleming, P. and Sewell, G. (2002) 'Looking for the Good Soldier, Svejk: Alternative Modalities of Resistance in the Contemporary Workplace', *Sociology*, Vol.36(4): 857–873

Foucault, M. (1991b) 'Governmentality' in G. Burchell, C. Gordon and P. Miller (eds) *The Foucault Effect: studies in governmentality*. Brighton: Harvester Wheatsheaf: 87–104

Foucault, M. (1991a) 'Politics and the Study of Discourse' in G. Burchell, C. Gordon and P. Miller (eds) *The Foucault Effect: studies in governmentality*. Brighton: Harvester Wheatsheaf: 53–72

Foucault, M. (1988b) 'The Political Technology of Individuals' in L. H. Martin (ed.) *Technologies of the Self*. University of Massachusetts Press: 145–162

Foucault, M. (1988a) 'Technologies of the Self' in L. H. Martin (ed.) *Technologies of the Self*. University of Massachusetts Press: 16–49

Foucault, M. (1986) *The Care of the Self: The History of Sexuality, Vol.3.* (trans. Robert Hurley). New York: Random House

Foucault, M. (1985) *The Use of Pleasure: The History of Sexuality, Vol.2.* (trans. Robert Hurley). New York: Random House

Foucault, M. (1984) 'What is Enlighthenment?' in P. Rabinow (ed.) *The Foucault Reader*. New York: Pantheon Books: 32–50

Foucault, M. (1982) 'The subject and power' in H. L. Dreyfus and P. Rabinow (eds) *Michel Foucault: beyond structuralism and hermeneutics*. Brighton: Harvester Wheatsheaf: 208–226

Foucault, M. (1980c) *Language, Counter-Memory, Practice*. New York: Cornell University Press

Foucault, M. (1980b) 'Truth and Power' in C. Gordon (ed.) *Power/Knowledge: Selected Writings 1972–1977 by Michel Foucault*. Hemel Hempstead: Harvester: 109–133

Foucault, M. (1980a) 'The eye of power' in C. Gordon (ed.) *Power/Knowledge: Selected Writings 1972–1977 by Michel Foucault*. Hemel Hempstead: Harvester: 146–165

Foucault, M. (1979) *The History of Sexuality. Volume 1: An Introduction* (trans. R. Hurley). London: Allen Lane

Foucault, M. (1977) *Discipline and Punish: The Birth of the Prison* (trans. A. Sheridan). London: Allen Lane

Foucault, M. (1965) *Madness and Civilization* (trans. R. Howard). London: Tavistock

Foucault, M. and Martin, R. (1988) 'Truth, Power, Self: An Interview with Michel Foucault' in L. H. Martin (ed.) *Technologies of the Self*. University of Massachusetts Press: 9–15

Fraser, N. (1996) 'Michel Foucault: A Young Conservative?' in S. J. Hekman (ed.) *Feminist Interpretations of Foucault*. Pennsylvania: Penn State University Press: 15–38

Frenkel, S., Korczynski, M., Shire, K. and Tam, M. (1998) 'Beyond Bureaucracy? Work Organisation in Call Centres', *International Journal of Human Resource Management*, 9(6): 957–979

Freud, S. (1930 [1963]) *Civilisation and Its Discontents*. London: Hogarth Press

Freud, S. (1923) 'The Ego and the Id' in S. Freud (1984), *On Metapsychology*. Harmondsworth: Penguin: 1984: Vol.11

Freud, S. (1922 [1955]) *Group Psychology and the Analysis of the Ego*. London: Hogarth Press

Freud, S. (1920) 'Beyond the Pleasure Principle' in S. Freud (1984), *On Metapsychology*. Harmondsworth: Penguin: 7–64

Freud, S. (1914) 'On Narcissism: An Introduction' in S. Freud (1984), *On Metapsychology*. Harmondsworth: Penguin: 67–102

Frost, L. (2005) 'Theorizing the Young Woman in the Body', *Body and Society*, Vol.11(1): 63–85

Frosh, S. (1991) *Identity Crisis: Modernity, Psychoanalysis and the Self*. Palgrave: Macmillan

Frosh, S., Pheonix, A. and Pattman, R. (2003) 'Taking a stand: Using psychoanalysis to explore the positioning of subjects in discourse', *British Journal of Social Psychology*, 42: 39–53

Fukuyama, F. (1992) *The End of History and the Last Man*. Harmondsworth: Penguin

Furedi, F. (2004) *Therapy Culture: Cultivating Vulnerability in an Uncertain Age*. London: Routledge

Furlong, A. and Cartmel, F. (1997) *Young people and social change: individualization and risk in late modernity*. Buckingham: Open University Press

Gandy, O. (1993) *The Panoptic Sort: A Political Economy of Personal Information*. Boulder: Westview

Gardiner, M. (1996) 'Alterity and ethics: a dialogical perspective', *Theory, Culture and Society*, Vol.13(2): 121–143

Garratt, S. (1998) *Adventures in Wonderland: A Decade in Club Culture*. London: Headline

Gee, J. P., Hull, G. and Lankshear, C. (1996) *The New Work Order*. St. Leonards, NSW: Allen and Unwin

Gendlin E. (1987) 'A philosophical critique of the concept of narcissism: the significance of the Awareness Movement' in D. M. Levin (ed.) *Pathologies of the Modern Self*. New York: New York University Press: 251–304

Giddens, A. (1999) *Runaway World: How Globalization is shaping our lives*. London: Profile Books.

Giddens, A. (1994) 'Living in a Post-Traditional Society', in U. Beck, A. Giddens and S. Lash, *Reflexive Modernization*. Cambridge: Polity Press: 56–109

Giddens, A. (1992) *The Transformation of Intimacy*. Cambridge: Polity Press

Giddens, A. (1991) *Modernity and Self-Identity: Self and Society in the Late Modern Age*. Cambridge: Polity Press

Giddens, A. (1990) *The Consequences of Modernity*. Cambridge: Polity Press

Giddens, A. (1984) *The Constitution of Society*. Cambridge: Polity Press

Giddens, A (1981) *A Contemporary Critique of Historical Materialism*. London: Macmillan

Giddens, A. (1979) *Central Problems in Social Theory*. London: Macmillan

Giddens, A. (1976) *New Rules of Sociological Method*. London: Hutchinson

Giddens, A. and Pierson, C. (1998c) *Conversations with Anthony Giddens: Making Sense of Modernity*. Cambridge: Polity Press

Gill, R., Henwood, K. and McLean, C. (2005) 'Body Projects and the Regulation of Normative Masculinity', *Body and Society*, Vol.11(1): 37–62.

Gilpin, R. (1987) *The Political Economy of International Relations*. Princeton: Princeton University Press

Glass, J. (1993) *Shattered selves: Multiple personality in a postmodern world*. New York: Cornell University Press

Goffman, E. (1971) *Relations in Public*. London: Penguin

Goffman, E. (1961) *Asylums*. Harmondsworth: Penguin

Goffman, E. (1952) 'On Cooling the Mark Out: Some Aspects of Adaptation to Failure', *Psychiatry*, 15(4) 451–463

Golding, P. (2000) 'Forthcoming features: information and communications technologies and the sociologies of the future', *Sociology*, Vol.34(1)

Goldthorpe, J. H. (1998) 'Rational Action Theory for Sociology', *British Journal of Sociology*, 49(2): 167–192

Goleman, D. (1998) *Working With Emotional Intelligence*. London: Bloomsbury

Goleman, D. (1996) *Emotional Intelligence: Why it Can Matter More Than IQ*. London: Bloomsbury

Golomb, E. (1992) *Trapped in the Mirror: Adult Children of Narcissists in Their Struggle for Self*. New York: HarperCollins

Gordon, C. (1991) 'Governmental rationality: an introduction' in G. Burchell, C. Gordon and P. Miller (eds) *The Foucault Effect: studies in governmentality*. Brighton: Harvester Wheatsheaf: 1–51

Gordon, C. (1987) 'The soul of the citizen: Max Weber and Michel Foucault on rationality and government' in S. Whimster and S. Lash (eds) *Max Weber: Rationality and Modernity*. London: Allen and Unwin: 293–316

Gorz, A. (1982) *Farewell to the Working Class*. London: Pluto

Grunberger, B. (1989) *New Essays on Narcissism*. London: Free Association

Grunberger, B. (1979) *Narcissism: Psychoanalytic Essays*. New York: International Universities Press

Haiken, E. (2000) 'Virtual Virility, or, Does Medicine Make the Man?', *Men and Masculinities*, Vol.2(4): 388–409

Hakim, S. (2004) *Key Issues in Women's Work*. London: Glasshouse Press

Hall, S. (1992) 'The Question of Cultural Identity' in S. Hall, D. Held and T. McGrew (eds) *Modernity and its Futures*. Cambridge: Polity Press: 273–326

Hall, S. (1989) 'Encoding/Decoding' in S. Hall, D. Hobson, A. Lowe and P. Willis (eds) *Culture, Media, Language*. London: Hutchison

Hall, S. and Jefferson, T. (eds) (1976) *Resistance Through Rituals*. London: Hutchison

Hannah, M. (1997) 'Imperfect panopticism: envisioning the construction of normal lives' in G. Benko and U. Stohmayer (eds) *Space and Social Theory: Interpreting Modernity and Postmodernity*. Oxford: Blackwell: 344–359

Haraway, D. (1997) *Modest_Witness@Second_Millennium.FemaleMan©_Meets_OncoMouse™ Feminism and Technoscience*. London: Routledge

Harvey, D. (1989) *The Condition of Postmodernity*. Oxford: Blackwell

Hay, C., O'Brien, M. and Penna, S. (1994) 'Modernity & Self Identity: the "hollowing out" of social theory', *Arena Journal*, Series No.2:45–76; reprinted in C. Bryant and D. Jary (eds) (1996) *Anthony Giddens: A Critical Assessment*. London: Routledge

Hebdige, D. (1979) *Subculture: The Meaning of Style*. London: Methuen

Heelas, P. (1996) 'Introduction: Detraditionalization and its Rivals' in P. Heelas, S. Lash and P. Morris (eds) *Detraditionalization*. Oxford: Blackwell: 1–20

Heelas, P., Lash, S. and Morris, P. (eds) (1996) *Detraditionalization*. Oxford: Blackwell

Hekman, S. J. (2000) 'Beyond Identity: Feminism, identity and identity politics', *Feminist Theory*, Vol.1(3): 289–308

Hekman, S. J. (ed.) (1996) *Feminist Interpretations of Foucault*. Pensylvania: Penn State University Press

Held, D. (1995) *Democracy and the Global Order*. Cambridge: Polity Press

Henley, J. (2005) 'Founding principle called into question', *Guardian* (November 8, 2005): 19

Henwood, F., Kennedy, H., Miller, N. (eds) (2001) *Cyborg lives?: women's technobiographies*. New York: Raw Nerve

Hermans, H. J. M. (ed.) (2002) 'The dialogical self' (special issue), *Theory and Psychology*, 12(2).

Hermans, H. J. M. (1999) 'The polyphony of the mind: A multi-voiced and dialogical self' in J. Rowan and M. Cooper (eds) *The plural self: Multiplicity in everyday life*. London: Sage: 107–131

Hermans, H. J. M. and Kempen, H. J. G. (1993) *The Dialogical Self: Meaning as Movement*. London: Academic Press Limited

Hey, V. (2005) 'The Contrasting Social Logics of Sociality and Survival: Cultures of Classed Be/Longing in Late Modernity', *Sociology*, Vol.39(5): 855–872

Hirst, P. (1981) 'The genesis of the social', *Politics and Power*, Vol.3: 67–82

Hochschild, A. (1983) *The Managed Heart*. Los Angeles: University of California Press

Hotchkiss, S. (2002) *Why is it Always About You? Saving Yourself From the Narcissists in Your Life*. New York: Simon and Schuster

Houston, S. (2002) 'Reflecting on Habitus, Field and Capital: Towards a Culturally Sensitive Social Work', *Journal of Social Work*, 2: 146–167

Hoy, D. C. (ed.) (1986) *Foucault: A critical reader*. Oxford: Blackwell

Hughes, J. (2005) 'Bringing emotion to work: emotional intelligence, employee resistance and the reinvention of character', *Work, Employment and Society*, Vol.19(3): 603–625

Hutton, P. H. (1988) 'Foucault, Freud and the Technologies of the Self' in L. H. Martin (ed.) *Technologies of the Self*. University of Massachusetts Press: 121–144

Jacoby, R. (1980) 'Narcissism and the Crisis of Capitalism', *Telos*, No.44 (Summer, 1980): 58–64

Jacoby, R. (1975) *Social Amnesia*. Hassocks: Harvester

Jagger, E. (2001) 'Marketing Molly and Melville: Dating in a Postmodern, Consumer Society', *Sociology*, Vol.35(1): 39–57

Jameson, F. (1984) 'Postmodernism, or the cultural logic of late capitalism', *New Left Review*, No.146: 54–92

Jamieson, L. (1999) 'Intimacy transformed: a critical look at the pure relationship', *Sociology*, Vol.33: 477–494

Jamieson, L. (1998) *Intimacy: Personal Relationships in Modern Societies*. Cambridge: Polity Press

Jay, M. (1994) *Downcast Eyes: The Denigration of Vision in 20th Century French Thought*. Berkeley: University of California Press

Jones, S. G. (1998) 'Introduction' in S. G. Jones (ed.) *Cybersociety 2.0: Revisiting Computer-Mediated Communication and Community*. London: Sage

Jordan, T. (2002b) 'Totalities and Multiplicities: Thinking About Social Change' in T. Jordan and S. Pile (eds) *Social Change*. Oxford: Blackwell: 273–316

Jordan, T. (2002) 'Community, everyday and space' in T. Bennett and D. Watson (eds) *Understanding Everyday Life*. Oxford: Blackwell: 229–270

Jordan, T. and Taylor, P. (1998) 'A sociology of hackers', *Sociological Review*, Vol.46(4): 757–780

Keat, R. and Abercrombie, N. (1991) *Enterprise Culture*. London: Routledge

Kellner, D. (1991) 'Introduction' in H. Marcuse, *One Dimensional Man* (1964 [1991]) Boston: Beacon Press

Kelly, P. and Kenway, J. (2001) 'Managing Youth Transitions in the Network Society', *British Journal of the Sociology of Education*, 22(1): 19–33

Kernberg, O. (1986b) 'Further Contributions to the Treatment of Narcissistic Personalities' in A. P. Morrison (ed.) (1986) *Essential Papers on Narcissism*. New York: New York University Press: 245–292

Kernberg, O. (1986a) 'Factors in the Psychoanalytic Treatment of Narcissistic Personalities' in A. P. Morrison (ed.) (1986) *Essential Papers on Narcissism*. New York: New York University Press: 213–244

Kernberg, O. (1975) *Borderline Conditions and Pathological Narcissism*. New York: Jason Aronson

Kinnie, N., Hutchinson, S. and Purcell, J. (2000) '"Fun and Surveillance": The Paradox of High Commitment Management in Call Centres', *International Journal of Human Resource Management*, 11(5): 967–985

Kirkup, G., James, L., Woodward, K. and Hovenden, F. (eds) (2000) *The gendered cyborg: a reader*. London: Routledge/Open University Press

Klein, M. (1988 [1975]) *Envy and Gratitude and Other Works 1946–1963*. London: Virago

Klein, M. (1956) *New Directions in Psychoanalysis*. New York: Basic Books

Klein, M. (1952) *Developments in Psychoanalysis*. London: Hogarth Press

Klein, N (2000) *No Logo*. London: Flamingo

Knights, D. and McCabe, D. (2000) '"Ain't misbehavin'?": Opportunities for Resistance Under New Forms of "Quality" Management"', *Sociology*, Vol.34(3): 421–436

Kohut, H. (1986 [1966]) 'Forms and Transformations of Narcissism' in A. P. Morrison (ed.) *Essential Papers on Narcissism*. New York: New York University Press: 61–88

Kohut, H. (1971) *The Analysis of the Self*. New York: International Universities Press

Kohut, H. (1977) *The Restoration of the Self*. New York: International Universities Press

Koskela, H. (2003) '"Cam Era" – the contemporary urban Panopticon', *Surveillance & Society*, 1(3): 292–313 (http://www.surveillance-and-society.org)

Koskela, H. (2002) 'Video surveillance, gender and the safety of public urban space: "Peeping Tom" goes high tech?', *Urban Geography*, 23: 257–278

Kovel, J. (1988) *The Radical Spirit*. London: Free Association

Kovel, J. (1982) *The Age of Desire*. New York: Pantheon

Kovel, J. (1980) 'Narcissism and the family', *Telos*, No.44 (Summer, 1980): 88–100

Krishnamurti, J. (1970) *The Krishnamurti Reader*. London: Arkana

Kristeva, J. (1984 [1974]) *Revolution in Poetic Language*. New York: Columbia University Press

Kunzru, H. (2004) *Transmission*. London: Hamish Hamilton

Lacan, J. (1977) *Ecrits: A Selection*. London: Tavistock

Lacan, J. (1975) *The Seminar of Jacques Lacan, Book 1 (1953–4)*. Cambridge: Cambridge University Press

Laing, R. D. (1967) *The Politics of Experience and the Bird of Experience*. Harmondsworth: Penguin

Laing, R. D. (1960) *The Divided Self: A Study in Sanity and Madness*. London: Tavistock

Laing, R. D. and Esterson, A. (1970) *Sanity, Madness and the Family*. London: Tavistock

Lasch, C (1995) *The Revolt of the Elites*. New York: Norton

Lasch, C. (1991 [1979]) *The Culture of Narcissism: American Life in An Age of Diminishing Expectations*. New York: Norton

Lasch, C. (1984) *The Minimal Self*. New York: Norton

Lasch, C. (1981) 'The Freudian Left and Cultural Revolution', *New Left Review*, 129: 23–34

Lasch, C. (1974) *Haven in a Heartless World: The Family Besieged*. New York: Norton

Lasch, C. et al. (1979) 'A Symposium: Christopher Lasch and The Culture of Narcissism' in *Salmagundi* (Fall, 1979)

Lash, S. (1999) *Another Modernity, A Different Rationality*. Oxford: Blackwell

Lash, S. (1994) 'Reflexivity and its Doubles: Structure, Aesthetics, Community' in U. Beck, A. Giddens and S. Lash, *Reflexive Modernization*. Cambridge: Polity Press: 110–173

Lash, S. and Friedman, J. (eds) (1992) *Modernity and Identity*. Oxford: Blackwell

Lash, S and Urry, J. (1994) *Economies of Signs and Space*. London: Sage

Latour, B. (1993) *We Have Never Been Modern* (trans. Catherine Porter). Cambridge, Mass.: Harvard University Press

Lawler, S. (2005b) 'Disgusted Subjects: the making of middle-class identities', *The Sociological Review*, 3(3): 429–446

Lawler, S. (2005) 'Introduction: Class, Culture and Identity', *Sociology*, Vol.39(5): 797–806

Leadbeater, C. (2004) *Up the Down Escalator: Why the Global Pessimists are Wrong*. Harmondsworth: Penguin

Lerner, B. (1999) 'The Killer Narcissists', *National Review* (May 17, 1999)

Levin, D. M. (ed.) (1987) *Pathologies of the Modern Self*. New York: New York University Press

Lipovetsky, G. (2005) *Hypermodern Times*. Cambridge: Polity Press

Lockard, J. (1997) 'Progressive politics, electronic individualism and the myth of community' in D. Porter (ed.) *Internet Culture*. London: Routledge: 219–232

Lupton, D. (2000) 'The embodied computer/user' in D. Bell and B. M. Kennedy (eds) *The Cyber Cultures Reader*. London: Routledge: 477–487

Mackay, H. (2002) 'New media and time-space reconfiguration' in T. Jordan and S. Pile (eds) *Social Change*. Oxford: Blackwell: 139–184

Mahler, M. S. (1979 [1958]) 'Autism and Symbiosis: Two Extreme Disturbances of Identity' in *The Selected Papers of Margaret S. Mahler*, Vol.1. New York: Aronson: 261–279

Mahler, M. S., Pine, F. and Bergman, A. (1975) *The Psychological Birth of the Human Infant: Symbiosis and Individuation*. New York: Basic Books

Marcuse, H. (1955) *Eros and Civilisation: A philosophical inquiry into Freud*. Boston: Beacon Press

Marcuse, H (1964 [1991]) *One Dimensional Man*. Boston: Beacon Press

Martin, R. (1988) 'Truth, Power, Self: An Interview with Michel Foucault' in L. H. Martin (ed.) *Technologies of the Self*. University of Massachusetts Press: 9–15

McCahill, M. (2001) *The Surveillance Web: The Rise of Visual Surveillance in an English City*. Devon: Willan Press.

McCallum. E. L. (1996) 'Technologies of Truth and the Function of Gender' in S. J. Hekman (ed.) *Feminist Interpretations of Foucault*. Pennsylvania: Penn State University Press

McCarthy, C. (2000) 'Reading the American Popular: suburban resentment and the representation of the inner-city in contemporary film and TV' in D. Fleming (ed.) *Formations: A 21st-Century Media Studies Textbook*. Manchester: Manchester University Press

MacDonald, K. (1999) *Struggles for Subjectivity*. Cambridge: Cambridge University Press

McGrew, A. (1992) 'A Globalized Society?' in S. Hall, D. Held and A. McGrew (eds) *Modernity and its Futures*. Cambridge: Polity Press: 61–116

McKinlay, A. and Taylor, P. (1996) 'Power, Surveillance and Resistance: Inside the "Factory of the Future"', in P. Ackers, C. Smith and P. Smith (eds) *The New Workplace and Trade Unionism*. London: Routledge: 279–300

McLuhan, M. (1964) *Understanding Media: The Extensions of Man*. London: Routledge

McNay, L. (1999). 'Gender, habitus and the field: Pierre Bourdieu and the limits of reflexivity', *Theory, Culture and Society*, 16(1): 95–117

McNay, L. (1994) *Foucault: A Critical Introduction*. Cambridge: Polity Press

McNay, L. (1992) *Foucault and Feminism: Power, Gender and the Self*. Cambridge: Polity Press

Melucci, A. (1996) *The Playing Self: Person and Meaning in the Planetary Society*. Cambridge: Cambridge University Press

Mestrovic, S. (1999) *Anthony Giddens: The Last Modernist*. London: Sage

Mestrovic, S. (1997) *Postemotional Society*. London: Sage

Miller, A. (1986) 'Depression and Grandiosity as Related Forms of Narcissistic Disturbances' in A. P. Morrison (ed.) *Essential Papers on Narcissism*. New York: New York University Press: 323–347

Miller, D. and Slater, D. (2000) *The Internet: An Ethnographic Approach*. Oxford: Berg

Miller, P. and Rose, N. (1990) 'Governing economic life', *Economy and Society*, Vol.19(1): 1–31

Mitchell, W. and Green, E. (2002) '"I don't know what I'd do without our mam": Motherhood, identity and support networks', *The Sociological Review*, Vol.50(4): 1–22

Morley, D. (1980) *The 'Nationwide' Audience: Structure and Decoding*. London: British Film Institute

Morris, M. (1988) 'The pirate's fiancée: feminists and philosophers, or maybe tonight it'll happen' in I. Diamond and L. Quinby (eds) *Feminism and Foucault: Reflections on Resistance*. Boston: Northeastern University Press: 21–42

Mouzelis, N. (1999) 'Exploring post-traditional orders: Individual Reflexivity, "pure relations" and duality of structure' in M. O'Brien, S. Penna and C. Hay (eds) (1999) *Theorising Modernity*. London: Longman: 83–97

Nilan, P. and Threadgold, S. (2005) 'Reflexivity and Habitus: Youth Futures in Australia, Fiji and Indonesia', *unpublished paper*.

Norris, C. (2002) 'From personal to digital: CCTV, the Panopticon, and the technological mediation of suspicion and social control' in D. Lyon (ed.) *Surveillance as Social Sorting: Privacy, Risk and Digital Discrimination*. London: Routledge: 249–281

Norris, C. and Armstrong, G. (1999) *The Maximum Surveillance Society: The Rise of CCTV*. Oxford: Berg

O'Brien, M. (1999) 'Theorising modernity: Reflexivity, identity and environment in Giddens' social theory' in M. O'Brien, S. Penna and C. Hay (eds) *Theorising modernity*. London: Longman: 17–38

O'Brien, M. (1998) 'The Sociology of Anthony Giddens: An Introduction' in A. Giddens and C. Pierson, *Conversations with Anthony Giddens: Making Sense of Modernity*. Cambridge: Polity Press: 1–27

O'Brien, M., Penna, S. and Hay, C. (eds) (1999) *Theorising Modernity: Reflexivity, Environment and Identity in Giddens's Social Theory*. London: Longman

O'Connor, P. (2006) 'Young People's Constructions of the Self: Late Modern Elements and Gender Differences', *Sociology*, Vol.40(1): 107–124

Payson, E. (2002) *The Wizard of Oz and Other Narcissists: Coping with the One-Way Relationship in Work, Love, and Family*. Julian Day Publications

Phillips, A. (2002) *Promises, Promises: Essays on Literature and Psychoanalysis*. London: Faber and Faber

Phillips, T. and Western, M. (2005) 'Social Change and Social Identity: Postmodernity, Reflexive Modernisation and the Transformation of Social Identities in Australia' in F. Devine, M. Savage, J. Scott and R. Crompton (eds) *Rethinking Class: Culture, Identities and Lifestyle*. Basingstoke: Palgrave Macmillan: 163–185

Pile, S. (2002) 'Social change and city life' in T. Jordan and S. Pile (eds) *Social Change*. Oxford: Blackwell: 1–48

Plummer, K. (2000) 'Symbolic Interactionism in the Twentieth Century' in B. Turner (ed.) *Blackwell Companion to Social Theory*. Oxford: Blackwell

Plumridge, L. and Thomson, R. (2003) 'Longtitudinal qualitative studies and the reflexive self', *International Journal of Social Research Methodology*, Vol.6(3): 213–222

Poster, M. (1990) *The Mode of Information*. Cambridge: Polity Press

Pringle, R. (1988) *Secretaries Talk*. London: Verso

Pulver, S. E. (1986) 'Narcissism: The Term and the Concept' in A. P. Morrison (ed.) *Essential Papers on Narcissism*. New York: New York University Press: 91–111

Putnam, D. (2000) *Bowling Alone*. New York: Simon and Schuster

Radice, S. (2001) 'All in the mind', *Observer* magazine (March 4, 2001): 49–50

Ramazanoglu, C. (1993) 'Introduction' in C. Ramazanoglu (ed.) *Up Against Foucault: Explorations of Some Tensions between Foucault and Feminism*. London: Routledge: 1–25

Ramazanoglu, C. and Holland, J. (1993) 'Women's Sexuality and Men's Appropriation of Desire' in C. Ramazanoglu (ed.) *Up Against Foucault: Explorations of Some Tensions Between Foucault and Feminism*. London: Routledge: 239–264

Ransom, J. (1993) 'Feminism, difference and discourse: the limits of discursive analysis for feminism' in C. Ramazanoglu (ed.) *Up Against Foucault: Explorations of Some Tensions Between Foucault and Feminism*. London: Routledge: 123–146

Ravenhill, M. (2005) 'The trouble with television is that it can't stop shoving liberal values down our throats', *Guardian* (November 11, 2005)

Reay, D. (2005) 'Beyond Consciousness? The Psychic Landscape of Social Class', *Sociology*, Vol.39(5): 911–928

Reay, D. and William, D. (1999) ' "I'll be a Nothing": Structure, Agency and the Construction of Identity Through Assessment', *British Educational Research Journal*, 25(3): 343-354

Redman, P. (2002) 'Love is in the air: romance and the everyday' in T. Bennett and D. Watson (eds) *Understanding Everyday Life*. Oxford: Blackwell: 51–90

Reeve, A. (1998) 'The panopticisation of shopping: CCTV and leisure consumption' in C. Norris, J. Moran and G. Armstrong (eds) *Surveillance, Closed Circuit Television and Social Control*. Aldershot: Ashgate: 69–87

Reynolds, S. (1998) *Energy Flash: A Journey Through Rave Music and Dance Culture*. London: Picador

Rhodes, J. (2005) *Radical Feminism, Writing and Critical Agency*. New York: SUNY Press

Richards, B. (1989) *Images of Freud: Cultural Responses to Psychoanalysis*. London: Dent

Riesman, D. (2001 [1961]) *The Lonely Crowd: A Study of the Changing American Character*. London: Yale Nota Bene

Robertson, R. (1992) *Globalization: Social theory and global culture*. London: Sage

Rojek, C. (1995) *Decentring Leisure: Rethinking Leisure Theory*. London: Sage

Rojek, C. and Turner, B. (2000) 'Decorative sociology: towards a critique of the cultural turn', *The Sociological Review*, 4(48): 629–648

Rose, N. (2000) 'Community, citizenship and "the Third Way"', in D. Meredyth and J. Minson (eds) *Citizenship and Cultural Policy*. London: Sage: 1–17

Rose, N. (1996c) 'Authority and the genealogy of subjectivity', in P. Heelas, S. Lash and P. Morris (eds) *Detraditionalization: critical reflections on authority and identity*. Oxford: Blackwell: 294–327

Rose, N. (1996b) 'Assembling the modern self', in R. Porter (ed.) *The History of the Self*. London: Routledge: 224–248

Rose, N. (1996) *Inventing Our Selves: Psychology, Power and Personhood*. Cambridge: Cambridge University Press

Rose, N. (1990) *Governing the Soul: the Shaping of the Private Self*. London: Routledge

Rosenau, J. (1990) *Turbulence in World Politics*. Brighton: Harvester Wheatsheaf

Rowan, J. and Cooper, M. (eds) (1999) *The Plural Self: Multiplicity in Everyday Life*. London: Sage

Sampson, E. (1981) 'Cognitive psychology as ideology', *American Psychologist*, 36: 730–743

Savage, M., Bagnall, G. and Longhurst, B. (2005) 'Local Habitus and Working Class Culture' in F. Devine, M. Savage, J. Scott and R. Crompton (eds) *Rethinking Class: Culture, Identities and Lifestyle*. Basingstoke: Palgrave Macmillan: 95–122

Schiller, H. (1976) *Communication and Cultural Domination*. New York: M. E. Sharpe

Schofield, B. (2003) 'Re-instating the Vague', *Sociological Review*, Vol.51(3): 321–38

Schutz, A. (1964) *Collected Papers II: Studies in Social Theory*. The Hague: Martinus Nijhoff

Schutz, A. (1962) *Collected Papers I: The Problem of Social Reality*. The Hague: Martinus Nijhoff

Scott, S. and Scott, S. (2001) 'Our mother's daughters: autobiographical inheritance through stories of gender and class' in T. Cosslett, C. Lury and P. Summerfield (eds) *Feminism and Autobiography: Texts, Theories, Methods*. London: Routledge: 128–140

Sedgwick, P. (1972) 'R. D. Laing: Self, Symptom and Society' in R. Boyers and R. Orrill (eds) *Laing and Anti-Psychiatry*. Harmondsworth: Penguin:

Sennett, R. (1999) *The Corrosion of Character*. New York: Norton

Sennett, R. (1977) *The Fall of Public Man*. Cambridge: Cambridge University Press

Sennett, R. and Cobb, J. (1972) *The Hidden Injuries of Class*. Cambridge: Cambridge University Press

Shilling, C. (1993) *The Body and Social Theory*. London: Sage

Showalter, E. (1987) *The Female Malady: Women, Madness and English Culture 1830–1980*. London: Virago

Simmel, G. (1950 [1903]) 'The metropolis and mental life' in *The Sociology of George Simmel* (trans. and ed. K.H. Wolff). New York: The Free Press: 409–424

Simon, B. (2005) 'The Return of Panopticism: Supervision, Subjection and the New Surveillance', *Surveillance & Society*, Vol.3(1): 1–20 (http://www.surveillance-and-society.org/articles3(1)/return.pdf)

Simons, J. (1995) *Foucault and the Political*. London: Routledge

Skeggs, B. (2005b) 'The Making of Class and Gender through Visualizing Moral Subject Formation', *Sociology*, Vol.39(5): 965–982

Skeggs, B. (2005a) 'The Re-Branding of Class: Propertising Culture' in F. Devine, M. Savage, J. Scott and R. Crompton (eds) *Rethinking Class: Culture, Identities and Lifestyle*. Basingstoke: Palgrave Macmillan: 46–68

Skeggs, B. (2003) *Class, Self and Culture*. London: Routledge

Skeggs, B. (2002b) 'Mobile selves?: authority, reflexivity and positioning' in T. May (ed.) *Qualitative Research: Issues in International Practice*. London: Sage

Skeggs, B. (2002a) 'Techniques For Telling The Reflexive Self' in T. May (ed.) *Qualitative Research In Action*. London: Sage: 349–374

Skeggs, B. (1997) *Formations of Class and Gender*. London: Sage

Sklair, L. (1991) *Sociology of the Global System*. Brighton: Harvester Wheatsheaf

Sprengnether, M. (1990) *The Spectral Mother: Freud, Feminism and Psychoanalysis*. New York: Cornell University Press

Standage, T. (1998) *The Victorian Internet*. London: Weidenfeld and Nicholson

Stenson, K. (2000) 'Crime control, social policy and liberalism' in G. Lewis, S. Gewirtz and J. Clarke (eds) *Rethinking Social Policy*. London: Sage

Stevens, R. (1983) *Erik Erikson*. Milton Keynes: Open University Press

Sweetman, P. (2003) 'Twenty-first century dis-ease? habitual reflexivity or the reflexive habitus', *Sociological Review*, 51(4): 528–549

Taylor, P. and Bain, P. (2003) 'Subterranean worksick blues: humour as subversion in two call centres', *Organization Studies*, 24:9: 1487–1509

Taylor, P. and Bain, P. (2004) '"India calling to the far away towns": the call centre labour process and globalization', *Work, Employment & Society*, Vol.19(2): 261–282

Taylor, P. and Bain, P. (1999) '"An Assembly Line in the Head": Work and Employee Relations in the Call Centre', *Industrial Relations Journal*, 30(2): 101–17

Taylor, P., Hyman, J., Mulvey, G. and Bain, P. (2002) 'Work organization, control and the experience of work in call centres', *Work, Employment & Society*, Vol.16(1): 133–150

Theodore, N. and Peck, J. (1999) 'Welfare-to-work: national problems, local solutions?', *Critical Social Policy*, Vol.19(4): 485–510

Thompson, E. P. (1993) *Customs in Common*. Harmondsworth: Penguin

Thompson, J. B. (1995) *The Media and Modernity: A Social Theory of the Media*. Cambridge: Polity Press

Thompson, P., Callaghan, G. and Van den Broek, D. (2004) 'Keeping Up Appearances: Recruitment, Skills and Normative Control in Call Centres' in S. Deery and N. Kinnie (eds) *Call Centres and Human Resource Management*. Basingstoke: Palgrave: 129–152

Thomson, R., Henderson, S. and Holland, J. (2002) 'Critical Moments: Choice, Chance and Opportunity in Young People's Narratives of Transition', *Sociology*, Vol.36(2): 335–54

Thrift, N. (1990) 'Transport and Communication 1730–1914' in R. A. Dodgshon and R. A. Butlin (eds) *An Historical Geography of England and Wales* (2nd edition). London: Academic Press

Tocqueville, A. (1968 [1835–1840]) *Democracy in America*. Glasgow: Collins

Toennies, F. (1957 [1887]) *Community and Society* (trans. and ed. C. Loomis). New York: Harper and Row

Toynbee, P. (2003) *Hard Work: Life in Low-paid Britain*. London: Bloomsbury

Tracy, S. J. (2000) 'Becoming a character for commerce', *Management Communication Quarterly*, 14(1): 90–128

Tsang, D. (2000) 'Notes on queer "n" Asian virtual sex' in D. Bell and B. M. Kennedy (eds) (2000) *The Cybercultures Reader*. London: Routledge

Tucker, K. H. (1998) *Anthony Giddens and Modern Social Theory*. London: Sage

Turner, B. S. (1992) *Regulating Bodies: Essays in Medical Sociology*. London: Routledge

Turner, B. S. (1984) *The Body and Society: Explorations in Social Theory*. Oxford: Blackwell

Turner, T. (2003) 'I Shop Therefore I Am', *New Internationalist*, 355: 13–15

Urry, J. (1989) 'The End of Organized Capitalism' in S. Hall and M. Jacques (eds) *New Times: The Changing Face of Politics in the 1990s*. London: Lawrence and Wishart

Valadez, J. and Clignet, R. (1987) 'On the Ambiguities of a Sociological Analysis of the Culture of Narcissism', *The Sociological Quarterly*, Vol.28(4): 455–472

Vidal, J. (2003) 'Two worlds prepare for a showdown in a Mexican nest of vipers', *Guardian* (September 6, 2003)

Wacquant, L. (1999) 'Logics of urban polarization: the view from below' in R. Crompton, F. Devine, M. Savage and J. Scott (eds) *Renewing Class Analysis*. Oxford: Blackwell: 107–119

Walkerdine, V. (1988) *The Mastery of Reason*. London: Routledge

Walkerdine, V., Lucey, H. and Melody, J. (2001) *Growing up Girl: Psychosocial Explorations of Gender and Class*. Basingstoke: Palgrave

Wallerstein, I. (1991) 'The lessons of the 1980s' in *Geopolitics and Geoculture*. Cambridge: Cambridge University Press

Walter, T. (2001) 'Reincarnation, Modernity & Identity', *Sociology*, Vol.35(1): 25–38

Walzer, M. (1986) 'The Politics of Michel Foucault' in D. C. Hoy (ed.) *Foucault: A Critical Reader*. London: Routledge: 51–68

Weber, M. (1930) *The Protestant ethic and the spirit of capitalism* (trans. Talcott Parsons). London: Allen and Unwin

Whitaker, R. (1999) *The End of Privacy: How Total Surveillance is Becoming a Reality*. New York: The New Press

White, M. T. (1986) 'Self Relations, Object Relations, and Pathological Narcissism' in A. P. Morrison (ed.) *Essential Papers on Narcissism*. New York: New York University Press: 144–164

Whitford, M. (2003) 'Irigaray and the Culture of Narcissism', *Theory, Culture and Society*, Vol.20(3): 27–41

Widick, R. (2003) 'Flesh and the Free Market: (On taking Bourdieu to the Options Exchange)', *Theory and Society* 32(5–6): 679–723

Wiley, J. (1999) 'No body is "doing it": cybersexuality' in J. Price and M. Shildrick (eds) *Feminist Theory and the Body*. Edinburgh: Edinburgh University Press

Willis, P. (1977) *Learning to Labour*. Farnborough: Saxon House

Wilson, E. (1999) 'Worrying Trend', *Guardian*, G2 (August 2, 1999) (http://www.guardian.co.uk/health/story/0,,282167,00.html)

Winnicott, D. W. (1974) *Playing and Reality*. Harmondsworth: Penguin

Winnicott, D. W. (1965) *The Maturational Process and the Facilitating Environment*. London: Hogarth

Winnicott, D. W. (1964) *The Child, the Family and the Outside World*. Harmondsworth: Penguin

Wittel, A. (2001) 'Toward a network sociality', *Theory, Culture & Society*, 18(6): 51–76

Woodward, K. (2002) 'Up close and personal: the changing face of intimacy' in Jordan and Pile (eds) *Social Change*. Oxford: Blackwell

Woodward, K. (1997) 'Introduction' in K. Woodward (ed.) *Identity and Difference*. London: Sage

Wynne, B. (1996) 'May the Sheep Safely Graze?' in S. Lash, B. Szerszynski and B. Wynne (eds) *Risk, Environment and Modernity: Towards a New Ecology*. London: Sage

Yar, M. (2003) 'Panoptic Power and the Pathologisation of Vision: Critical Reflections on the Foucaultian Thesis', *Surveillance & Society*, 1(3): 254–271 http://www.surveillance-and-society.org)

Young, M. and Wilmott, P. (1957) *Family and Kinship in East London*. London: Routledge and Kegan Paul

Zylinska, J. (ed.) (2000) *The cyborg experiments: the extensions of the body in the media age*. London: Continuum

Index